Sometimes the Lord uses a person knowing that they will be obedient no matter the cost, and he will use them in powerful ways. Such were the likes of King David, Moses, Smith Wigglesworth, William J. Seymour of the Azusa Street revival, Jonathan Edwards, and the list goes on. Lonnie Frisbee was one of those instruments the Lord used in mighty ways in the late 1960s to the end of the 80s and beyond. I hope that after reading this book, you will be inspired to say "yes" to the Lord when he calls your name for a task—one that he wants you to complete. My friend with Improbable People Ministries says that God uses improbable people for impossible tasks. That's Lonnie Frisbee. My wife and I knew Lonnie for many years, through triumphs and failures. Through it all, his heart and mind was always stayed upon the love of his God and the work of God's kingdom. Enjoy the book!

—Steven Zarit
Vineyard Ministries International General Manager, 1986–1994

Every movement of the Holy Spirit has its strengths and weaknesses. Why? God uses man. The Jesus People movement changed my life forever. I tasted, experienced, and absorbed an entirely new and different culture to Christianity. Lonnie Frisbee was a forerunner and trailblazer of this amazing movement where Jesus Christ was kept central. I am so grateful for Lonnie's sacrifice and the wake he helped create with signs and wonders following. Blessings to all who read this series of books and become trailblazers as well.

—Dr. James W. Goll
Founder of God Encounters Ministries and International Best-Selling Author

Reading through this second book on Lonnie's life, I am more taken than ever with the incredible anointing on his ministry and the simplicity, sincerity, and even rawness of his story. I have loved learning about God's work in and through this bold and courageous ambassador of his kingdom. This story of God's ceaseless favor on his life in spite of Lonnie's pain and rejection is such a paradox. It is also a great invitation that God is extending to us. Lonnie's life is a testimony of God's faithfulness to use "whosoever will . . ."

—Robby Dawkins
Pastor at The Vineyard Church, Urbana

Lonnie Frisbee was a Holy Spirit man who understood the heart and nature of God and one of the most amazing prophetic and apostolic revivalists of our day and age. He carried an anointing of "electric power" that cross-pollinated to many streams and networks of churches, impacting countless individuals in America and the nations. I was privileged to meet and know Lonnie for a brief period of time in my life as a young adult, but what he imparted to me was life-changing! I accredit much of what I know and understand in power gifts of miracles and healing to my time of impartation with this 20th century legend. Lonnie truly was a man after God's own heart!

—Jeff Jansen
Author and Founder of Global Fire Ministries International

As Lonnie's older brother, I had the opportunity to see up close how Lonnie flowed with the Holy Spirit in a *real* relationship with the Father and the Son of God. Obedience is better than sacrifice.

—Stan Frisbee

There is a lot of anointing on this book! I had the privilege of being part of Lonnie's life and ministry. Neither of us could have imagined all of the wonderful things we would see as God poured himself out. Lonnie was a good friend, father, and Elijah to me. I'm forever grateful.

—Peter Crawford
Lonnie Frisbee's 1978 Missionary Partner

I was asked to write a short endorsement for this book about Lonnie Frisbee. I feel like I could write two chapters. Lonnie was one of the most anointed, the most controversial, and the most conflicted people and had the most radical stories of the Jesus movement and beyond. I asked him one time why we didn't hang out. He said, "Positive poles repel one another. The Lord probably wants to give you a ministry," and just walked away. What do you say to that? Well, par for the course. My wife Donna and I were both at church on Mother's Day in 1980 when Lonnie shared. The church was very ripe for revival—God used Lonnie Frisbee as the match that ignited a firestorm that went around the world. Thousands came to know Jesus as Savior, and thousands were also introduced to the gifts of the Holy Spirit! Sometimes we don't know what we have until it's gone. Rest in peace, Lonnie. God knows you deserve it.

—Billy Minter
Pastor of Church at the Well

We were blessed to be friends with and mentored by that radical evangelist and missionary Lonnie Frisbee, who was used by God to bring great impartation to our lives. Lonnie's impact directly influenced our ministry, and we are still preaching in many different and often dangerous parts of the world. When we recently ministered in St. Denis, Paris, France, which has 160 mosques in that one area of the city alone, we remembered Lonnie and how he was always reminding us of the need to shine the light of Christ into the dark places of the earth. God lit that place and the people "Frisbee style," with Holy Ghost fire to evangelize the region!

—Bryan and Mercedes Marleaux
Founders of Grace World Mission

Not by Might,
Nor by Power

The Great Commission

Also in this series:

Not by Might, Nor by Power: The Jesus Revolution

Not by Might, Nor by Power: Set Free

Not by Might, Nor by Power

Jesusfolket är här

The Great Commission

Lonnie Frisbee
with Roger Sachs

NOT BY MIGHT, NOR BY POWER: THE GREAT COMMISSION

Lonnie Frisbee with Roger Sachs

© 2016 by Freedom Publications

First Edition

Reprint 2020

Freedom Crusade
P.O. Box 2583
Santa Maria, CA 93457

www.freedomcrusade.org
www.lonnierayfrisbee.com
info@lonnierayfrisbee.com

Cover photo courtesy of KQED-TV, San Francisco. Used by permission.

ISBN 0-9785433-2-7

Printed in the United States

Dedicated to the Lord of the harvest

TABLE OF CONTENTS

FOREWORD xiii

PREFACE xvii

A LONNIE INTRODUCTION 1

ONE: Forever Young 19

TWO: Commissioned..27

THREE: Ready, Set, Go! 41

FOUR: South Africa 55

FIVE: Like a Mighty Wind...69

SIX: A Fire Was Lit...79

SEVEN: Onward..95

EIGHT: Riley..105

NINE: They Screamed, "Lonnie!" 111

TEN: A New Season...125

ELEVEN: Mother's Day 1980...137

TWELVE: The Vineyard 153

THIRTEEN: Jehovah Love...173

FOURTEEN: A New Wave..191

FIFTEEN: A Team of One Hundred 203

SIXTEEN: Marwan 219

SEVENTEEN: Trouble in River City......................................235

EIGHTEEN: Devil's Food Cake 249

POSTSCRIPT...257

ENDNOTES 261

Foreword

In life experience and personality, Lonnie and I couldn't have been more different when we first met about forty-eight years ago. I had grown up in a very loving and stable Norwegian Lutheran family, served four years in the Air Force, and was completing a BA in Biblical Studies. I was relatively shy and had never taken a drug in my life. I worked hard to prove to God that I had been worth saving (a Lutheran thing).

Then there was Lonnie. Tragically, he was almost destroyed in his childhood by the very adults who should have been models of God's love. After rejections, beatings, being born with a clubfoot, and ongoing sexual molestation and pain, he finally experienced the reality of Jesus when he was eight, thanks to the influence of his grandmother. But he still struggled to find value and meaning in everything, from dancing on TV to experimenting with LSD and other drugs, winding up in Haight-Ashbury in San Francisco. Finally, at eighteen, he had a radical and supernatural encounter with Jesus that changed everything—including exponentially the lives of literally millions of people.

He was a hippie; I was not. And there he was, sitting on a stool at Calvary Chapel Costa Mesa in 1969, surrounded by an overflow crowd of young hippie-ish people, talking about Jesus. Long beard, long hair, slight build, wearing a kind of tunic, his eyes sparkling. He wore a constant and genuine smile and spoke with gentle, but powerful authenticity. In retrospect, it looked a bit like what could have been a scene out of *The Lord of the Rings*—especially at the end of the meeting when all heaven broke loose.

A short while later, the Holy Spirit gave us a connection, a friendship, and partnership. Though four years older, I felt like the young learner. I'd led Bible studies, been a youth director, and led many to the Lord and into the baptism in the Holy Spirit, but much of my experience had been *about* Jesus. Ministering with Lonnie was like being *with* Jesus!

Being anywhere with Lonnie wasn't safe. In all my past experience with ministry, the leaders had meetings, planned the events, and pretty much knew what was going to happen and when. In between meetings or big events, life was lived "normally." I was a Christian, a "Spirit-filled" Christian, and sought to live a godly life in Christ. But Lonnie made no distinction between a meeting and the rest of life. Every moment of every day seemed to be set apart, an opportunity. I began to feel a bit like the poor disciples who never knew what was coming when they were with Jesus.

I didn't like scary. When it was time for lunch, I "shut down" my spiritual antennae and had lunch. But Lonnie never seemed "off." In the middle of anything, he might simply go speak to someone, share the gospel, and pray—oblivious to embarrassment. Something always seemed to happen. People would begin to tremble or weep or pray. And it was often loud!

I still don't like scary, but God used Lonnie to teach so many of us that the depth and power of God's love, the love that sent Jesus to Earth and the cross and resurrection, transcends human fear. Perfect love, we're told, casts out all fear. Lonnie, above all, was chosen by God to demonstrate that love, love that utterly transcends self-consciousness and self-centeredness and replaces it with Jesus-consciousness.

I went on to plant churches (called Vineyards) and pastor for the next forty years, seeing Lonnie from time to time. My wife, Joanie, and I were heartbroken when Lonnie died in 1993. Despite his heart for God and gifts, his ongoing struggles with personal sin led to his premature death. I didn't know all the details, and I was initially angry with him. Not only was his life taken, but his testimony was compromised. However, I've come to repent over my judgment, as I recognize how the enemy tried to destroy Lonnie from his birth, how his early beatings and rejection and molestations set him up for the failures that opened the door to the fatal consequences. In that regard, Lonnie also leaves us with another crucial lesson: no matter our personal wounds, weaknesses, and histories, we are all responsible to seek and embrace God's great grace and power for forgiving, for healing, and for life choices. We can learn from the painful mistakes of others.

In understanding these things, with all my heart I thank God for his gift of Lonnie in my life and to the church. Lonnie modeled discipleship for me in a way that freed me from my self-consciousness, in a way that demonstrated the living and active power of God as we traveled together from Africa to Asia to Europe and saw miracles of grace and literal healing. His teaching via the demonstration of the life of Jesus taught me and provoked me to risk much more than the safety that comes with just good teaching and culturally current worship.

Lastly, our call is not to be like Lonnie. We have each been given unique gifts and callings, our own personalities and opportunities. Lonnie's most important example is that of constantly surrendering to Jesus' invitation to an intimate love relationship in order to fulfill God's purposes for each of us.

May this book be used to encourage you to risk being like Jesus in love and action by the power and anointing of the indwelling Holy Spirit and to see Jesus live his life in and through your uniqueness.

I love you, Lonnie, with all my heart, and thank you for being a vessel of grace as we share in the joy of fruit that remains to God's glory. See you soon.

Kenn Gulliksen

Preface

This is the second volume of the life story of Lonnie Frisbee. Everything about Lonnie has a supernatural component attached. It baffles people to this day, both friend and foe, of which Lonnie has plenty of both. The first book in this three-part series focused on Lonnie's role in the Jesus People movement of the late sixties and early seventies. This well-documented Christian revival caught the attention of the whole world by 1971, and it is estimated that by 1977, ten years after this phenomenon began, two million new born-again believers came into the Christian faith. It was the largest ingathering of souls in the history of the United States, overshadowing the Great Awakenings of the eighteenth and nineteenth centuries. In addition, out of this revival an entirely new denomination of Calvary Chapel churches emerged, which presently has over a thousand churches worldwide.

In the first book written in his own words, Lonnie walked us through his involvement as a hippie preacher reaching out to his counter-cultural friends during a radical season of American history—with Vietnam raging, drugs, rebellion, massive rock concerts, and student protesters taking to the streets. From eyewitness accounts, film, and other media, Lonnie Frisbee is credited with being the most significant catalytic personality who sparked the "Jesus People Revolution," as *Time* magazine named the revival. Nevertheless, as time marched forward, the "organized church" more or less completely wrote Lonnie out of their history for a variety of reasons, but mainly due to unsubstantiated allegations of his sexuality.

In this second book, which picks up the story in 1977, Lonnie leaves Calvary Chapel to "live by faith" as a missionary. It is another great story, filled with the undeniable supernatural acts of God and featuring the command of Jesus to "go" to all the nations of the world, preaching the gospel. It is the call of the Great Commission in the Bible, to which Lonnie dedicated his entire life. Lonnie shares how God sent him and a missionary friend, Peter Crawford, to South Africa and around the world. It was the beginning of another major move of God, which eventually touched the entire continent of Africa.

Then on Mother's Day 1980, Lonnie brought an anointing back from South Africa, and God poured it out on a church that met in a high school gymnasium—Calvary Chapel Yorba Linda. Another revival was eventually birthed in America, and another modern-day denomination emerged, presently called the Association of Vineyard Churches. The Vineyard presently has over a thousand churches worldwide.

How could one young controversial hippie be so radically used by God? And who is telling the truth about his involvement in church history? What about the other allegations? I think we owe it to Lonnie to allow him to speak for himself. Like I mentioned in the first book's introduction, Lonnie was one of the most gifted public speakers in the world, but was definitely not a writer. As a missionary who worked closely with Lonnie, I have been charged by Lonnie with the task of being the ghostwriter to help him tell his own story. For most of the three years prior to his death in 1993, we recorded his story on paper, tape, and film. I now present to you this second volume of Lonnie Frisbee's life and adventures in God. It is truly amazing!

Roger Sachs

A Lonnie Introduction

Do you know that in life you might find yourself in some very unlikely relationships? God is an absolute expert at throwing curve balls in this particular arena. I (Lonnie) found myself in such a relationship with an older couple named Fred and Ruth Waugh. They are from Riverside, California, but I actually met Fred in Denmark back in the early seventies. I was on my very first mission trip with a team of young, "on fire" believers in the midst of the Jesus People revival. It was a short but life-changing trip for me with plenty of action—but I had no idea how strategic and important this man Fred and his wife would become in my life and ministry for decades to come.

Fred Waugh is a very successful businessman and a totally committed Christian. He and his wife, Ruth, have always been real involved with their local church as well as with other Christian activities. Fred first began to explain the things of the Holy Spirit to John Wimber in Fred's office back in 1963, way before John was in the ministry. He later became a counsel to me on my mission board. It was Fred and Ruth who helped develop and communicate the vision for South Africa. They held on to the vision with me in all of my exploits. My missionary partner and I went on an around-the-world ministry trip in 1978, and for the eight months we were gone, this couple held a prayer meeting every week. Ruth baked a cake, and they opened their home, took up offerings for us, and stood in prayer for the mission. When you're traveling for eight months with someone, you need prayer every day because sometimes you want to skin your partner alive. Fred and Ruth have always held down the fort for me, and I love and appreciate them very much.

One evening in 1991 at a Freedom Crusade mission meeting in Tustin, California, I asked Fred and Ruth to share whatever they wanted to a group of us so that we would have video and audio documentation for this book. Fred was sixty-eight years old at the

1

time. The following short story is a bridge between two major seasons of my life, and Fred and Ruth walked with me through it all. Here are Fred's remarks almost word for word, with a few whispered interjections from Ruth.

"A DIVINE INTERVENTION"
by Fred Waugh

I'm not sure where to begin. First of all, the things I'm going to share were not a result of Fred Waugh, but a work of the Holy Spirit. My wife and I were privileged to have been a small part of what God has been doing over these years, and it's a real joy and pleasure to be able to share these things. I think it's good for us at times to recount the blessings of God and how he has moved in such miraculous ways. It builds our faith for the future. I believe that we are in a situation where a new wave is coming. We need to recognize that and to prepare ourselves. Lonnie asked me if I would share some of the beginnings of our involvement with him and the ministry. This goes way back, as Lonnie mentioned.

I was a businessman, a conservative Episcopalian, and so for me to get linked up with a long-haired hippie—well, that *had* to be divine intervention. As a matter of fact, when I first encountered these long-haired people, I was somewhere in Hollywood. I remember being up there, driving down Hollywood Boulevard and seeing these men with long hair, and I just had absolute contempt for them. Looking back, I think I actually saw Lonnie in Riverside years before we ever met. Here was this long-haired kid carrying a Bible. That was almost insult upon insult, as far as I was concerned. For me, it was 180 degrees from what one would expect in terms of a Christian. Long hair for men was supposed to be an abomination. At least that was my training.

I remember one time I was on the freeway with a very good friend of ours, Dr. Frost. We were headed to a meeting in Santa Barbara to share the good news of Jesus and the power of his Holy Spirit. We were on the freeway in my new Cadillac, fish sticker on the back window, talking and talking about the things of the Lord. An old rattletrap car pulled up alongside us. It was loaded with a bunch of these hippies with their long hair. I saw them look at us with kind of a strange look. My first impulse was to thumb my nose at them, but as I started to do it, it was like the Holy Spirit cut me off at the knees and spoke to my spirit, saying, "What if they saw the fish on the back of your car and knew what it meant?" Oh boy, talk about being cut down. I was humbled. I no more than had that thought when the kid next to the window picked up a Bible and pointed at it. He gave me the "One Way Jesus" sign. I immediately recognized—I really, really had an attitude problem.

Shortly after that in just a matter of weeks, we attended a convention down in Palm Springs. It was a Christian Business Men's Committee convention. A black man was the speaker at the morning meeting. We had heard this man before. In fact, he had attended one of our Bible studies in our home, so I knew him well. His primary message was that it's not skin that separates us—it's sin. But for some reason, instead of sharing his usual stuff, this day his message was to parents, and there were a lot of parents in the crowd. We're talking about two thousand businessmen and their wives.

He said, "A lot of you parents are sending your kids to hell because you can't look past the long hair."

Boy, that cut me deep. I realized that I was one of those. The whole "long hair" scene so turned me off that I couldn't even be civil to them.

The minister said, "If that's your condition, I want you to stand to your feet, and I want to pray for you."

Here were two thousand people assembled, and the Holy Spirit said to me, "You better stand up." So I stood up. There were probably three or four people out of the two thousand who were on their feet.

The speaker prayed for us and a miracle took place. I walked out of that auditorium, located our car, and at the first traffic signal that we hit on our way downtown for lunch, I saw three or four hippies on the street. As we stopped, waiting for the signal to change, we got into a conversation with these kids and had an opportunity to share Jesus with them. I pulled over, and when we finished sharing with these young hippies, one of them turned to me and said, "Since this convention has been in town, we haven't been able to walk the streets without getting buttonholed by Christians." He looked me right straight in the eye and said, "You know what? You're the first one who has made sense to me." An hour before, I wouldn't have even been caught talking to him, let alone sharing Jesus.

That was in January. The following March or April, around Easter vacation, I was invited to go with a group of businessmen to Denmark. We had been involved with a ministry called the Inner Church Renewal Ministries, headed up by Ray Bingham. The ministry's primary purpose was to share the reality of the Holy Spirit with the more traditional churches—pretty much working with the Catholics at that time. We had been involved with them in a number of their meetings before Ray asked me to go with him to Denmark.

Ray had met a young man who was involved with Campus Crusade for Christ. This particular young man had been filled with the Holy Spirit, which included speaking in tongues. This put him at odds with some of the doctrinal positions of his particular denomination. It was like with other situations where Christian organizations and denominations try to put the Holy Spirit into that "box" Lonnie often talks about. You can't box up God, but you can certainly grieve the Holy Spirit. Thank God many churches and ministries are more open now. However, at that time the gifts were not permitted, so this young man went out into the San Fernando Valley by himself to the malls and witnessed to kids who were just

4

hanging out. He eventually put together rallies in one of the theaters up there, gathering over a thousand kids.

Out of this group, there were seventy-five who accepted an invitation to Copenhagen, Denmark. The second International Sex Fair in Copenhagen was being put on by some of the darker forces of the secular world. Our group was invited by other Christians in Europe to go stand against the fair and to share our faith with the kids of Copenhagen. At that time, Denmark was the primary mover as far as pornography goes, before it was quite so prevalent here. Drugs were also a huge problem in Denmark. So we accepted the invitation.

We were at the airport with these seventy-five kids. They were all pretty clean-cut, but there was one kid with very long hair who slipped in. This was Lonnie Frisbee. It was 1970, and Lonnie was just twenty years old. For reference, I was forty-seven at the time. He was on Kenn Gulliksen's honeymoon. A woman back home had been aware of this trip and bought two tickets for Kenn Gulliksen and his wife, Joanie, as a honeymoon gift. However, Joanie couldn't make it because of her work schedule, so she prayed and thought that it was important for Lonnie to be on this trip and gave her ticket to him.

We went to Copenhagen and were there for Easter week. Right away, there were miracles on the streets. Our kids would work the fair and the streets during the day, and each evening we would assemble at a different church for a rally. It was absolutely amazing! God moved dramatically, and lots and lots of young people got saved! Lonnie led the way.

When we first arrived in Denmark, the local churches were all at odds with each other. However, by the last night that we were there, the churches in Copenhagen all came together. There was a breaking that, I believe, was really the beginning of a tremendous renewal for all of Scandinavia. The things that took place afterward you can almost date back to that time when the churches' hearts were broken for souls and unity. They humbled themselves and

5

came together, and from that point on, God really started to move. Many, many exciting things happened, but again, from my perspective, I wouldn't have been involved at all with those kids if God hadn't changed my heart the way he did that day in Palm Springs.

THE WHOLE LOAD

When we came back from Denmark, our priest at All Saints Episcopal Church knew that I had made the trip to share my faith there, and he asked me to speak with our congregation about what happened in Denmark. It was so far out for Episcopalians, so I told him what we were doing over there was "not exactly Episcopalian." They aren't known to go out on the streets and pray for people and things like that.

I said, "I better have lunch with you and share what took place. Then if you want me to share with the congregation, fine. I'll be happy to do that."

I gave him an account and his response was, "Fred, you're a layman. Denmark is a long ways away. You can get up there and share things with our people that I can't. I want you to give them the *whole* load."

I said, "Okay. If that's what you want, that's what we'll do."

A few Sundays later, I spoke at all three services and shared the fantastic and miraculous things that took place with those young people in Copenhagen. I finished sharing, and I think the priest gave the first altar call that had ever been given in that church. When he came to dismiss the service, he said, "I felt like there were a number of you who would like to know more about what Fred has been talking about. If you would, I'd like to have you come to the front."

That morning twelve people came forward. When we were in Denmark, we used a "four steps to peace with God" leaflet as a method to share the gospel with the Danish people. When these people came forward, I felt impressed to lead each one of them through those steps. Twelve people committed their lives to Christ

6

that day. They have been twelve very significant people throughout the years in that congregation. It has really been amazing to witness.

Well, one of the individuals who came forward was the Dean of Women from Rubidoux High School, which is in one of the harder areas of the Riverside community. We had been involved in a small home group with this woman and her husband. One of her fellow teachers had a young teenage son named John whom they had just discovered was involved in drugs. He was fifteen years old, had been pushing drugs for a couple of years, and was already in trouble with the law. His mother was a teacher and his stepfather was the representative for the California Teacher's Association. These were the kind of people who could not handle this kind of situation, so they brought this young man to me. We tried to talk with him, but really hadn't had much result.

The Sunday morning I was speaking in the church, this young man came. We had developed somewhat of a friendship by this time, and he knew that I was going to be speaking. He was one of the young people who committed his life to Christ that morning, which was really exciting for us! I wanted to give John something to remember his decision by, so I went out and bought him a neat little Oxford New Testament made of really fine leather. I wrote in it and put the date so he would remember the day he committed his life to Christ.

About a week later, his mother called on the phone and said, "John has taken off, stolen a motorcycle, gone to San Diego, and was caught by the police. He's now in juvenile hall. Will you go down to see him?"

Oh boy! I went down to juvenile hall, and they had these stalls where you could share with the kids. They brought John in, and I tried again to talk with him. However, the whole time he just sat looking at the ceiling, tapping his foot. When he got up to leave, I noticed one thing: He had that New Testament I bought him in his back pocket. It was all   crumpled up, and he had been sitting on it.

It was a mess! But I thought it was beautiful—he still had it. It was with him.

I thought to myself, "What are we going to do with this kid? I've got to get him with some young people who have been through the same problems he's been through."

My first reaction was to try to take him up to the San Fernando Valley and introduce him to the kids who went to Denmark. I mentioned this to our friends Bill and Lois Wade, who had just recently started attending Calvary Chapel in Costa Mesa.

Calvary Chapel baptismal service at Corona del Mar

They said, "Why don't you bring him down to Calvary Chapel?"

This was when Calvary was just beginning. Lonnie had come, and they were growing by leaps and bounds and had built the little chapel. Lonnie was speaking every Wednesday night, and there were well over a thousand people showing up to hear him each week. You had to get there at four or five o'clock if you wanted to get a seat inside. Otherwise, you were outside on the patio looking through the windows.

I had been so impressed with Lonnie in Denmark, so I set a date and said to John, "How about coming with us?"

He "sort of" agreed to come.

I said, "Okay, John. I'll pick you up Wednesday evening and take you down to Costa Mesa, and we'll see what's going on."

This was in August. August in Riverside is like 118 degrees in the shade. When I pulled up in front of John's house, he reluctantly came out wearing a big army jacket with the hood pulled up. He was trying to hide himself, really. He was all bundled up, and we couldn't figure it out, but conceded, "That's the way it is." So we

8

took him to Calvary Chapel just the way he was. We got in and managed to find good seats.

They started singing, and John was sitting there with the hood over his head trying to block the world out. As the huge crowd started to sing and worship the Lord, something happened. The atmosphere became electric. The kids in those days put their arms around one another while swaying

Lonnie (center, right) at a baptismal service at Corona del Mar

back and forth in the rows. You could see and feel the love of God. The energetic crowd cheered and applauded the original songs and the talented young musicians. Before long, I saw John take his hood off and tap his foot. Then he was clapping. Then he put his arm on the one next to him and started swaying back and forth with everyone.

That night, Chuck Smith announced a baptismal service at Corona del Mar. As we walked out of the service that night, I asked John if he'd like to go to that baptismal service Saturday afternoon. He didn't answer me.

Two days later, his mother called and said, "What's this about John being baptized Saturday?"

"Well, I don't know!"

She said, "John said he's going to be baptized on Saturday." For Episcopalians, being baptized is a *very* important event. His mother continued, "We would like to come and bring some friends. It's such a special thing."

I agreed, and that Saturday about noon we had a caravan from Riverside that went down to Corona del Mar to view the baptism.

We got there, and kids were *everywhere*. It was right at the entrance to the bay where the huge rocks are. Our group sat up on the rocks, observing all of this. Lonnie was there baptizing. Chuck Smith was there. There was a huge crowd of the candidates for baptism and countless onlookers. John was baptized that day. It was glorious! Children of the Day and Love Song were there worshipping in the midst with their guitars. Hundreds and hundreds of people were singing, "Come to the Water." Our people were so

Entrance to Pirate's Cove, Corona del Mar

moved, they could hardly handle it!

We had carpooled to Corona del Mar, so all of the cars were parked back at our ranch. Ruth had fixed some dessert. There must have been a dozen people there that night. We gathered in the house and sat around on the furniture and the floor, sharing with each other. John had his little New Testament with him. Ruth happened to spot him, so she said, "John, why don't you read something for us out of your New Testament?" John opened it up to Romans chapter 6, where Paul talks about being buried with Christ in baptism and then resurrected.

John's stepfather looked at him and asked, "John, how did you find that?"

"I just opened it up and started reading."

About two weeks later, his stepfather committed his life to Christ.

We started a caravan to Calvary Chapel every Wednesday night, regular as clockwork. This went on for several weeks. One day, as I was driving down the freeway, the Holy Spirit really started speaking to my heart. He said, "This shouldn't just be happening at Calvary Chapel; this should be happening in every church in the land. Invite Lonnie to come to All Saints."

I thought, "That's a good idea." I found out that Lonnie would speak at other meetings besides his Wednesday evening service, so I went and talked to Chuck Smith. I said, "If you respond to it, we'd like to ask Lonnie to come up on Sunday night."

10

Chuck said, "That sounds really great. When do you want to start?"

"Not before next Sunday."

He said, "That's fine with me, if it's all right with Lonnie."

I had talked to our priest first of all, before I went down to Chuck. Our priest said that, as far as he was concerned, it would be okay with him, as long as the two or three of us that had been going down to Costa Mesa in the caravan sponsored Lonnie, explaining, "If people start throwing rocks around here, I want them to throw them at you and not at me."

We talked to Lonnie and invited him to come up to Riverside, and he agreed to come. Lonnie had been written up in *Time* magazine, and they used a picture of this long-haired hippie in the article, so we took that picture and made flyers and passed them all over town, and people came. Lonnie brought the soon-to-be-famous group Love Song to do the music. That first night we had about seventy-five people attend, and three young people committed their lives to Christ. One of them was the daughter of the chairman of the board of our church government. This young girl went to our priest after she committed her life to Christ and said, "I had a date on Monday to go drop LSD with some kids, but I don't need to do that now." Her life was drastically changed.

As a result, our vestry said, "Look, we don't want you as individuals to be sponsoring this. We are going to do it as a church."

Like I said, the first night we had seventy-five, but the meetings grew like wildfire. We used to pass out a Good News Bible and a little packet for the kids to remember their commitment. In the first year, we passed out over a thousand Bibles to young converts. They came and went, but we got to a point where the church was literally standing room only. It was a tremendous thing that not only changed the lives of the kids in our community, but it revolutionized our church. The older people didn't necessarily relate to all that was going on, because it was far from an Episcopalian liturgical service. It was fashioned after a service at Calvary Chapel. However, the impact that it made is still being felt in our church and in our community today.

After a year and a half or so, Lonnie felt a call to Scandinavia, and as a result, we had to make some changes. Greg Laurie was invited to come out and be the minister of our Sunday night fellowship. Eventually, we thought it would be better for the hundreds of committed young Christians to be involved with the total church responsibility including the finances. We talked it over with our priest and decided that we would go down and talk to Chuck Smith. To make a long story short, Calvary Chapel decided to sponsor them in their own building, and those meetings evolved into what is now Harvest Christian Fellowship. The last figures I heard, they minister on Sunday to something like ten thousand. It is one of the largest churches in America, and Pastor Greg Laurie is still doing a tremendous job as the pastor. Praise God!

When we first started our Sunday night fellowship, we didn't feel like we had the freedom to pray with the young people to receive the Holy Spirit. We would invite them forward and have a prayer of commitment. Then after the service was over, we'd take them all to our home. We'd have a caravan from the church up to our house, and that's where we'd pray for them to receive the baptism of the Holy Spirit. In the relatively short time that we had them, I know of at least twelve or thirteen young men who have gone into the ministry full time as a result of our Sunday night fellowship. This is in addition to the launching and wonderful works of Harvest Ministries. It's really been exciting over the years.

Just a month or two ago, I received a letter from a young man who said, "You probably won't remember me, but I was going through my address book and ran across your name. I want to express my appreciation to you for touching my life. I came to All Saints as a drugged-out hippie and didn't actually commit my life to Christ at that point. I attended a number of the meetings and then went back to a school in Missouri. I eventually committed my life to Christ. It was the impact of All Saints and the Sunday night fellowship at your house that changed my life. I'm now a pastor in Newport, Oregon, and involved in the Youth Renewal Ministries in a denominational church. I just wanted to write and share this. You opened your hearts and arms to me and touched my life, which has been radically changed. I'm now in the ministry."

That has been repeated any number of times. It was nothing that we did. I was just the doorkeeper, the guy who greeted the kids. Lonnie was the minister. It gave us an opportunity to really touch Riverside and to change the atmosphere for the young people there. In fact, that was the vision that the Lord gave me. He gave me a vision of Landis Hall, the largest hall in Riverside at that time. In my vision it was filled with young people praising God. That was not only fulfilled literally, but Raincross Square was also filled with young people and praise. We really thank God—it was all because of him! He gave us the privilege of having a small part in it.

My friends Fred and Ruth have been an example of the older generation getting involved and serving the Lord, going on the streets sharing Christ, opening their home, demonstrating their faith as a family, interceding for missions, going to the nations themselves, and just simply being faithful and obedient servants of God in every way. From the very beginning of my missionary journeys, Fred was there. We met in Denmark and have joined in a vision for the Great Commission to this very day, traveling around the world together and doing missionary work in Colombia, Brazil, and South Africa. God has truly blessed our friendship!

I want to close this introduction by honoring my unlikely friends, Fred and Ruth, with a word of thanks and heartfelt gratitude for all their labor of love for me and Jesus our King. I am so blessed to have partnered with them. It is truly remarkable what God has done, and believe me, it is not by might, nor by power, but by my Spirit, saith the Lord!

LONNIE FRISBEE

Special Note:

I received a phone call in early 2016 from Marwan Bahu, who said, "You should film and interview this couple who were close to Lonnie. I was just at their house, and we had a great meeting."

"Who are they?"

"Fred and Ruth Waugh."

"WHAT?! Lonnie and I filmed them at a mission meeting in 1991, and they were pretty old back then!"

Marwan said, "Yeah . . . well, they just moved back to Riverside from Texas. They are both ninety-four now and still going strong! They had a houseful of mostly young people and were telling us great Lonnie stories. Ruth has an awesome anointing on her—and, of course, so does Fred. It was so cool!"

I took our whole crew and reunited with this amazing couple. We spent a week at their home in Riverside, CA, listening to stories and filming another interview—this time twenty-six years *after* the one Lonnie shared above (only now with great lighting and multiple professional cameras!) Praise God for Fred and Ruth!

Roger Sachs

"Not by might, nor by power, but by my spirit, saith the LORD of hosts."

Zechariah 4:6

ONE

Forever Young

I LOOKED OUT of my hotel room window at a huge crowd of mostly young people gathering below. I was in Gothenburg, Sweden, on the last leg of an around-the-world mission trip. It was the late seventies. As I continued looking down from our very modern high-rise hotel room, I could see literally thousands of people assembled around a nearby stadium, all lining up to see Bob Dylan live during a sixties music revival. It was reported that Dylan was drawing fifty thousand fans to his concerts. Suddenly, the Lord put a prayer in my head. He dropped it down into my mind so that I was very disturbed. Often when God wants to get one's attention, it's not necessarily a blessing. He can disturb the king in his sleep! He has disturbed kings many times, like when the handwriting on the wall said, *"MENE, MENE, TEKEL, UPHARSIN"*: "Thou hast been weighed in the balances, and found wanting."[1] So the Lord dropped this prayer down in my head: "Bring down the idol. Save Bob Dylan. Bring down the idol. Save Bob Dylan."

I was taking Danny Lehmann on his first overseas mission trip. It was actually the first time that he had ever been on any mission journey. Decades later he would be the missions director of the Youth with a Mission (YWAM) base in Honolulu, where he trained and sent out thousands of young people to hundreds of nations around the world on short and long-term mission trips. However, on that day we were together in Gothenburg, Sweden, and we had been invited to a Teen Challenge tent ministry with about fifteen hundred Swedish kids participating. Bob Dylan was also in town for a two-day music festival, and in my hotel room that first day, the Holy Spirit continued to speak to me about him.

The Lord said, "Bob Dylan is an idol to the young people. The wrong kind of idol."

19

Now, I understand teenagers or young people idolizing singers, but the Lord said, "Bring down the idol. Save Bob Dylan." I could clearly hear those words in my mind over and over.

I must mention that I am a Dylan fan. I honestly thought that God was going to have me go find Bob Dylan and lead him to Christ. Of course, we often naively interpret the will of God. So all day long on the day of the concert, I walked around Gothenburg looking for Bob Dylan on the streets. I would get temporarily encouraged in my mission because people would catch my eye and then come over to me and say, "Are you part of Bob Dylan's band?" and I thought, "I must be getting warmer!" Everybody was asking me that same question all over the place. I walked and walked for hours, hoping to find Dylan and lead him to Christ.

You know, some people would think that all of this would be a total waste of time: looking for a rock star on the sidewalks of a huge foreign city. However, I believe it was not a waste. I could feel the leading of the Holy Spirit concerning my involvement with Bob Dylan. Nevertheless, that day I did not run into Bob Dylan on the street and miraculously lead him to Christ. But that's what was in my mind. That's what my effort was. After a while, it was finally time for the concert.

Like I said, we had about a thousand to fifteen hundred Swedish Christians in our tent meeting directly across the street from the auditorium that evening. I started out by saying, "I realize that most of you would like to be across the street. I don't blame you, because I'd rather be hearing Bob Dylan sing folk songs from the sixties than listening to me." I admitted it.

"But," I said to them after the sermon, "let's do something different now."

I had everyone turn around, raise their hands toward the auditorium, and say together, "Bring down the idol! Save Bob Dylan! Bring down the idol! Save Bob Dylan!" We kept chanting this. There was a powerful, escalating buildup—it was amazing.

Suddenly, it felt as if a huge ball of white fire went flaming out like a cannon ball from the tent meeting. I could feel the anointing of God all over me. I screamed at the top of my voice: "SPEAK IN TONGUES!" and they all started to speak in tongues and have a wonderful, intoxicating time before the Lord!

While the meeting was still going strong, while we were all caught up in the presence of God, I slipped outside through the back of the tent, led of the Holy Spirit. There were thousands and thousands of people gathered for the concert across the boulevard. Many were still outside because Dylan did two concerts. He packed out the auditorium twice, so there were people there that night who hadn't heard him yet.

I heard the Lord say, "Go around here," and I obeyed him.

He said, "See that door right there? Go through that door." *This was wild!* Again he said, "Go through that door."

I opened it up . . . and walked right into the concert. Dylan was in a black jumpsuit with lightning bolts going down both sides. Everybody had BIC lighters lit throughout the whole auditorium. It was very ethereal. He had white makeup on his face in contrast to the black jumpsuit and silver lightning bolts. He was singing, "Forever Young." It was so positive, so unlike Dylan.

Within a relatively short period of time after that night, a member from the Vineyard Christian Fellowship was called out in the middle of the night to go share the Lord with a certain woman. She was Dylan's girlfriend. Bob Dylan was in love with her; this beautiful black girl was the one he wrote "Precious Angel" about. Dylan subsequently also received Christ into his life during this time period. Thousands of angels threw a party in heaven like it says in the Word.

"Coincidentally," as a side note, the pastor who led Dylan to Christ was himself led to the throne of grace by a person who "yours truly" led to Christ years before (so I was told). In addition, this pastor was involved directly with a ministry that I would shortly be working with in a major way: the Vineyard Christian Fellowship. So again, a person I led to Christ led a future pastor to the Lord, and then that pastor led Dylan to the Lord. This was after our Scandinavian trip. Isn't that interesting? I absolutely love Dylan's first Christian album, *Slow Train Coming*, and especially the song "Gotta Serve Somebody."

Because Dylan didn't work out in an evangelical fundamentalist setting, the rumor within the body of Christ was that he had fallen away from God. What's he supposed to do, though, go on a Full Gospel Business Men's speaking tour? Or sing, "*Ohhhhhh—He touched me*" at his concerts? And anyway, how can you go away from the Lord? "If I go to the top of the highest mountain, you are there. If I go down to the very depths of the sea, you are there, my Lord!"[2] God is everywhere and can see into the heart of a man to know where he truly is. God is very patient, and his loving-kindness never fails. We should also remind ourselves that none of us are finished products yet.

I am convinced that the Holy Spirit of God had a divine purpose in directing me to walk the sidewalks of Gothenburg, Sweden, all those years ago, diligently looking for Bob Dylan. I don't think that God led me in vain. There is a spiritual connection. I have been interceding for Bob Dylan for years. He faces pressures that most of us could not imagine. The Lord has poured out tons of grace upon me. Who am I to judge another? Love never fails, my brother, and Jesus is the one who can keep us "forever young" in an eternal kingdom!

This reminds me of several other improbable "coincidences" where I was indirectly involved in something that God was doing at the time. When you press into God, you will start to notice more and more of these coincidences along with answered prayers, divine appointments, and outright miracles. Pretty soon, it becomes *totally* impossible for something to be mere coincidence. Let me give a couple more short examples that are very special to me in which the Lord used me. Since we were talking about my experience with Bob Dylan, these coincidences also involve a few of my favorite celebrities. Believe me, only God can do these things, and to him be all the glory!

DONNA

I was listening to Donna Summer one day, and a Christian "brother" (in the presence of several other believers) said to me, "You're listening to worldly and heathen music!"

I told him, "I'm praying for Donna Summer's salvation," which was not true at all. I lied to them just to get that judgmental Christian off my back.

Later I told my missionary partner, John Ruttkay, that I had lied to a bunch of people about praying for Donna Summer's salvation. "John, I've never prayed for her salvation, so let's get down on our knees and pray for her (and a little forgiveness for lying)."

So we started to pray that Donna Summer would have the chains of darkness broken around her and that the Lord would bring her into a revelation of his Son. We were in Europe then. A short time after that, we heard that Donna Summer had met the Lord.

Well, I was on my way to a funeral in New York, flying with a friend, and on the way to the airport in the car, I said, "You know, Jack, I think the Lord is calling me to minister to Donna Summer. Now that she's saved, I also have a burden to intercede for her. I feel like I was part of bringing her in and that I should continue praying for her life and growth as a child of God."

I believe intercession has to be one of the highest callings in the body of Christ, and yet at the same time, one of the most thankless jobs. (By the way, when I talk about the "body of Christ," I am referring to every *truly* born-again believer in the world.) When we got to the airport, lo and behold, there was Donna Summer, standing there in a full-length mink coat, wearing diamonds that stood out against her beautiful, long black hair. I was so shocked to see her! Shocked, but not shocked, if you know what I mean. I immediately walked up and started to talk to her, which frightened her quite a bit. I walked past her entourage and started to talk with her, and she started having a panic attack. I had unknowingly broken through her comfort zone by being so bold.

However, it just so happened that Donna was on my plane. She was sitting in first class, and pretty soon the Lord spoke to her. She came to the back from her seat, looked around in the rear section of the plane, and found me out of hundreds of people in a packed out 747. She had me come up to first class and sit with her. We spent the whole flight to New York talking about the things of God. It was a very high moment in my life. Not just high in the sky, but high in the Spirit because I really felt like I was a part of her salvation and continuing Christian experience. What a beautiful princess she is!

TRUE REVIVAL

So that was my indirect involvement with Bob Dylan and Donna Summer. One night Blair from the TV show *The Facts of Life* came into our meeting, and the Lord gloriously baptized her with the Holy Spirit. Donna Summer brought her to the church that night. Another time I was getting ready to do a Bible study in Beverly Hills and decided to take a walk. I was just walking with the Lord and suddenly came across Johnny Rivers. We began talking as we continued along. Come to find out, he was attending my Bible study that evening. He shared with me how he had found Christ. I absolutely love divine appointments.

I'm reminded about one last short story relating to celebrities. Back when I met Johnny Rivers, at that particular time there was a great move of the Spirit among show people. The star dancer and singer from *Dreamgirls* got born again. He had been living a gay lifestyle, so his salvation started a real move of God among show people on Broadway. Because of one person coming to the Lord, putting his sins before the throne under the lordship of Christ, all of these show people came to the Lord and were born again. In New York as well as Hollywood, God began to move among the wives of some of the more notorious rebels, which included Gavin MacLeod of *The Love Boat*. It is so glorious when God reaches in amongst us regardless of our station or status in life. He knows how to get the "big ones." A true revival, like the one we were so blessed to experience in the Jesus People movement, is one that goes from "the guttermost to the uttermost!"

THE LORD OF THE HARVEST

My personal call to the Great Commission began after a visitation that I received in Tahquitz Canyon as a young eighteen-year-old hippie in the sixties. I was saved as an eight-year-old child, but it was ten long years later in 1967 when God called me to serve him. I saw a radical open vision. I was in the mountains near Palm Springs, when suddenly I saw thousands and thousands of people in the valley of decision. As the Lord lifted up my eyes, I saw a huge harvest field of people like a wheat field. In this visitation the power of the Holy Spirit surrounded me. Then I saw a light from heaven come down and ordain me, and I heard a voice say, "Go in my name for I have touched your lips with a coal of fire that burns ever before the presence of God. Proclaim to the people that I am coming back soon!"

From that moment on, my life changed. During the Jesus People revival, we saw with our own eyes thousands of people come to Christ. It was absolutely glorious! One photo published in *Eerdmans' Handbook to Christianity in America* captured exactly what I saw in a portion of the vision. In addition to thousands in the valley of decision, I saw a multitude of young people being baptized in the ocean. The vision became *reality* in less than three years! By 1971, the "Jesus Revolution," as *Time* magazine labeled the phenomenon, was broadcast on TV and the radio and in newspapers, magazines, documentaries, and books across the world. I was so blessed to be a part of it. Believe me, it was the highlight of my life! But now I want to grab hold of a powerful vision that a very prophetic man had. Bob Jones, a special friend, saw an end-time revival that will bring one billion souls into the kingdom of Christ in a final outpouring before his return. We are talking about the second coming of Jesus Christ. It is coming soon!

So as I open up this next chronicle of my life story, I want to dedicate it to the Lord of the harvest and to the Great Commission.

This next volume focuses on the command of Jesus to "GO!" God sent me literally around the world in 1978 to preach the gospel, which, for me, became such an important and foundational season of time. That journey set the pace and the focus for my entire life and ministry from that time on.

My greatest joy is to see people get radically transformed by a loving God and be adopted into an eternal kingdom!

Jesus declares—

"Say not ye, There are yet four months, and then cometh harvest? Behold, I say unto you, Lift up your eyes, and look on the fields; for they are white ALREADY to harvest! Pray ye therefore the Lord of the harvest, that he will send forth laborers into his harvest."[3]

TWO

Commissioned

SINCE WE ARE speaking and considering visions: God visited
a young man back in 1956. A twenty-year-old student was traveling
around the Bahamas, when he had a radiant vision from the Lord.
Loren Cunningham saw waves breaking over the earth. As a huge,
giant wave swelled up to crest and break, the wave suddenly became
thousands of young people sharing the good news of Jesus to all the
nations of the world. Therefore, from that vision the Lord birthed
Youth With a Mission, more commonly known as YWAM, which
has placed an emphasis on the Great Commission. So beware,
world, there is a great wave coming in these end times and a huge
harvest of souls being prepared.

Just as God called and raised up Gentile leadership to provoke
the Jews unto jealousy, so God has raised up para-church
organizations like Teen Challenge and YWAM to stimulate the
church to action. For too long the people of God have ignored the
Great Commission. While many *do* take this command seriously, for
the most part Christian churches do not design their budgets around
missions or pray for other countries or intercede for souls around the
world. However, God is not limited to any denomination, particular
leader, or popular doctrine. Don't think for a minute that God is
going to allow one puny denomination to bear the whole revelation
of the kingdom of God. And don't think for a minute that God is
going to give one clever teacher all the truths that are in the
mysteries of the Godhead. Nevertheless, I believe that God is
provoking, stimulating, wowing, drawing, and speaking revelation to
people about the importance of the Great Commission.

In Loren Cunningham's vision he saw thousands of young
people carrying the banner of Christ. They criticized YWAM in the
early years of the ministry. How can you trust young people? The

27

accusation was mainly implying, "How do you keep them from immorality when you have so many young people together?" You don't. And yet Loren lifted up the standard of holiness and sanctification in his camp. Young people *can* fit in God's structure pretty easily when they're in love with him! Also, God showed him that young people have a simple faith and believe in God in ways that older people usually cannot. Today, there are YWAM bases in over a hundred countries, with thousands of young missionaries serving around the world. I would say that Loren Cunningham has stimulated the Great Commission more than anyone through the obedience to the vision that the Lord gave him.

THE GREAT COMMISSION

And Jesus came and spake unto them, saying, All power is given unto me in heaven and in earth. Go ye therefore, and teach all nations, baptizing them in the name of the Father, and of the Son, and of the Holy Ghost: Teaching them to observe all things whatsoever I have commanded you: and, lo, I am with you always, *even* unto the end of the world.[4]

In 1977, I was on my second tour as one of the pastors at Calvary Chapel in Costa Mesa. During my first tour of duty, I had started a work in All Saints Episcopal Church in Riverside, CA, which developed into Harvest Ministries with Pastor Greg Laurie. I led Greg Laurie to the Lord when he was seventeen years old at Harbor High School. So I started the church in All Saints, then Greg took it over and began pastoring it. They have something like ten thousand members in the church now—praise God! I will be sharing a radical story about All Saints Episcopal Church and the call to missions later. But to back up, I was on staff at Costa Mesa, and after pastoring a year and listening to everybody's problems, my problems started to become bigger than the peoples'. Listen, don't go for the lie that everybody is called to the five-fold ministry. You know, you've heard of the five-fold ministry: *pastor, pastor, pastor,*

pastor, and pastor. It seems like the traditional church requires everybody to be a pastor. That's like wanting every part of the body to be a mouth, which would get old real quick! It's not all about pastoring. I hated pastoring! I hated pastoring simply because I'm not a pastor. I'm an evangelist. I'm a worker. I need to get out there and be with the people. I can't sit and listen to how many times people have committed adultery. *Hello!* You know, it can weigh you down.

The Lord has different kinds of callings, and he certainly placed a different one on me. On one hand, I realize how totally blessed I've been to be a part of several significant moves of God in the world. However, on the other hand, I can say from experience that there is much tribulation that comes along with the "callings" of certain people. It can break you. It's actually designed to break you because God loves to use broken people. If you are broken in this life, you might not be able to find a place in it 'cause you don't fit in. It's like a square peg in a round hole. So where people don't fit into this world, God has a place for them—in the family of God! And for people who don't fit in, he has a special place and a special purpose! You know what that is? That purpose is doing the work of the Lord that nobody else is concerned about at all.

AFRICA

One day I was watching a *Wild Kingdom* episode on TV about Africa. During one of the frequent commercial breaks, Marlin Perkins came on with a pitch for Mutual of Omaha Insurance. There were video shots of remote Africa in the background of the commercial with, you know, lions and elephants and cheetahs. Suddenly, the power of God through the presence of the Holy Spirit fell on me and filled me from the tip of my toes to the top of my head. The presence of God was so strong that it felt like my hair was on fire!

Lonnie and Marian

Then God spoke to me and said, "I'm going to send you to Africa. You're to quit your job and go to Africa."

So I told this to a sister who was with me, Marian (actually, I was engaged to Marian at the time). I said, "The Lord told me that I have to go to Africa." Then I started making secret preparations in my heart to go.

Soon after this, Pastor Chuck Smith came up to me and asked, seemingly out of nowhere, "How would you like to go to Africa?"

I told him that I would pray.

Chuck said, "Yes, why don't you pray about going to Africa," but he was probably thinking, "Yeah, that's where we'll send him. We'll send him to the edge of the world!"

Nevertheless, I had the bishop of the Calvary movement mentioning to me that I should pray about going to Africa. It was a powerful confirmation that went deep. It absolutely could not have been a coincidence. I already had the witness of the Holy Spirit to forsake my routine in Southern California and go to Africa. So now after Chuck approached me, I definitely became convinced that God was calling me to Africa at that particular time.

In the old days back in the forties, they used to say, "Better be careful. If you trust God in all this mumbo jumbo, you'll either end up in a mental institution—twinkin' and blinkin'—or in Africa, getting bit by Tsetse flies!" It was everybody's worst nightmare to be sent to Africa! Well, that's exactly what happened to me!

Once I agreed to obey the call, the leaders at Calvary Chapel laid hands on me in the presbytery and officially commissioned me out to Africa. Believe me, I was very excited! However, you can imagine my shock when, on the very next pay period, I reached in my mail slot to get my paycheck, but it wasn't there. I went down to accounting and was just a "little bit" upset!

The accountant said, "Pastor Chuck says you're living by faith now."

What?! I was flabbergasted. Calvary Chapel was sending me out to go to Africa . . . but they weren't going to pay for it! Chuck was sending me out by faith, without financial help at all. The huge church that I helped establish (practically from scratch) did not support me. I was very frustrated, but still felt called to Africa and determined to go. Thus began another faith journey.

I had a lot of free time, about a five-month period, between quitting Calvary and going to Africa, and my money ran out. I was just twenty-seven years old and had nothing. I had five cents in my pocket. I lived in my grandmother's house that I inherited and had two roommates, one being Peter Crawford. Peter wanted to be on the team to Africa along with a couple of other brothers. Both of my roommates had jobs and helped pay the bills, but none of us had enough resources for a mission trip to Africa. I woke up one morning and said to Peter, "We *must* take action or else the trip will all be lost." I felt an urgency to do something. So we went down to Costa Mesa Travel dressed up in our suits and ordered tickets around the world. We excitedly told the travel agent, "We are being sent out as missionaries from Calvary Chapel Costa Mesa and by Pastor Chuck Smith."

The travel agent said, "Oh, that's wonderful!"

It turned out that there was a new program set up by one of the airlines. We could go around the world anywhere in one direction for a year for $1,900 a piece. So we booked for Mexico, Venezuela, Colombia, Brazil, South Africa, Kenya, Israel, and Denmark, and then we decided to finish off our trip by going to meetings across the United States.

I remember looking up at the clock and noticing that it was 10 a.m. right as the travel agent was complimenting us on traveling so young.

She said, "We attend Calvary Chapel, and I even enrolled my daughter in Maranatha Academy."

I was suddenly struck with terror because I didn't know how I was going to pay for those tickets. I didn't have the money! The money wasn't even close to being in view. You know, the Bible says that God owns the cattle on a thousand hills, so I glanced back at the clock on the wall and challenged the Lord: "God, you have to sell a couple cattle quickly!"

Nevertheless, putting aside our fears, Peter and I mapped out our big grandiose plans and sat there with the agent, adding in this and that. The total came to five thousand dollars and some change. We walked out of Costa Mesa Travel, thinking, "Wow, the trip of a lifetime! This is incredible! We're going everywhere!" But then—you know how the drill goes—reality set in. We had three days to pay for the tickets, and so it was back to, "How are we going to come up with that kind of money?"

We ordered the tickets on a Monday morning. Three days later, I woke up kind of early and realized we had to pay for the trip that day. I moved very, very slowly. I was lethargic, you know, because we didn't have *any* of the money. I felt like just going back to bed. Peter and I were discussing this dilemma when the phone rang. It was the church secretary.

"Hi, Lonnie, this is Dee. Guess what?"

"What, Dee?"

"There's a check here made payable to Lonnie Frisbee for twenty-five thousand dollars!"

"No, Dee, come on! I'm not in the mood for this kind of joking. We ordered some tickets and need to pay for them *today!* We need five thousand bucks and don't have any money, and I'm not in the mood for jokes—period."

"But Lonnie, no, no, no. Seriously! I've never seen this many zeros on a check. I'm trying to count them all here. It's twenty-five thousand dollars made payable to *you!*"

"We'll be right down!" I screamed.

We jumped in Peter's car and sped across Santa Ana over to the offices of Maranatha Music where Dee's office was. We walked in and blurted out to Dee, "Let's see that thing!"

Sure enough, it was a cashier's check for twenty-five thousand dollars from the owner of an oil company.

The donor had wanted to remain anonymous, but I tracked him down from information on the check and a couple of phone calls. I was finally able to meet with him in order to thank him and ask why he mailed me such a mind-blowingly generous check. In 1977, twenty-five thousand dollars was a lot of money! It still is. I'll keep him anonymous, but he said he heard me share about my vision to go to Africa on a Teen Challenge radio program. He is a Christian man and said the Lord told him, "Send that young man, Lonnie Frisbee, twenty-five thousand dollars."

I asked him if he remembered approximately when the Lord spoke that to him, and our oilman friend shared with me, "The Lord told me to send you twenty-five thousand dollars, and I said, 'Okay, I will.' That was Sunday evening after listening to the Teen Challenge program. On Monday morning I went to my office, sat down, and typed out the check. Then I put it into my check writer and pushed the button to send it through. The check writer just chewed up the whole check. It was completely ruined. I said to myself, 'I *knew* it was the devil!' Then the Lord spoke clearly to me again, 'No, no, that was me! Make out another one and put it in there!' So I made out another check, ran it through the machine, signed it, and sent it in late Monday morning."

What a total blessing this obedient man was! It turned out that he was making out this check and sending it in at the *exact* same time that we were sitting in the travel agency by faith, racking up a five-thousand-dollar tab! There is no such thing as coincidences in the kingdom of God! In addition, we actually received the provision in the mail *exactly* when the money was due. On the very day! Another coincidence? Come on, this stuff is impossible without God being totally real! We joyfully paid the travel agency for the tickets. The

Lord definitely sold more than a couple cows that day! Thank you, Jesus! How fast God can put a little spring back into our step!

There is even a short story behind the Teen Challenge radio program, which played such a huge role in this miracle provision. In addition to Peter Crawford, my other roommate was Mike McCoy, who worked for KYMS, a Christian radio station called "The Gift of 106." Mike had been praying for our mission all along and started talking to the station manager about the trip to South Africa. So the station manager said, "Why don't you guys come down and do the Teen Challenge show?" The Teen Challenge host had to be out of town one evening, and it was a live radio show. They all knew that I could fill in for the program because for a season I had my own short spot on the radio. It was on that one and only Teen Challenge

program that our precious oilman heard me share about my vision to go to Africa. As a result, a millionaire had a visitation from the Lord, who told him, "Send that young man twenty-five thousand dollars." I'll never forget the emotions and gratitude and awe of God that welled up in my spirit as a result of this experience in a million years!

Right after this last-minute miracle happened, I was asked to fill in for Greg Laurie one evening because he was on vacation. Back during that time period, Greg used to have a regular meeting at Calvary Chapel on Monday evenings. Peter Crawford *definitely* remembers that evening very well and sums it up in the following personal account.

"YOU GO OUT THERE"
by Peter Crawford

Greg Laurie had gone to Hawaii with Chuck Smith that week, and so Chuck had asked Lonnie to come fill in on Greg's Monday evening meeting. The place was packed. There were at least fifteen hundred people there, if not more. We had gotten all of the Maranatha musicians together who had been friends of Lonnie. Oden Fong was there, and Tommy Coomes, and most of Love Song. All the old Maranatha music people were there too, and they played to the huge crowd, who loved it.

Then Lonnie said to me, "Okay, Peter, you go out there and tell them what we're doing."

By the way, this was my first time ever speaking in public. So I walked out there in front of around two thousand people, got on the stage, and knew what I wanted to say, but my lips were stuck to my teeth. My mouth just went completely dry. I couldn't speak! I couldn't do anything. Finally, I managed to say, "Well, we're going to South Africa to take it over for the kingdom of God!"

In spite of my lips being stuck on my teeth, we gave a short presentation to the crowd. I spoke along with some other people who we thought would be going on the team, and then Lonnie came to the rescue and took over. It was a great meeting with awesome music and, of course, Lonnie's anointed stories and preaching. We took an offering, and about three thousand dollars came in.

In addition, we told everyone that Maranatha Music, a branch of Calvary Chapel, had offered to take care of all the financial dealings for our mission. For a five-dollar or more donation, people would receive a copy of the Maranatha *Praise 2* album. We were also told that we could have all the money from those sales for our mission. Over the next few days, another couple thousand dollars came in. All the money, including our twenty-five-thousand-dollar donation, was given to Maranatha Music, since the church leaders were responsible for distributing our funds while we were on our trip. So in a matter of just one week, we went from no dollars to around thirty thousand dollars! Just like that— *instant provision!* And it came right when we needed it!

BILLY GRAHAM AND T. L. OSBORN

So Peter and I (Lonnie) were fully funded, energized, and, believe me, full of faith! Before I first went to Africa, the Lord said, "I want Billy Graham to lay hands on you, and I want T. L. Osborn to lay hands on you." Almost immediately, we saw in the newspaper that Billy Graham was doing a crusade in Las Vegas right at that time. Coincidence, coincidence! So Peter and I went to Las Vegas, which is a comparatively short drive from LA, to the Billy Graham crusade.

When we arrived, I called the Billy Graham organization and said, "Hi, this is Lonnie Frisbee from Calvary Chapel, and I would like to meet with Billy Graham. I want him to lay hands on me."

The response was: "Hahahaha! Oh, excuse me, Mr. Frisbee, you gotta be kidding!" That's what they said, "You gotta be *kidding.*"

"No, I'm not kidding."

And they said, "Sorry."

So I waited twenty minutes and called back. "Yes, this is Lonnie Frisbee, and I would like to be able to make an appointment with Billy Graham. I'm going to Africa and want him to lay hands on me."

"Hahahahaha! Do you know how many people are trying to meet with Billy Graham? Every star on the strip is calling."

So I waited a little longer and then made another telephone call. I shouted *really* loud into the phone, "What are you running over there? A *circus*? I want to talk to your top man in charge, and I want to talk to him NOW!" And they let me!

The man who came on the phone just so happened to be a man I had helped in his first LA tent meeting a few years back named Ralph. He agreed to meet with me and said, "Lonnie, you brought Love Song with you to my meeting. You came and sat in the front row and listened to me preach and didn't charge anything. Right now, I'm the only black evangelist in the Billy Graham organization. You're going to South Africa. You got it made in the shade, brother! Come meet me tonight in front of the podium about a half hour before the meeting."

So we met with our evangelist friend Ralph in front of the podium later that day before the service. The Las Vegas auditorium was already nearly full with thousands of people. Peter handed Ralph a printed article with our pictures on it and a short statement about our vision for the South Africa mission.

Ralph said, "Well, just a minute. I'm going to take this up and show it to Billy," and he went up on the platform and showed the article to Billy Graham.

Billy Graham briefly chatted with Ralph, looked at our pictures, and said, "Oh, I'd like to meet with them. Have them come and sit over here in the security area, and I will meet with them right after the meeting."

So we were escorted to the front row seats next to the stage. When the meeting was over, they took us downstairs into a security area in a long hallway, and there we met with Billy Graham. He was with his wife, Ruth, and several associates.

Lonnie and Peter with Billy Graham (far right)

He had just finished preaching to thousands of people, or actually, if you count the TV broadcasts, millions of people. As he walked up, it was almost like an aura was surrounding him, like a tangible field of the presence of God. Peter said it was like a ten-foot circle was glowing around him.

We told him, "We're going to South Africa. We're being sent by Chuck Smith and Calvary Chapel. Do you know anybody there? Can you give us any clues on what to do?" Because at that point we had no ideas at all.

Billy Graham said, "I was there and remember knowing a man named Bishop Zulu, probably in the Anglican Church. You could look him up. But let me pray for you."

So he and his associate evangelists gathered around us. Billy Graham put his large hands on us and prayed, "Father, I just pray that you would open doors for these young men beyond what they could ever possibly imagine and that you would go before them and bless their trip to South Africa."

We were almost speechless, but both managed a simple, "Amen in Jesus' name." What a total blessing!

And so Billy Graham laid hands on me in Las Vegas and prayed for our mission. I had already met with T. L. Osborn and asked him to lay hands on me for missions and evangelism. For anyone who is not familiar with the biblical practice of the "laying on of hands," it is a pretty big subject throughout the entire Bible, but mostly in the New Testament. Jesus himself laid hands on people when he healed

them, commissioned them, imparted gifts, and so on. That's what I was wanting from these two great leaders in the body of Christ, and I felt mightily led of the Holy Spirit to receive an impartation and blessing from them.

Now, T. L. Osborn was somewhat of a country bumpkin from Pocasset, Oklahoma. He said to me when we first met, "I went as a young man, as a ploughboy, to a William Branham meeting, and there were thousands of angels flying above my head, singing a song: 'You could do this, you could do this, you could do this,' and I walked out of that meeting with one of the greatest miracle ministries of our time." T. L. Osborn drew hundreds of thousands of people to his meetings. He's been one of the most successful evangelists around the world. I've seen him pray for people and their legs lengthen five inches. No jerking or manipulating the length. You know, I don't believe in manipulation. If God's gonna do the real thing, let's believe God to do the real thing! Let's not present a hoax or manipulate people into thinking something's going on when it really isn't. I absolutely refuse phoniness in the ministry. T. L. Osborn is one of my heroes of the faith, and I was honored when he too laid hands on me and prayed for our missionary calling.

THE TABLE WAS SET

It turned out that it was just Peter Crawford and me on the team—and, of course, Jesus! So the table was set, and we were about to embark on a totally new chapter of our lives. I knew this trip was radical and God-breathed. I sensed it in every fiber of my being. We were definitely called, set apart—and commissioned!

Have you ever felt the internal excitement and mixture of emotions just before stepping out into some unknown future? Many of you know what I'm talking about. I was feeling it all and knew that God was sending us to the uttermost parts of the earth to proclaim his goodness and love. It was exciting and life changing just getting us to this launch point. Only God knew what more would be waiting for us around the world!

THREE

Ready, Set, Go!

SO THERE WE WERE, two young men going off on this tremendous adventure with God around the world. We picked up our tickets and prepaid our house payments and other bills for about eight months.

The first part of our trip started in Mexico. We met a wealthy señorita in Mexico City whose ministry was distributing Bibles to prisoners. We gave her part of our suitcase full of Bibles for her labor of love to help minister in the prisons there.

It was also in a Mexico City hotel that I was in the shower, totally soaped up, trying not to use all the water (being a good hippie) because we had a water shortage in the United States. So I was soaped up, shampooed up, with soap on my face, and the hotel turned the water off for two hours—just before I could rinse off! So here's a little practical word to missionaries: If you can rinse, *do it!* I mean, I had soap in my eyes, soap all over my body, and I had to run quickly and jump into bed before freezing. It was the middle of winter. So if you have an opportunity to rinse, rinse. Enjoy the hot water while it's there, but remember, leave a little for your brother!

Also, my life was almost taken when I was caught in a hotel elevator that started going up before I was able to get out, pulling half of my body up while the other half was caught in the door! I never thought it possible to be killed in an elevator (it was an old Mexican elevator). It closed on me and started pulling me apart. Persecution had come to greet us spiritually and *physically*. It almost killed me!

VENEZUELA

Then we went to Venezuela, mainly to Caracas. Our time in the city was mostly socializing and absorbing the culture. Peter had old

41

college friends there, and we had several wild parties and outings along with a few personal guided tours of the surrounding area. We were also able to spend some time on the beach and enjoy the beautiful tropical food and see the simple ways of the peasants. I saw some of the most extreme poverty I'd ever witnessed in my life on the hills of Caracas, where the city was divided between the wealthy and the poor. I also became aware of the civil disorder in Venezuela. I could feel it in the spiritual atmosphere.

While we were there, Peter fell in love with a beautiful Venezuelan girl. Peter spoke fluent Spanish, so they would talk for hours. He had a real challenge on his hands. He knew beyond a shadow of a doubt that God had ordained and sent us on this journey, yet here was a huge temptation. This gal was everything a young, single, twenty-four-year-old American could possibly dream of! She was flawless, full of life, and absolutely beautiful.

Peter confided in me, "Lonnie, she is a perfect Natalie Wood look-alike, don't you think? Better yet, she is Natalie Wood with a spicy Latin flair!"

Many of the educated young women of South America are very free and outgoing in every way. After a couple of parties with maybe a little too much wine, she could not understand why Peter would not sleep with her. Believe me, it was only the grace of God that allowed him to keep his sanity and focus on what was really going on. The Spirit of God showed him that he would be jeopardizing our mission as well as dishonoring this gal. It was difficult, but he passed the test!

COLOMBIA

Soon we were off to Colombia. We flew into Bogotá, and the customs agent in our line was literally tearing apart everyone's luggage, apparently looking for drugs. Cocaine smuggling was big then, and this particular agent was more thorough than any of the others. Our line was absolutely crawling along compared to the rest of the lines. Peter was carrying a separate suitcase with about two

42

hundred Bibles in addition to the other luggage that we both had. As time dragged on *forever*, we became increasingly worried about this customs guy tearing us apart also. Finally, we reached the agent. Peter, who, as mentioned, speaks great Spanish, decided to offer up the suitcase full of Bibles first.

The agent said, "What are these?"

"These are Bibles."

"Are these Christian or Protestant Bibles?" In his understanding he probably meant, "*Catholic* or Protestant."

Peter truthfully replied, "These are Christian Bibles."

"Really!" He picked one up. They were New American Standard Bibles in Spanish. The agent said, "Well, look at this."

Peter replied, "Hey, would you like that? You can have that one."

The agent lit up. "Really? Wow! My own copy of the Bible. Thank you very much!"

Then he held the Bible up and called attention to all of the other customs agents up and down the line: "Look! These guys gave me a Christian Bible! Check it out!" He kept flashing this little red Bible and saying, "Look! A Christian Bible!"

Our excited customs agent suddenly blurted out, "Okay," and he just waved both of us right on through the checkpoint without even looking in another bag. We zipped up the Bible suitcase and walked right into Colombia. It was amazing!

Colombia was a total trip. We took a taxi from the airport to downtown Bogotá, found a hotel, checked in, and then hit the streets. Immediately, all these strange people were coming up to us, saying, "Hey! You want to buy some emeralds? *Psst!* You want some coke? *Psst!* You want some grass?"

As soon as we walked out on the street, that's what it was like. We were going, "No, no, no! We don't want any of that."

Finally, a young guy about our age named Francisco came up and also said, "Hey, do you guys want to buy some coke or anything?"

We said, "No."

By this time we were getting disgusted with this barrage, so Peter said, "But listen, we hear that Colombia has some of the world's best coffee. If you will just take us to a coffeehouse, we'll buy you a cup of coffee. You can sit down and talk to us and tell us what's going on in Bogotá."

So Francisco took us to a little coffeehouse, and we drank coffee and explained to the guy that we weren't there to buy drugs. We weren't there to buy emeralds or any kind of contraband. We were there to proclaim the kingdom of God.

Francisco asked, "What's that?"

Then we explained the gospel of Christ, how Jesus took our place on a cross, and Francisco's need to repent and receive that resurrection power in his life.

He was really listening. I could feel the Holy Spirit opening our new friend up, so we took him back to our hotel room and prayed for him, cast a demon out, and then Francisco got baptized in the Holy Spirit. It was glorious!

However, pretty soon the staff at the hotel confronted us, saying, "What are you doing? That guy's a drug dealer." They really scolded us for bringing a drug dealer into the hotel. Nevertheless, Francisco ended up getting born again. Praise God!

Years later on another trip, I was actually getting robbed in Bogotá by a group of young thugs when I heard someone yell out, "Wait a minute! I know this guy. Look, don't do anything to him!" It was Francisco. He probably saved my life that night, and I'm continuing to trust that Jesus eternally saved Francisco back in that hotel room in 1978.

CHILDREN OF THE PROSTITUTES

This first time in South America, I went out walking on the streets of Bogotá, Colombia, at three o'clock in the morning. What a stupid thing to do! I'd tell anybody off if they were walking around on the streets of Bogotá at three o'clock in the morning. But what did I know? Anyway, when I was out, I started to see little children, as young as three years old, sleeping in piles in the alleys beside trash cans like kitties. They were sleeping in piles! I'm talking about dozens of kids. They were sleeping in the alleys in the rain next to garbage pails—little children, four, five, and six years old. I lie not. I immediately asked somebody, "Who do these children belong to?"

They said, "They're the children of the prostitutes." In Spanish they said it: "*Son los hijos de las prostitutas.*" They don't practice birth control in Colombia since they are a Catholic nation in orientation. The poor people don't have any effective way of preventing pregnancy, so when a prostitute gets pregnant, she gives birth and dumps the child on the street as soon as the baby is weaned. In Colombia there are hundreds of children living on the streets and in alleys. It is unthinkable, but true.

I said, "Oh, God." Here we have millions of dollars in our churches' budgets. I went to these kids. I tried to—I don't know what I was trying to do. I was trying to touch them. I felt like if I could touch them, I could help them. You know, they were sleeping in piles! When I got near, they reacted like animals with wild eyes. Some of them ran up ladders to the roofs of the buildings around us. They *all* ran away from me just like alley cats.

I prayed to the Lord, "Wouldn't it be wonderful if somebody would start an orphanage here for these poor prostitutes' children?"

The Lord said to me, "Lonnie, what a wonderful idea!"

I ran all the way back to my hotel, jumped into my little bed, pulled the covers over me, put the pillow over my head, and cried out, "Ahhh, ahh, ahh, ahh, ahh!" because I didn't want to hear it.

The Lord said, "What a wonderful idea that you just had to start an orphanage for these poor orphans here in Colombia. What a wonderful idea!"

Ahhh, ahh, ahh! I didn't think it was such a wonderful idea after I said it. However, I soon realized that I couldn't start an orphanage in Colombia, because I had to go preach in South Africa. And that was the truth. Nevertheless, the seed was planted in my heart. I have been interceding for those children in Colombia ever since. This very second, there are little children in unbelievable circumstances trying to survive any way they can. *Please* pray for homeless kids everywhere.

MEDELLIN

Then we traveled to Medellin, Colombia, the cocaine cartel capital of the world. This was during the time when Pablo Escobar was the reigning Medellin drug lord who eventually controlled 80 percent of the global cocaine market. His cartel was smuggling over seventy tons of cocaine a month into the United States. We are talking *billions* of dollars of cocaine that went out of Medellin.

In Medellin we went into a prison. Calvary Chapel had adopted a Canadian missionary couple, Don and Georgia Rendle, who had moved to Colombia with their teenage kids and started a radical prison ministry. We were ministering to murderers and revolutionists and all kinds of strange people there in the prison. We brought medicine also. We soon discovered that the warden was taking all the money. He had a nice convertible, flashy clothes, and young blondes hanging on his arm. He looked more like a pimp than a prison warden. If you got arrested and thrown in prison in Colombia and didn't have wealthy parents, you were as good as dead. They fed the inmates this gruel, a grayish mop water with turnips floating on the top—like something out of *Oliver Twist*. The neglect of basic human needs in that prison was unbelievable!

We met some of the cocaine cartel leaders who the government had imprisoned. The cartel had not yet gained its billion-dollar power, but it was raising its head like a dragon while we were there. The "connected," rich prisoners had a soda fountain and a hamburger restaurant built in the prison. The cartel lords owned it. They paid for the soda fountain to be stocked with ice cream. One of the incarcerated cocaine lords treated me to an ice cream in the fountain that he built. He was a very nice man, and he was sorry that he was caught—but that's all. No conscience. So a wealthy

Colombian cocaine lord in prison could not only build ice cream fountains, but could still control his drug businesses from inside the prison. We saw some of the upper class in prison, but we also saw a *huge* pitiful sea of misery and destitute poverty.

At one point, we were locked into a patio where there were cutthroat murderers, homosexuals dressed up like women, and hundreds of prisoners begging and trying to touch us. Peter Crawford had a panic attack. He started hyperventilating and losing control of his ability to walk. He shook violently all over his body and became practically paralyzed. Then he cried out to God to have mercy because he was gripped by the fear that he was never going to get out of that place alive. However, I want to point out something scriptural here: We went in on authority and we came out on authority. We went in by faith and we came out by faith. Even though you might have periods of time when your confidence and faith might break down, the Lord is with you. And Pete did not have to stay in that prison with death, poverty, and sickness. This would be a good place to share a few of Peter Crawford's own personal reflections of that prison experience.

"A GLIMPSE OF HELL"
by Peter Crawford

Don and Georgia had been successful in leading maybe twenty to thirty men to the Lord there in the prison, so we went with them and spoke at a meeting. I interpreted for Lonnie. We prayed for a lot of the men in there. Some of them got baptized in the Holy Spirit, and others we were just able to be friends with and pray for them.

Then we went on a tour of the prison after the meeting. There were guys there whose entire life's possessions consisted of a pair of boxer shorts, a T-shirt, a spoon, and a toothbrush on a string around his neck. That was all they owned. As we walked around from cellblock to cellblock, I had never seen such faces of desperation in my entire life, and I still have never seen what I saw in that Colombian prison anywhere. There were people who were just helplessly hanging out from behind iron bars. They have become unforgettable and permanent snapshots in my mind of total dejection.

In this Colombian prison, if you wanted anything, you had to pay for it. These were mostly poor people who had been thrown in prison, so they didn't have any clothes to speak of. The food that they got, the normal slop that they were feeding them, was brought up in two big fifty-five gallon, stainless-steel barrels. The soup looked like dirty dishwater with little pieces of salad and maybe a green onion or something like that floating on top, and the color of the water was all gray. Then maybe the prisoners got a piece of moldy bread or a potato. I mean, it was terrible. If somebody was tougher than you and liked your shoes, they'd just take them. Or they'd take your pants. Or they'd kill you! So these guys were dirty and grimy, half dressed, and basically without hope.

We went into another cellblock, and I ended up getting locked in. It was one of the most frightening experiences I'd ever had in my life. I had never been around people that hopeless. It was just that I was so alive and these people were so dead, and they surrounded me. They were attracted to me and were pressing in from all sides—a huge crowd—I mean, out farther than you could see. I couldn't see Lonnie or the Rendles anymore; we got separated. The prisoners started talking and begging and putting their hands on me. I was not prepared to be completely surrounded by people in that condition. I was the only one who got stuck in there until they finally got me out.

AN ESCAPE

Like Pete indicated, some prisoners hid a toothbrush and a cup in their underwear because everything was robbed from them when they first arrived. You could have somebody killed for two dollars and fifty cents in that prison. While we were putting on a little recorded Maranatha concert in that Medellin prison, somebody was stabbed with an ice pick. It was beyond insane. We met the converted "Birdman," a famous revolutionary who allegedly killed hundreds of people during an upheaval in Colombia. He was one of the most feared men in the prison, but had become one of the kindest, most loving new creations I ever had the privilege of meeting. He permeated Jesus Christ from his life and his eyes. I'll never forget him. He was a well-known murderer, but under the lordship of Christ had become a gentle lamb, serving the people of God in the prison and helping the Rendles. I decided then that if I ever shared about what I saw in that Colombian prison that I would remember the Birdman of Medellin.

Days before we arrived in Colombia, a nineteen-year-old American had escaped from the prison. He had tried to smuggle cocaine, so they caught him and put him in prison. Over a period of time during his incarceration, this nineteen-year-old prisoner had become a very close friend of the missionaries and especially to the Rendles' teenage children because he was an American.

The son's father, who had a lot of money, arranged for him to escape. He paid the money to someone in the system, possibly the warden, because the family in America had become desperate about the plight of their young son. The father realized that without any help from home the boy's life was in extreme danger. He made trips to Colombia, but how could they care for him from America? How could they even reach into where their boy was? So they arranged an escape.

And he did escape, however, it was a set up. The army was waiting for him in a village, and they destroyed his body with machine gunfire. They shot him so many times that he couldn't even be recognized. The son of the missionary read it in the paper and saw a picture of the mutilated corpse in the headlines. The authorities had made an example out of him. They weren't going to let America get away with anything, so they slaughtered the nineteen-year-old American. It took a lot for the missionary children to recover because they had been close friends. Very sad story.

After a couple of trips to the prison, we ended up taking money out of our budget to buy penicillin for the teenage boys who had been raped in prison and were dying from syphilis. The prison opened the gates to the prostitutes every Sunday. The prostitutes would come in the prison, infect the prisoners, and then the older men would rape and infect the boys. There were some boys as young as fourteen years old who were dying because all they needed was a shot of penicillin. Some of these children had been thrown in prison as young teens for things like stealing bread, and then they were raped in prison. We brought in thirty injections of penicillin because this particular prison had no medical clinic. Venereal disease was rampant, and we had to inject the kids ourselves. It was something to remember! We made four visits to that prison in Medellin. I'll never forget those desperate *children* in prison.

STARSHIP HELMETS

In Colombia we also saw solid gold religious artifacts dedicated to the gods of cocaine. The ancient worshippers wore solid gold hats that came down over their ears like Venetian starship helmets. At one place we were brought into a room guarded by armed soldiers with machine guns. Inside they were playing piped-in lute music from Colombian Indian whistles. They turned the sound up and turned the artificial lights on. From the ground up in the large room, there were treasures and artifacts of solid gold with glittering light reflecting off, creating a shiny, orange glow. Immediately, I was very aware of the ancient heathen spirits who ruled over the religion of the idols.

Colombia has millions of precious people, but there is a huge war battling over their souls. We could see it, feel it, and even experienced some of it ourselves. In this battle between light and darkness, which is so "in your face" in Latin America, we need to focus on the one true light—Jesus, the light of the world!

What we need to do more than anything is put on the helmet of salvation detailed in the Bible, not Venetian starship helmets of gold. Listen to God's instructions to us:

> For we wrestle not against flesh and blood, but against principalities, against powers, against the rulers of the darkness of this world, against spiritual wickedness in high places. Therefore take up the whole armor of God, that you may be able to withstand in the evil day, and having done all, to stand. Stand therefore, having girded your waist with truth, having put on the breastplate of righteousness, and having shod your feet with the preparation of the gospel of peace; above all, taking the shield of faith, with which you will be able to quench all the fiery darts of the wicked one. And take the helmet of salvation, and the sword of the Spirit, which is the word of God; praying always with all prayer and supplication in the Spirit.[5]

BRAZIL

Then we moved on to Brazil, and this was the introduction to a country that I would fall in love with and that would always be an important part of my life. It was on this first major missionary journey when I received a burden for Brazil. We came in on Carnival, which is a huge celebration in Rio de Janeiro that has been celebrated in Brazil for hundreds of years now. Carnival is a world-famous spectacle with music and dance, parades filled with rainbows of brilliant color, endless energy, and beautiful people. It is amazing! At the same time, there's a lot of heathenism and revelry practiced.

It was actually a few days after Carnival when we arrived. Nevertheless, people were still running around in their costumes and bathing suits—I mean, there were bathing suits and costumes *everywhere*. Carnival never really stops in Rio. This great city was just a stopping point that we had from Colombia to South Africa, and I suggested that we just blow on through Brazil. Peter Crawford knew better. So we ventured into Rio to have the total culture shock of the trip, with its topless beaches and super outgoing people. However, in spite of the party atmosphere, the first thing we were greeted with was the news that three sailors had been shot *right* in front of our hotel room after we arrived!

A thief had murdered a nineteen-year-old black boy, an American sailor in port during an official visit with President Jimmy Carter. Three sailors who were part of the president's entourage were shot, but only one fatally. We had just left Colombia where a nineteen-year-old American was brutally killed, and then greeted in Brazil with another nineteen-year-old American gunned down, this time in a robbery. How quickly a young life can be snuffed out and how vitally important that each of us is prepared for eternity. The Bible declares that death *is* our last enemy, but Jesus conquered the grave and has made a way past death for all who will come to him!

As we were recovering from jet lag, we discovered that there were two medical nurses from the States staying next to us in the German hotel we had chosen. We happened to come out of our room at the same time and said, "Where are you gals from?"

"California. We're missionaries."

I said, "We're Christians too. Where do you go to church?"

"Calvary Chapel in Costa Mesa."

Wow! It just so happened that the nurses were meeting a couple of other sailors from the president's ship. We decided that we didn't like that, so we went with them as chaperones on their dates with the sailors. I felt like a brooding hen, but the young sailors were cool, and as a result of that, we were invited onto the presidential vessel, which housed five thousand men. We started eating our meals with the Americans, going on the ship every day. We discovered a ministry among Americans, because they were brokenhearted about their friend being killed. They had a big funeral on the ship for him, and then they sent the body back to America.

In March 1978, our journey through Central and South America came to an end. We said goodbye to all our new friends in Rio, especially to the American sailors and marines guarding President Jimmy Carter on his good-will mission to Brazil. What an eye-opening adventure this first leg of our trip had been. The Lord showed us so much in Mexico, Venezuela, Colombia, and then Brazil. The needs of the people were and still are overwhelming. They are overwhelming for both rich and poor. I could actually feel the powerful dark principalities over the nations and was so aware of the war going on in the spirit realm, a war that attempts to enslave mankind and keep people away from Christ, our Redeemer. I was also reminded that the warfare for each of us in this life is real, and the stakes are high. The stakes are our eternal destinies.

On the upside, we had made so many new friends along the way and had powerful divine appointments. Ministry can be brutal and hard sometimes, but God always mixes in just the right amount of fun, adventure, and agape love! I was and am *so* grateful that Peter Crawford talked me into staying over in Rio instead of quickly jetting off to our next destination. Brazil stayed in me. Nevertheless, I knew in my spirit that our next destination was the main event of our mission. I had fallen in love with Brazil, but in my heart I was already saying, "Africa, here we come!"

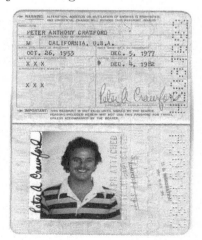

FOUR

South Africa

ON ALL MY missionary journeys over the years, people have often asked how I muster up genuine faith for any upcoming trip. The answer is that no matter how broke I might be or how crazy the circumstances, I simply visualize myself on the plane, and it happens. There I am, looking out the window! When God ordains a mission, he makes it happen. Me visualizing myself on the plane heading to a particular destination is the tool I use to bolster my faith, and then the Holy Spirit takes it from there. It works for me!

So Peter and I boarded our jet to Johannesburg, South Africa, from Rio, and I was so excited to actually be "in the air" on my very first visit to Africa. On this long flight from Rio, a young gal named Hildegard was seated next to us, and pretty soon we learned about her

unfortunate adventures in South America. She had been robbed in Peru and lost her passport and all her money, basically everything she had. However, after much intrigue, the South African Embassy finally helped her get a return ticket to South Africa. We talked to our new friend all the way across the Atlantic Ocean. She was a very sweet gal who lived near Cape Town. When we landed in Johannesburg, we said a quick goodbye to this brand-new friend, and Peter wrote down her address, which turned out to be in Durbanville. He insisted on handing her a twenty-dollar bill. She didn't even have food money and was still a long way from home with a connecting flight the next day.

Before we left on our mission, I met a young guy back in California who was from South Africa named Steven Boschoff. His father was a doctor in Johannesburg, and Dr. Boschoff had agreed to pick us up at the airport and to host us "in country." What a neat man! For a couple days we felt like jet-lagged zombies. After somewhat recovering, we rented a little VW Bug and started to explore Africa. Peter almost had a heart attack driving on the wrong side of the road! Over there they call the traffic lights "robots," and almost every junction is a fast-moving traffic circle with all the cars going in the "wrong" direction full speed away, looping to the left clockwise. It takes a little practice to survive, believe me!

The initial feelings, impressions, and sensations of Africa that I experienced are hard to put into words. First of all, I had this sense of vastness, of everything being huge. I could literally feel an open heaven with God's love for Africa tingling in the air. I could almost reach up toward the clouds and touch it—all of creation and beauty, along with danger and adventure. It was an "alive" feeling more than anything else. At the same time, I could feel and see the pain and poverty and hear the cries of God's children. It happens every time I set foot on that continent. I tap into the pure love and compassion of Jesus—and it is addictive. I have gone back to Africa at least once every year for fifteen years or so. I love Africa with all its wonders!

In addition, I had no concept of "white Africa" or anything at all about South Africa, its history, geography, or politics. I must have slept through geography class or whatever in high school, but I was getting a quick firsthand education in 1978. In the past when I thought about missions to Africa, somehow I pictured that I would be ministering to black Africans, maybe like Reinhard Bonnke does. There is a video of one single Reinhard Bonnke meeting in Nigeria with over a million people attending. It is amazing! But on this trip, it soon became clear that God was sending me primarily to the white South Africans. I didn't even know there was a large white population in Africa with modern cities and highways. In spite of the bad press, I personally discovered the South Africans to be a very loving people overall—both white and black.

The two official languages of South Africa are English and Afrikaans. I love the accent of the people when they speak English. There are lots of other languages there too, like Zulu, Tsonga, and Sotho, along with regional dialects. The history of the country is quite interesting, which I won't get into, but the Afrikaans language originated from Dutch. I think Afrikaans is such a beautiful-sounding language, although I don't understand a single word. Almost all of the whites, as well as millions of black South Africans, speak both English and Afrikaans. One of the perks of being a missionary is being able to absorb all of the different cultures along with the unique and super interesting people. Each one of the fifty-four countries on the African continent definitely has plenty of uniqueness to absorb.

I knew about racial prejudice back home in America, but it was definitely on steroids in South Africa. In 1978, apartheid was in full force, and the division between black and white, as well as the division between black and black, were undeniably visible and very shocking to me. Like I said, I thought the Lord was calling me to black Africa. I didn't realize he was also calling me to the white supremacists! But he was, and Jesus is the one who wants to break down the walls between all of us. I was soon to learn that the most rejected minority is the multiracial population of Africa, called the *mulattos*, or "colored." The whites reject them and the blacks reject them, but I think they are one of the most beautiful people groups in the world. I have black friends and brown friends and white friends and everything in between. I can hear the line in the John Lennon song: "One thing I can tell you is you got to be free—*come together right now over me!*" Poor John had the right idea.

PETER'S VISION

My friend Peter Crawford is a very gifted and spiritual person. Practically my whole ministry has been a demonstration of the gifts of the Spirit, and we both *strongly* believe in dreams and visions. In fact, Peter shared a powerful vision with me before we even got to South Africa. Back in the fifties and sixties, there was a long-running TV show called *Bonanza*. It was an old western adventure series about a ranch up in Nevada owned by Ben Cartwright and his three sons. At the beginning of each weekly program, a huge map of the *Bonanza* ranch would come on the screen and a little flame would start to burn in a section of the map. The flame quickly began to flare up, spreading outward until the entire map was consumed in fire, all while the familiar theme song blasted away.

In the vision, instead of the *Bonanza* homestead, Peter saw a map of Africa, which slowly zoomed in on South Africa. Next, it zoomed in even closer to Cape Town and then out of Cape Town. A flame just like the flame on the *Bonanza* map started to burn the map that he was seeing. It spread in two directions from Cape Town, going up the Indian Ocean coastline and then right up the middle of the country. There were two main branches of fire, and they quickly spread north and came together in the top part of South Africa. The entire map was then consumed in flames. At that time Peter felt like the Lord was saying, "I'm going to start a revival, and it's going to burn along these corridors. It's going to burn this nation up with the love and mercy of God because I am a consuming fire!" His vision encouraged both of us as we began our adventure, though neither of us would know the full meaning and impact of the vision for months and even years to come.

THREE WEEKS OF NOTHING

Once we were ready to start ministering, we didn't really know what to do. I only knew I had this message inside that was from God. Our host, Dr. Boschoff, would suggest, "Why don't you check out this church?" or "How about that church?" in an attempt to discover an open door to minister to people in South Africa. Nevertheless, every church we visited was a cold shoulder and a closed door. We heard about a group called the Walk, which came out of a controversial ministry founded by John Robert Stevens back in the States. They practically mocked us and said, "The day of the traveling evangelists is over. Go home!" It was very discouraging.

We heard about a church in Pretoria, a city close to Johannesburg, so we drove up there to visit Hatfield Baptist Church. We met with the assistant pastor in his house, where he questioned us for quite a while. Then he asked about our music preferences, specifically if we liked "Christian rock." We said we *loved* Christian rock and all kinds of contemporary Christian music. That got us blackballed from there. Apparently, this particular church had a bad experience with "super loud" Christian rock.

For three weeks absolutely nothing happened. We continued exploring South Africa, meeting people, visiting churches, and it definitely wasn't all wasted time. Then during the week of Good Friday, which fell on March 24th that year, we happened to be back in Pretoria and found out that Hatfield Baptist Church was having a special Good Friday service. Peter and I decided to attend. We didn't plan on meeting with any of the leaders again and simply wanted to honor and remember the price Jesus paid to rescue each of us. That Friday evening meeting was a divine appointment for me like no other and was absolutely off the scale.

The Bible indicates that often it is better for someone else to tell a story than oneself, especially if it is praiseworthy or something one might have a tendency to boast about. I have my shortcomings, but I always point to the One who makes it all happen. I'm going to have Peter Crawford share from his perspective about that meeting at Hatfield Baptist Church along with its aftermath. We audiotaped Pete's account almost like a travel journal. He is an eyewitness and much more of a "detail guy" than myself, and in this case, you need to hear the details. Only God could have orchestrated what happened, and only *he* deserves all the praise and all the glory!

"A NATION IN A DAY"
by Peter Crawford

Lonnie and I went back to that Baptist church on Good Friday of 1978. There were well over a thousand people in church, with many weeping and on their faces in prayer. The presence of God was so thick it practically overwhelmed me. Lonnie immediately said, "This is where we're supposed to be!" We found a seat, which was kind of in the middle of the large church. I mean, the entire time we were there, it was like this fullness and sweetness of God's presence was everywhere. That evening, the church had set up several microphones spaced out in the aisle so that anyone could share what Jesus meant to them or a good word from God on this special day of remembrance.

It was refreshing to see a congregation that actually put into practice and encouraged the biblical exhortation in 1 Corinthians 14 that they could all share a word, song, or revelation from God. However, none of the microphones were near our seats. Nevertheless, pretty soon Lonnie stood up and started out with: "Thus saith the Lord!" and paused for a second.

Immediately, the senior pastor, who was way up in the front of the church, cut in and said, "Brother, would you mind stepping to one of the microphones in the aisle over there so that what you share everybody can hear? We would love to be blessed."

Lonnie replied, "I don't need a microphone! I have a microphone voice! THUS SAYETH THE LORD!" Then he belted out this prophecy. I can't remember the whole word, but it was along the lines of, "The day of the superstar in the body of Christ is over. Just as my loving presence is heavy upon you right now, so I am going to pour out my Spirit upon every open and willing heart!" The word was much longer, but what hit me the most was that the presence of God in the room was magnified to a level that I had never felt before. It was beyond goose bumps! I hope that it was recorded, but I just remember the senior pastor leaning over to the assistant pastor and saying something in his ear.

Soon after the meeting, we were invited over to the assistant pastor's house for the second time. This time he said, "So—what are you guys doing here again?"

Lonnie said, "Well, we just really feel that God has called us to South Africa, and he sent us with a message about the individual priesthood of the believer. You know, that God is not only going to use your Billy Grahams and your T. L. Osborns, but he's going to put his anointing on every single believer. Every single believer is capable of being a minister of the gospel. He sent us with that message for South Africa."

The pastor said, "Look, we have a national leadership meeting Tuesday morning. Why don't you guys stay over with us and come to the meeting? You can share that message with the leadership."

So we stayed and celebrated Easter with them in Pretoria. Over the weekend we met an American missionary family connected to the church, and they treated us to hamburgers. It was so cool to have a little touch of America so many thousands of miles from home.

Then on Tuesday morning, we went to the leadership meeting. Now remember, for three weeks nothing, absolutely nothing at all was happening for us. Then here we were showing up at an elders' meeting at ten o'clock in the morning. We walked in, and pastors and leaders from every city in the nation were sitting there. So Lonnie shared with them. First, he gave them some credentials: "I've been with Chuck Smith. I was involved with the Jesus movement, and I was with Bob Mumford, and I was with . . ." He gave them quite a Who's Who. "And this is the message that we have and why we came."

After about an hour, they said, "Brother, we really believe that God has sent you. We want to invite you to come to our churches."

And just like that, God gave us the entire nation. The Bible asks, "Can God make a nation in one day?" In our case God opened the door to a nation in one hour! At that point we had to decide: "We can go here, here, and here, but we can't go there." I mean, we actually had *way* more invitations than we could possibly accept in the time that we had left. In one hour God had given us a totally open door to South Africa!

ON THE WINGS OF AN ANGEL

Right after that radical meeting with pastors from all over South Africa, Peter Crawford and I (Lonnie) received a long distance phone call from the States. It was our old roommate in California, Mike McCoy.

"Guess what, Lonnie?"

"What?"

"I was watching TV, and the Billy Graham crusade from Las Vegas came on. They are just airing it now. It's from the crusade a couple months ago when you guys went to Vegas and met Billy Graham. It was actually the Sunday morning meeting. You left after the Saturday evening meeting and came back here to Santa Ana, but Billy Graham came on the next morning and said, 'Last night I met two young men who are going to South Africa, and I really think that their mission is from God.' Lonnie, he asked everybody to pray for you. Isn't that wild!"

It turned out that they did not edit out that part of Billy Graham asking everyone to pray for us in the Las Vegas crusade when it was televised. We had met with Billy Graham in early February, and it was televised almost two months later, which, coincidently, is the Easter season of 1978. So right about the exact same time that we were sitting in an elders' meeting in Pretoria, South Africa, Billy Graham was on national television asking *millions* of people to pray for the two young men from California! Come on—you *cannot* make this kind of stuff up! God took those prayers on the wings of an angel right down to South Africa and opened up a nation to us from one end of the country to the other in the matter of an hour!

KRUGER NATIONAL PARK

When you're a visitor in Africa, you definitely want to see some of the animals. You know: lions, elephants, giraffes, rhinos, and cheetahs, to name a few, which we saw year after year on the TV show *Wild Kingdom* with Marlin Perkins. As we started going through the ministry invitations and then sorting out our schedule, our new friends at Hatfield Baptist Church arranged personal guides for us to check out Kruger National Park. It is a huge wildlife reserve, 220 miles long and around 50 miles wide, about the size of Wales in the British Isles. It has everything and then some. Our guide and friend from the church, Sippy, drove us in a Land Rover to the famous reserve. Sippy turned out to be quite the practical joker and a real joy. A little fun and adventure before a hectic schedule of back-to-back ministry and meetings was definitely in order. Off we went— safari style!

It was quite a drive of a couple hundred miles or so just getting to Kruger, which is northeast of Pretoria. We stayed in a hotel just outside of the park. The next day we drove into the colossal reserve and eventually saw a couple herds of animals, but not that much otherwise. We kept driving and driving down this long winding asphalt road for miles and miles without seeing much of anything. Then we saw a little dirt road that was blocked off by a big old log.

We were getting really tired of not finding the wildlife, so we all agreed to take a little unauthorized side tour. We pulled over, got out of the car, lifted up the log, drove through, replaced the log, and took off down this narrow dirt road inside of Kruger National Park.

Pretty soon, the dirt road wound around, went up, and then dipped down into huge gullies with wide-open vistas. We had to ford streams and things like that; it was very cool and a much better adventure. At one point we came up on a bunch of workmen, who stood up and turned to look at us. I could read their minds: "What are these crazy white people doing out here in this national park on our dirt road in the middle of Africa?" We just waved at them with big smiles and kept driving. It was a riot!

I remember coming around a curve and spotting three adult giraffes just standing there behind some trees. I said to Sippy, "Stop!

I want to take some pictures." So I got out of the car with my camera and slowly started walking toward the huge giraffes. I went quite a distance past a clump of trees, looking for the best angle to capture these guys on film. The giraffes were chomping away on some leaves way up high and not paying attention to me at all—so far, so good. I felt like some great white hunter stalking his prey! The guys stayed back by the car and were just watching and waiting for me to get my shots.

Suddenly, I heard Sippy screaming at me, "Lion! Lion! Lonnie, there's a lion!"

I spun around in a panic and started running like crazy. My heart literally about jumped out of my chest. I had previously walked around a huge grove of trees, but now I ran full blast through the trees, taking a short cut back to the car. Then even *more* suddenly, right in front of me at eye level was this huge spider about the size of my head in the middle of this massive spider web. Believe me, I had to slam on my brakes and almost ran right into him. I lie not! It was freaky scary! I hate spiders, and this one looked like one huge man-eating spider that could give me nightmares for the rest of my life.

Then I heard Peter and Sippy laughing like crazy. There was no lion. Sippy had decided to play a little cruel joke on the great white American hunter. It took about half an hour for my heart to stop pumping massive amounts of blood into my brain. I got back into the safety of the Land Rover, and my "friends" were still cracking up.

"I'll get even with you guys later if I don't have an aneurysm! Just wait!"

We continued having fun cruising around and seeing different things in the park that we hadn't seen on the paved road. We saw some water buffalo, some hippos, and a few other animals, but to our disappointment, no elephants or cheetahs or *lions* that day!

However, pretty soon we came up on a whole troop of baboons out in the middle of the dirt road and all over. We stopped to check them out, and Sippy said, "Watch this!" We had a big bag of Starburst hard candy in the car, and he unwrapped a few, rolled down the window, and tossed out the candies. The baboons went absolutely crazy. What we didn't expect was that within a couple of

minutes, about fifty baboons completely swarmed our vehicle. We had to roll up the windows *real quick*. They were jumping all over. It was scary! Have you ever seen the fangs on a big male baboon? We did! We cracked a window and quickly threw out some more  candy with the wrappers still on and everything. A huge male was stealing all the candy from the females and ate the Starbursts, wrappers and all. We watched for quite a while. The hood of the car was covered with baboons intently looking at us, waiting for more candy.

With the windows rolled up, it got really hot inside the car almost immediately. Sippy said, "No problem. I'll turn on the air conditioner, and we'll just watch these guys."

The real problem was that on this Land Rover of ours, the air conditioner intake was right at the base of the windshield and two huge baboons were sitting right on the intake with their big baboon butts. So we ran the air, and pretty soon some nice, cool, Freon-generated airflow started to refresh us as we continued to watch the circus surrounding our car. Then all of a sudden, this super nasty baboon-butt odor was sucked into the ventilating system, creating an incredible refrigerated baboon stink. It was beyond unbelievable! We were trapped inside with the worst smell ever and fifty baboons all around us.

We kept screaming, "Oh man, we gotta get out of here! What are we going to do? We've got to get out of here!"

So Sippy started the car up, revved the motor, took the whole bag of candy, cracked the window again, and just tossed it. The baboons all scrambled and were tearing the bag apart in a huge free-for-all—and we got out of there! It took almost an hour to clear the smell out. It was so bad. I mean, it was *bad* bad!

Eventually, after lifting and replacing another big log, we got back out on the paved road. Later that day, we came up to one of the ranger stations. There were a bunch of cars there, and you could use a restroom and also buy drinks or souvenirs. We happened to overhear the rangers talking on their radios, saying, "There's a car with three or four guys that went down one of the side roads, and we're looking for them." We listened to this whole thing transpire on the radio. They were out searching for us! We silently chuckled to ourselves because we couldn't really say, "Hey, we're those guys! We confess!" We weren't going to admit to anything and possibly get fined, thrown in jail, or maybe "thrown to the lions!" Who knows? By the way, there really are hundreds and hundreds of lions and elephants in this world-famous reserve. Kruger National Park was a trip!

After that leadership meeting in Pretoria and our adventure in the great reserve, our mission around the world took on a brand new beginning with a fresh anointing that was being poured out. It was like sweet manna from heaven. I love it when the supernatural of God descends upon our lives. It's like we're suddenly walking in another dimension. Oh, that we could stay in that presence and walk in his dimension every moment of our lives! Come on people, taste and see that the Lord is good! We probably can walk in union with his presence every moment—in theory. But then, of course, God is working with "cracked pots," you know, earthen vessels with a few cracks here and there. In this process, he has adopted us at an unbelievable price, and then over our lifetimes, sprinkled with a little success here and there and many failures, he reshapes us into the likeness of his Son. He constantly looks deep into our hearts. Soon enough, when it's all said and done, we will see him face to face and "know him even as we are known."[6] It is one of the great truths of the Bible for every believer. In spite of our cracks and crevasses, Peter Crawford and I were riding high on the crest of a wave that was about to break and crash upon Africa!

FIVE

Like a Mighty Wind

WE CAME BACK to Pretoria and immediately began to gear up for our ministry trip. To my great pleasure, another new friend, Corne van Niekerk (pronounced Corn-ay), volunteered to be our guide throughout South Africa. We would become lifelong friends with this fun-loving man.

The first stop was Durban. We went to a Full Gospel Business Men's Fellowship meeting and started to proclaim the message of the priesthood of the believer. It was our main message and revelation that God had given me for our journey. I also shared stories from the revival back in California. We prayed for people, and it was a good meeting, but nothing earthshaking happened in Durban. God was getting our feet wet and warming us up for the upcoming flow.

Our next stop was way down south at a place called King William's Town. To get to this town, we had to pass through the Transkei, which was one of the "homelands." There are actually ten homelands in South Africa established by the government. They are like huge reservations, territories for the many different black tribes, which are smaller, self-governing nations within a nation for the black indigenous population. During the drive we were on a single-lane road going through major sections of South Africa. It was in the Transkei that I first saw lots and lots of "for real" African villages, with the mud huts, thatched roofs, and small fires burning everywhere. We drove right through many villages and could see many more villages in the distance. The reality of being in Africa flooded the car. It was exactly like I had always imagined!

Shortly after entering the Transkei, we saw this hitchhiker beside the road. He was a young white guy who turned out to be an honest-to-goodness South African hippie. There are not that many free-spirited hippies running around over there, because basically South Africa is a very conservative country. But this guy was one, with long hair and a big smile. There was just something about him. We felt the Lord telling us to pick him up, so we pulled over.

As we were visually taking in the new African landscape with the villages and people, the hitchhiker started to open up. He had been raised among a black tribe in a small village near where we were in the Transkei. He was a university student currently on vacation, heading out on a four or five-hour ride past the Transkei. Soon he admitted that he was tripping on LSD, though he didn't have to tell us—we could tell he was loaded. However, like I said, I really wasn't expecting to run across very many acidheads in South Africa, seeing that the people are, you know, "straight."

We stopped at a little restaurant and shared breakfast with our African hippie. I started to tell him about a few of my acid trips and experiences in the Haight-Ashbury, tapping into one of my favorite strategies: Identify with him at his level, get him laughing, get him comfortable, open him up, be real, have fun, and then . . . stab him with divine truth! It's called "fishing for men."

As the kilometers clicked by, we all started to tell him about the Lord, like a tag team. There was a lightness and real joy in the air. Remember, we had a captive audience to work on, so it was definitely entertaining and fun. He told us he didn't believe in God and that his father was an atheist. He didn't know anything about religion.

The Lord told me to open up to Isaiah 53 and start showing him about the prophecies that Jesus fulfilled. I read to him out of Psalm 22, where Jesus' crucifixion was predicted in detail.

He said that he could hardly believe that was in Scripture and thought it was a total set up. He was very skeptical and didn't believe the Old Testament prophecies could be fulfilled in the New Testament. He had dismissed the Bible as a bunch of fairytales for weak-minded people.

I shared that we were not on a religious trip, but that Jesus was a real person who likes to set people up in order to introduce himself because of his great love. I told him about my conversion and that my friends in the car also were Christians. We shared the gospel story in detail, and believe me, that five-hour drive through the Transkei seemed like only minutes! Still, there was nothing that I could say or do to persuade that young man about Jesus Christ. He was entertained, but he wasn't budging.

At the same time, he was slowly returning to planet Earth from "Never-never land," and as time went on, I noticed that he was not trying to escape at all. I could sense that this was definitely a divine appointment and that God was giving him into our hands. As we started to get near his destination, the presence of God began to fill the car. Every single one of us could feel it. The atmosphere was getting tingly.

I looked at our friend, who now had his eyes closed.

He looked up and turned to me and said, "I feel strange. I feel different all over. I've never felt this way before!"

I said, "Well, who have we been talking about? Jesus! That's Jesus you feel. Just call upon his name."

"I'm afraid!"

"Go ahead. Call upon his name and see what happens."

So he started to call upon the name of the Lord Jesus. Right at the same time on the little stereo in the car, the second chapter of Acts began singing the song "Hallelujah, He is risen!" The presence of God blasted into the car! It was perfect timing! We were all praising the Lord and getting filled with the Spirit. That young man was delivered from drugs, saved, filled with the Holy Spirit, and then he began to give utterance in tongues as he was baptized. People might not believe God would do that with a guy coming off a psychedelic trip—but he did!

It was just a radical Jesus People salvation right in the middle of Africa—one of those special unique divine appointments, an event along the road. We didn't even get his name or address or anything, but I believe in my heart that my South African hippie friend is on a brand-new road, on a real *live* trip, definitely going to the same destination as all of us who have surrendered to our King. We will meet again, my brother!

SHOOTOUT!

After this, we headed into some of the most beautiful areas in the world along the Indian Ocean coastline. We had so many churches lined up besides our initial connections in King William's Town that it would take forever to tell everything that happened during the next couple of months. In that first area alone, we were scheduled to speak multiple times in Port Elizabeth as well as King William's Town and onward. But before we really got properly started, we had to wait three days for the first meeting down there. The pastor of the church had all three of us staying in a *tiny* trailer. I mean, Corne by himself is a big man well over six feet tall. I had bumped heads with Peter a few times already, both in Central and South America. In spite of all the recent open doors, divine appointments, and adventures that God had already blessed us with, a major blowup was brewing in Africa in the confined space of this little trailer abode.

I haven't focused much on the reality of spiritual warfare on this first Africa mission. However, spiritual warfare is *very* intense concerning everything about Africa. The Bible declares that we are not to be ignorant of the enemy's devices, and one thing that I've noticed is that just before a huge blessing from God, a huge attack will often manifest. It can come in a million different packages. It also says in God's book that the enemy comes "to rob, kill, and destroy."[7] The devil and his demons know how to push our buttons. They know our weaknesses. We as believers need to wise up and put on the Ephesians 6 armor and "stand." Sometimes easier said than done. Nevertheless, we also know the end of the story: God wins! He is using everything in this life, including the warfare, to teach us how to become victorious sons and daughters. He is preparing us for a perfect eternal kingdom! We need to stay in touch with the big picture.

But back to the shootout, I'm going to quote Pete's perspective from his journal concerning this major blowup of ours inside the "O.K. Corral"—I mean, the "O.K. Tiny Trailer." Before you judge us too harshly, keep in mind that we are all "jars of clay."

FROM PETER'S JOURNAL

We finally got to King William's Town. It was the middle of the week, and they had set up meetings for Lonnie and me on the weekend. The pastor's name there was Ivan Vorster, and it was a Baptist church. They took us to stay at his house, but the place where Corne, Lonnie, and I actually lived for three days was this little eighteen-foot travel trailer that the pastor had out in his backyard. We all stayed out there and slept in it. By this time, Lonnie's and my relationship had gotten frayed. I mean, we'd been living and traveling together now for close to three months, and, you know, we were the last thing we saw before we went to sleep and the first thing we saw when we got up. We were starting to get on each other's nerves. It was hindering the flow of the Spirit, and so we sat out in this trailer for three days and fasted. It finally got down to a real fight between Lonnie and me that went something like this:

"I hate you!"

"Well, I hate *you*!"

"Well, I hate you more!"

"No, you couldn't possibly hate me worse than I hate you!"

"Well, get screwed!"

"Okay, well, *you* get screwed!" (We might possibly have used other terms to express ourselves, if you know what I mean.)

We really got into it. We were screaming and yelling at each other, and Corne, this nice, gentle, South African giant was sitting there, going, "I don't believe it! You guys are Christian *ministers*, and you're yelling that kind of stuff at each other?"

Lonnie said to him, "We're just speaking the truth in love, brother!"

Corne sat there for a while and seemed oddly impressed. "Well, I think I like it. You're being real with each other."

At one point in our screaming, I got the biggest rebuke of my life. I'll never forget it! I was accusing Lonnie with: "I have no idea how you even manage to get from point A to point B *EVER!*"

Lonnie responded, "I'll tell you how I do it, Peter. I do it by the power of the Holy Spirit!"

How could I argue with that? Plus, I knew in my spirit that it was true. The presence of God was sternly but lovingly rebuking me. For three days we just kind of worked on our "stuff."

We finally hammered out our issues, more or less. At the end of three days, we calmed down our ruffled feathers, prayed some more, and then it was off to the meetings.

We drove to the first church meeting in King William's Town. I just remember Lonnie telling the people, "Hey, God wants you to be his minister *now*! He doesn't want you to depend on Billy Graham or any other megastar. God wants *you*. This isn't against Billy Graham or any of those guys. This is just the fact that Billy Graham is the last of a generation. Anybody who wants to stand in God's way is going to get knocked down like some of the big TV

74

evangelists!" We shared that word and then said, "Now we want to pray for you."

The first person we prayed for was an eight-year-old boy, and as we started praying for him, he started gagging and choking. He couldn't breathe. Lonnie said, "Wow, interesting." He rebuked whatever was attacking the kid, and the boy got delivered from a demon. He was healed instantly in the name of Jesus, and then he could breathe! It caused quite a stir in the church. Another man who had been in the ministry for years but had backslidden was there, and we prayed for him also. God touched him and called him back into the ministry. An older woman in her sixties or seventies came up and said, "I've been going down to Cape Town regularly every six months to have my eyes worked on for cataracts. The Lord's touched them tonight, and my eyes are completely better now." Another lady got saved there. At this first small church meeting, we started to see dramatic healings, deliverance, a salvation, a marriage healed, and on and on. It was powerful, but still just a warm-up for some of the stuff that God did in other churches and meetings as we continued on.

· · ·

UPDATE

At this point in the story concerning our argument, I (Peter) want to insert a little updated reflection of Lonnie. It is now 2014 as I write this about our trip from my journals. It's hard for me to believe that it's been twenty-one years since Lonnie left us. I don't even remember the exact cause of the clash that we had in King William's Town. I listen to some of the audio recordings I made twenty-five and thirty years ago, and the memories come flooding back. We were *very* different personalities. Lonnie was definitely an artist, left-handed, creative, a mystic.

In fact, there's no doubt about it. Lonnie Frisbee was a mystic. He was a guy who could communicate with God and just hear his voice on a high spiritual level and then go higher and higher, a friend of God who could take you places you didn't think possible to go. How am I going to put this? He was a guy like the Beatles in one way. The Beatles broke up in 1969–70, and people didn't really catch up to their music until maybe twenty-five years later. Lonnie was that kind of a forerunner. We had spiritual conversations in the eighties that I didn't really see being fulfilled and commonly spoken about in the church until about 2005, maybe even 2008. He was a mystical guy who could see that far into the future concerning the things of God. You would be astounded and amazed just talking to him, because it was so incredibly anointed and supernatural most of the time. God did little and big miracles almost daily when you hung out with Lonnie. He definitely had his other moments, but it was an amazing thing to know Lonnie!

THE POWER OF GOD FALLS

So Peter and I (Lonnie) were back on track after our fight. We invited the lady who got saved at the service to come to our next meeting in East London the following weekend and told her that we would love to baptize her. She followed us to our meeting, and it was so special. East London was only about twenty miles from King William's Town. We stayed at a pastor's farm, which was right on the beautiful Indian Ocean coastline, with a river winding through the farm, spilling into the ocean. It is outrageously beautiful there!

The church we were invited to in East London was a medium-sized Baptist church with a seating capacity of probably around two hundred. However, they had made posters inviting people to attend

76

and hear "The American Evangelist Lonnie Frisbee." They publicized and distributed these posters all over, and twenty minutes before the meeting, the place was absolutely packed with way more than two hundred people. We tried to fit everyone in with more chairs. We put them in the aisles and in the front of the church and out the door. We had people looking in the windows. We started out the service by gloriously baptizing the lady from King William's Town in a little baptismal pool, but the people kept coming. I spoke for a while, but pretty soon we gave up and moved the meeting to a large fellowship hall, which probably held around four hundred people, all packed wall to wall.

After we settled into the new venue for a few minutes, I began sharing with the people. Here's how it works for me: a little Scripture, a little preaching, a little testimony, a little showbiz, and a **WHOLE LOT OF ANOINTING!** It's the only way. Without the anointing of God, we are wasting everyone's time.

Then I prayed. It was a simple prayer, but God decided to pour out a huge blessing on these four hundred hungry Baptists. It was absolutely incredible! There came a sound from heaven like a mighty rushing wind. I could hear it in the Spirit. I could hear it with my ears. You could actually see with your own eyes where the Holy Spirit began to blow and move on the people. Everyone was swaying together in unison. You cannot see the wind, and you cannot see the Holy Spirit, but you *can* see the impact. The Spirit of God was blowing across the room, and then back and forth in a big "S" pattern, and I could actually see entire groups of people waving like yielded wheat in the wind. It seemed to flow perfectly, almost like divine choreography.

I did not want it to stop! This brand-new experience continued to flow over the people back and forth, until I knew inside that something else was about to happen. Then the Holy Spirit fell on the *entire* room! The power of God hit all four hundred people at once. People were knocked to the floor. People were getting healed and delivered from all kinds of bondages. Many were being called into the ministry. Some were shaking violently, and others were completely out under the power of God for hours, oblivious to everything else around them. Some were crying, some were laughing. Hundreds of Baptists, who do not believe that the gifts of the Spirit are for today, were speaking in tongues. Hundreds and hundreds of people got baptized in the Holy Spirit simultaneously. It was an earthshaking, wonderful, remarkable experience! I will never forget it as long as I live. I was in total awe of the presence and power of God, and that meeting changed my life and ministry forever. We go from glory to glory, from mountaintop to mountaintop, according to God's love letter!

The meetings went on for at least three hours, and believe me, it sent minor and eventually major shock waves throughout South Africa. Some people and churches embraced what was happening with open hearts, and others rejected it as "not from God." News of that meeting went everywhere including Cape Town, where we would be heading next. But first, we returned to the beautiful farm right on the Indian Ocean. We picked some fresh strawberries and milked some of the cows. Have you ever tasted fresh milk on top of fresh strawberries? It is like dying and going to heaven. I'm sure heaven is going to have strawberries and fresh milk forever and ever!

SIX

A Fire Was Lit

WE HEADED SOUTH toward Cape Town. God had dramatically demonstrated that he was with us—big time! Thank you, Jesus, and thank you, Billy Graham! God poured out tremendous signs and wonders in meeting after meeting with increasing intensity. He had given us new friends and favor upon favor. However, there were still obstacles to overcome, big and little, like when we got totally lost in Cape Town, drove around most of the night, and were unable to find our contact. The three of us finally pulled over and slept in the car. It wasn't the first time for me, but very uncomfortable to say the least. Much worse than an eighteen-foot travel trailer for sure!

After a few phone calls, we were able to reach Derek Morphew. Little did I know that this man would become one of the very closest and dearest friends of my entire life. All I knew about him at the time was that a friend or relative of his had attended one of our meetings up north and then phoned to see if he could host us in the Cape Town area. It was also mentioned that he attended an Assembly of God church, and that was about all I knew. By phone, in the stiffness of the morning air, Derek walked us into his community, which was a suburb city outside of Cape Town named Durbanville. Soon we met Derek and his wife, Karen, and their young daughter. I instantly felt a connection with this great family and a wonderful peace in their home. They prepared a great meal for us with a couple bottles of good wine.

I recently asked to get a hold of Derek and family to record their version of our initial meeting and ongoing relationship. Like I said before, sometimes it is far better to get corroborating eyewitness accounts of important events and even seasons of time than to have just one man's perspective. Believe me, this meeting would soon affect thousands of people, major Christian denominations, and ultimately, the entire continent of Africa. That might sound a little grandiose, but it's true, and that's also why I want to get as many eyewitness testimonies from credible, key people as possible.

I believe Derek Morphew is the most credible witness and, in my view, the most connected leader in all of Africa. I didn't even know he was a leader when I first met him! What God did beginning with our trip in the late seventies was off the scale. Obviously, the Lord had been working in millions of lives long before we ever got there, and he will continue to work in everyone's lives long, long after we are gone—until he returns. Nevertheless, God is presently doing a mighty work in Africa, and unto him be all the glory!

"YOU CAN'T BE THE PASTOR!"
by Derek Morphew

I first met Lonnie in 1978. I think it was his first trip to South Africa. Just to give you the context, since most people know he was a key figure in the Jesus People revival in California, we had a very similar move in South Africa. There was a particular Assembly of God church that had been praying for revival. It was quite a conservative church. One day, the hippies arrived. Suddenly, there were men without shoes and girls who didn't always have on complete clothing. There was the same sort of reaction that Chuck Smith described, with some saying, "We don't need these people," and many other leaders saying, "This is the revival we've been praying for." Some tried to make them dress differently, but eventually they said, "No, we can't make them dress differently." Hundreds of young people were converted, and from there it became like combustion. There was a downtown boutique owned by one of the members of

80

the church, and most of the conversions of hippies happened there. Evangelists were born in that time.

Lonnie wanted to come meet the counterpart movement in our country, and he'd been up to Johannesburg and Pretoria and spoke in Hatfield Baptist Church, a growing charismatic church at the time. One of the pastors, Corne van Niekerk, knew who I was because my sister-in-law was a member of Hatfield and knew him. Corne phoned me and said, "There's this guy called Lonnie Frisbee who's from the Jesus People in California, and he wants to come to Cape Town to see what's going on there. We're looking for a host."

I said, "Sure, he can come stay with us."

So he came to stay at our home. What was interesting was that on Sunday morning as we were driving to our church service, Lonnie said, "When am I going to meet the pastor?"

"I am the pastor," I told him—and he wouldn't believe me.

He said, "You can't be the pastor!"—which I take as a bit of a compliment, now knowing Lonnie. Obviously, we hadn't matched his experience with a lot of pastors.

At the Sunday morning service, I invited him to speak. I can remember it was mostly a kind of exposition on justification through faith, that we are not saved by our good works, but by what Jesus has done. His message was probably fifteen to twenty minutes. It was good, but that's not what I remember really happening in the meeting.

After preaching, Lonnie said, "I'm going to invite all the kids twelve years old and younger to come and stand in the middle of the room." Then he prayed for the Holy Spirit to come. Well, the power of God fell on those kids, and they started falling down, weeping, and trembling. Then, of course, all the mothers started crying because they saw that

God was on their children. An hour or so later, we had to carry some of the kids to their parents' motorcars because they were so laid out that they couldn't walk.

That was the first time I saw Lonnie ministering, and really, the first time I saw power phenomena of that level. I was, by this stage, a Pentecostal pastor. I'd seen people speaking in tongues. Sometimes I'd seen people, when they were getting filled with the Holy Spirit, be really overcome, but it was an individual case here and there. But to see twenty to thirty kids just laid out like that was quite a new phenomenon for me.

That kind of began our relationship. Lonnie has subsequently come to South Africa almost every year for the last sixteen years, staying in our home, breaking bread with us. I became a close friend and confidant of his. Our children all grew up with him and still love him very much, as both my wife, Karen, and I do. Lonnie and Karen are both artists and have a very close relationship. Lonnie usually comes with a team of various sizes, and we have learned over the years to drop everything when Lonnie comes to town!

A BLOCK AWAY

As Peter and I (Lonnie) were getting to know our new friends, we asked them about the address we had in Durbanville for the world-traveling girl who had been robbed in Peru. Peter broke out his address book, and Derek said, "Yes, this house is a block away." What a "coincidence" to meet a lady in distress in Rio on our plane going to Johannesburg, South Africa, and then a month or so later on the other side of the country, to find out that she is a block away from where we are staying at Derek Morphew's house. Coincidence? *I don't think so!*

Peter called her up and said, "Hey, Hildegard, guess what? We're here, and we're staying just a block from you!"

She said, "Really? Let me bring you the twenty dollars."

"No, no, don't bring us twenty dollars. Why don't you take us around on a little sightseeing thing and be our tour guide while we are here in our spare time?"

So we connected with Hildegard and took her to everything we did. Between meetings she took us all over. She was so sweet. On one outing she took us to the Cape of Good Hope, which is where the Indian and the Atlantic Oceans come together. We went to the very end of the continent, up on the rocks, and could see the huge waves of the two oceans dramatically interacting. There are small Blackfoot penguins all along the rocky coast there. They are so interesting, and it was so strange for me to see them in a natural setting somewhere besides Sea World or some zoo. The Cape of Good Hope is rightfully called "the fairest cape in the whole world." God definitely knows how to create beauty, and the evidence is all over Africa!

We also drove up to Stellenbosch, which is beautiful wine country in its own right. It's just like Napa in California, where you can go wine tasting or maybe have a cheese and wine luncheon. There is a university community up there, and we did a meeting with the students. Hildegard also took us downtown, to the waterfront, and to the coastline and harbors. We went up on Table Mountain and all over the city. Cape Town has the feel of San Diego and is a wonderful modern city, but we could also see the reality of the racial segregation. Just outside of the city, there were these huge fenced-off townships. We heard about District Six, where sixty thousand black residents were forcibly relocated to other locations. I had a vision of bloodshed in the streets, which I shared in the meetings.

Hildegard went to all the meetings with us and was absolutely flabbergasted. She said, "Wow, I have to make a choice now! I know that there's a God. I've seen him in your meetings."

We don't know if Hildegard opened her heart to the King of Kings. She never said for sure, and we never force anyone. Neither does Jesus! But we do know that God sent us to her all the way from Rio de Janeiro. God then put us a block away from her home, just to say, "I'm real, Hildegard! I'll chase you from the ends of the earth if I have to because I love you! I have provided the way for you to spend eternity with me! I don't want us to be even a block away any longer. You need to choose me!" It was and is Hildegard's personal invitation to the kingdom of God. I pray that she did open up and make the best decision of her life: saying yes to Jesus. It is your invitation also. He loves each and every one of us as much as he loves our special friend Hildegard.

A SPIRITUAL CONNECTION

Between meetings, I was lying in my room, quite alone, and God began to open up a spiritual connection to me. You know, sometimes it can be heaven or sometimes it can be hell. At first I saw, as it were, a weather map over my bed. Then it was like I was looking up at a hurricane on some weather news broadcast. In the middle of this huge cloud that was rotating above me, there came a deep, dark hole that was sucking down. It was over my bed, and I was looking at it. The Lord was showing me the deepest, darkest judgment and the most terrible separation from God. He was showing me the wrath of God!

I was looking into that darkness. I saw it from every perspective. I'm an artist—I saw it from this perspective, and that perspective, and then another perspective. I saw it from all different synoptic types of perspectives. The Lord was showing me this great cloud going around and sucking down, and he reminded me that there was going to come a day when our world is going to experience the judgment and the wrath of God. I feel an urgency to share this even though it is not light, fluffy, or pleasant news. However, the Bible declares that the gospel is a sweet-smelling savor to those being saved, but an ugly stench of death to others. At least we will have done our job and have been the watchmen on the wall who warned the people of the coming wrath!

So God again alerted me to the reality and importance of the huge battle over the souls of mankind. We don't like to think about darkness and demons, hell and death, the wrath of God and eternal separation from his presence, but that is *exactly* why Jesus left heaven and became "one of us"—so that he could sweep us under his wing of protection and rescue us. We love that part of the story. It seems to me that overall, God *majors* in the good news and *minors* in the threat of eternal damnation in the lake of fire. Nevertheless, both revelations are vitally important. Listen! We are all dying. Get in touch with your mortality! It's not a matter of *if*, it's a matter of *when* and *how*. Ask God to reveal that heaven is real. He will! And with that resurrection power of the cross, Jesus will usher you into his kingdom. That is the good news! Just believe and receive—it's that simple!

OUTPOURINGS

In Cape Town we had one meeting after another. Some were with small youth groups and some with large churches. We got invited to white churches, black churches, and all kinds of churches throughout the area. That made me *real* happy! A pattern was becoming wonderfully evident: A huge outpouring of the Holy Spirit would occur everywhere we went! Just like in Derek's church, people were getting knocked to the floor, young and old, some getting major healings, lots of deliverance, and many people getting the baptism of the Holy Spirit with the evidence of speaking in tongues. It was wild, messy, shocking—but wonderful! Peter and I were just as amazed as everyone else.

Some of the kids had visions of angels and visions of Jesus and were in trances for hours. Some of the mothers got really concerned. This one lady charged up to me and said, "What did you do to my son? Stop it! Stop it now!"

I told her, "I didn't do anything to your kid. God did! I didn't start it, and I'm not going to stop it!"

Some of the mothers themselves hit the floor and started speaking in tongues along with their kids. The Holy Spirit was a new experience for most of these people. This was back when speaking in tongues was a big controversy. To many it still is. However, the outpouring of the Holy Spirit continued to happen in all different types of churches, especially Baptist churches, which totally blew my mind. How clever is our God!

OH MY SOUL

I especially remember this one black church. We got totally lost trying to find it and drove all over the place. We finally decided to go back to Derek's place, when all of a sudden, there it was! We accidentally found the church in our wandering around, but we were an hour and a half late. To several of the meetings we wore a coat and tie, and this was one of those times, so we cinched up, tucked in, and walked into the church. It was a pretty good-sized church with lots of people. They were patiently waiting for us and said, "Hi, brothers, you're on! We're ready for you now!"

The people were still in some powerful worship with a great band. So we walked up on stage and just watched as they were singing, "Bless the Lord, oh my soul, and all that is within me, bless his holy name!" They were singing that old familiar hymn in a wonderful "African-eze" style! The presence of God was on the entire place and on that song. They continued singing it until the reality of the words became the atmosphere! I never experienced anything quite like it! They powered through that one song over and over for about twenty minutes or maybe more. The anointing and presence of God simply increased and increased.

"Bless the Lord, oh my soul, and *all* that is within me, bless his holy name!" This church knew how to worship.

When the song wound down, and with the presence still hovering over us, I moved them right into a ministry time. We started praying for people, loudly proclaiming the priesthood of all believers, and getting words of knowledge. Pretty soon, I had everyone, starting with the youngest, make a huge circle around the entire church. The youngest kids looked like they were around four years old, and some of the adults were grandpas and grandmas. Peter and I started with the little kids, and as fast as we could lay hands on them—*boom, boom, boom, boom*—they would get filled with the Holy Ghost!

I remember everyone's hands would shoot up in the air, and the cute little four-year-olds would start screaming, shrieking, and speaking in tongues! It went all around the room like that! Many of the older people were crying out that they had been healed. We saw God do a lot of miracles, touch a lot of people's hearts and physical bodies, but mostly he would *completely* baptize them in the Holy Spirit. How wonderful it was to worship, fellowship, and serve together with our black brothers and sisters in Christ! What a joy!

A WORD OF KNOWLEDGE

I'll tell about one more thing that happened in one of the smaller youth group meetings in Cape Town. We would get supernatural "words" for people on a regular basis, but this is an example of one that really stood out. For reference, if God happens to show you something personal about someone that you could not possibly know about, the Bible calls that "a word of knowledge." It's one of the gifts of the Spirit. There were only about twenty kids at this particular meeting, and I had them sit in a big circle so we could talk. I don't remember exactly what I was sharing with everyone, but I remember looking over at this big black kid sitting across from me. Later we learned that his name was Charlie.

I pointed at him and said, "Suppose you have something wrong with your head that you haven't been able to tell anybody. It's your secret." That's all I said to him. I had no idea what it was all about, and we moved on.

Soon everyone stood up, and we started praying for people. These three girls got baptized in the Holy Spirit, and all three of them began speaking in tongues. Charlie was standing there, and the next thing I knew, he got knocked to the floor! We just assumed he was also getting baptized or touched by the Lord. After all, it was happening in all the meetings. However, he started flopping on the floor like a fish out of water! He was flopping and shaking, which then turned into convulsions and even more flopping.

We realized that Charlie was going through some kind of major deliverance. He tried to get up, but fell back down, knocking over a bunch of chairs and benches. He hit his head on one of the benches and was bleeding from his forehead.

I said to him, "Charlie, the Lord is delivering you from a demon. Just relax. Let God do the work, and you'll be fine—*Now, come out of him in the mighty name of Jesus!*"

While this was going on, Peter told the shocked kids, "Don't be alarmed. Just continue praying for Charlie!"

Their response was wonderful. All the kids started sincerely praying for Charlie, who, like I said, had been flopping on the floor. Have you ever caught a fish and dropped him on a dock? That was Charlie!

Within a matter of minutes, he was rising to his knees. Then he stood up with his hands raised to the heavens and was filled with the Holy Spirit! He joined in with the three girls speaking in tongues. Tears were flowing. They all continued to praise God in their new heavenly language. It was radical! It was bold! It was free! Believe me, if the Son has set you free, "YOU ARE FREE INDEED!"[8]

Afterwards, I asked Charlie, "Can you tell us what was going on?"

He told us, "Well, I have epilepsy. I've never told anybody about it. I hide it. Sometimes I would wake up in a gutter from seizures. One time I woke up on a bench in the back of a bus and was robbed. I've never told anybody about it. I keep it a secret as much as possible."

Wow! The Lord delivered and healed Charlie! He was eighteen years old. In the name of Jesus we cast out a spirit of epilepsy, and I believe with all my heart that Charlie has had the rest of his young life to live for Jesus free from his "secret."

We needed to head back up to Johannesburg because we were scheduled to fly to Kenya next in a few weeks. I had fallen in love with Cape Town and especially with the Derek Morphew family. We had so many special personal times together, with great meals, pasta, wine, deep conversations, and laughter—it was honestly the best part of the entire trip for me. The power of God falling on huge crowds is wonderful, believe me, **but love flowing amongst friends is hard to beat!**

AN OPEN DOOR

After Cape Town, Peter and I continued our trip heading north through South Africa. We drove up the middle of the country along the same path that the Dutch-speaking colonists took in their oxen-powered, covered wagons way back when. Our next stop was Bloemfontein, which is a pretty large city near the center of South Africa. The church we were initially invited to more or less "dis-invited" us, probably because of the incredible reports that were going out about the meetings. Of course, we had *instantly* become very controversial with all the speaking in tongues and different spiritual manifestations. Many churches and individuals were not quite ready for this kind of "wildfire."

However, that particular church did open the door for us to minister in one of their mid-week youth groups at someone's home in Bloemfontein. It was a Wednesday night, and we drove there to find a packed house filled with young people. It turned out to be a great meeting. We prayed for people, prophesied, taught about the gifts, and then the power of God hit that meeting so hard that it became like a zoo. We had piles of young bodies on the floor everywhere in the house. The presence of God was absolutely awesome, and it more than made up for getting disinvited by the main church.

UPDATE FROM PETER CRAWFORD

In 2014, I received a phone call from a man who asked me if I was the person who traveled with Lonnie Frisbee to Africa in 1978.

He said, "I know that Lonnie died, and I've been asking around trying to find the person who was with him back then, and I was given your name. If it was you, you're the only other one who I can talk to. Was it you?"

"Yes, that was me," I told him.

After telling me a little about himself, he said, "Lonnie and you did a youth meeting in Bloemfontein, South Africa, back in 1978. Do you remember me?"

"I don't remember you, sir, but I remember the meeting. It was just one of those special times that has stuck in my mind."

He said, "I just want to tell you that that night when you prayed for everybody, we were all down on the floor. There were ten of us guys in my little circle when Lonnie and you prayed for us, and nine of us went into full-time ministry after that. I've been taking mission teams to Pakistan over the last thirty years, and we have been leading thousands of people to Christ. The ministry I'm in has established over five thousand small home churches in Pakistan. It's still legal to be a Christian in Pakistan and still legal to hold crusades.

"You're kidding!"

"No, you probably had no idea, but nine of us went into full-time ministry out of that one small meeting. I just want to thank you!"

I was so shocked and amazed that some guy tracked me down, called me up out of the blue, and wanted to thank me thirty-seven years later for praying for him and his friends. We had no idea what the outcome of that meeting in Bloemfontein would be. Over three decades later, it turned out that our prayers were still affecting a whole Middle Eastern region. You never know what God can do even in a small meeting or what the outcome of some "chance" divine appointment might possibly be. Believe me, it was a fantastic phone call!

LIVE FROM PRETORIA

In 1978, as our final days in South Africa quickly approached, we returned to Pretoria and joined the Hatfield Baptist Church summer youth camp. Peter and I (Lonnie) shared a summary of our recent journey through the country and the mighty works of God. In one of the meetings, I decided to do a "live" audiotaped message in front of two hundred kids and young adults to send back to America to be broadcast on the radio. I shared about Peter's vision, and I shared the hitchhiker's amazing story going through the Transkei. Here is part of my report fresh from the field from the actual 1978 audiotape:

"This is Lonnie Frisbee giving a report from South Africa about the mission trip that we've been taking around the country. The Lord gave us the vision for this country a long time ago before we even came to Africa. The Lord promised us that he's going to sweep this land with revival, and he's going to touch the young people. It has really been a demonstration of the Holy

Ghost, as we saw here last night upon some of the children. We would go into the churches and say, 'Oh, let all the children come to the front of the church right now! We want to pray for them!' And as the children started coming forward—six, seven, eight, up to twelve years old—the kind of kids that in churches, you know, you wouldn't expect to be coming into Jesus Christ until maybe they got into high school or something like that, yet the Spirit of God was falling down on these little children. They were weeping and raising their hands up to God and being baptized with the Holy Spirit!

For those of you who don't believe in the baptism of the Holy Spirit, that's your tough luck! The Lord was filling all these little children with the power of the Holy Spirit. And guess what, folks? It was in Baptist churches all over South Africa. Praise God! We just want to give a glory report and to bless the Baptists in California. Bless all the Baptists who are listening to this radio show. We want to say that we're just seeing a great move of God and the Spirit of God among Baptist churches."

REVIVAL

During the final days of our time in South Africa, we continued to share the message of the priesthood of all believers and the "good news" of the gospel. We emphasized the new birth made possible by Jesus on the cross. However, we did not come in words alone, but like Paul declared, "My message and my preaching were not with wise and persuasive words, but with a demonstration of the Spirit's power."[9] It was just glory after glory after glory, as the intensity of God's presence increased in every meeting.

Everything we were seeing matched Peter's vision for South Africa before we even began ministering. Peter didn't know the geography of the country and had no idea of the history of South Africa. However, those paths that the flame in his vision took were the *exact* same paths that the European settlers took hundreds of years ago when they first settled in South Africa. The settlers went up the coast, and they also went up the center of the country. To me, the whole vision spoke of revival. A fire was lit in the land—revival had started! A nationwide breakout had begun in South Africa, and the people could see and feel the impact. It was all about breaking down walls between churches, races, denominations, individuals, and eventually between nations!

I feel just as privileged to be a part of this outpouring in Africa as I was in the Jesus People revival in California. Peter Crawford and I were just two young men, twenty-four and twenty-seven years old, without a clue of what to do in Africa. We just showed up. God took it from there and changed a nation. Praise be unto our King!

"For it was not by might, nor by power, but by his Spirit, saith the Lord!"

Lonnie ministering in Africa

SEVEN

Onward

AS THE FINAL days of our mission to South Africa approached, we began preparing ourselves for our next adventure in Africa. We would be flying into Nairobi, Kenya, and then on to Israel. Peter Crawford and I were riding high on a spiritual wave that we had supernaturally seen in the Spirit and had just experienced all over South Africa. We were full of joy and energy and felt like a million bucks. But don't you know that with every mountaintop, every radical victory, and with every great testimony, the spiritual forces of evil try to snatch the victory away. The Bible warns us about this with the reminder "not to be ignorant of the enemy's devices."[10] We know this and have experienced the warfare many, many times in the past. But in the midst of the "high," we often drop our guard and forget that the devil is real and definitely coming to "rob, kill, and destroy."[11] He is ruthless, a liar, a thief, and a murderer. He will take you out even if you have a little chink in your armor. He didn't like what we had just done in South Africa and was coming on hard after us. The lesson is: Pay attention and keep the full armor of the Lord on at all times, especially on the other side of a mountaintop victory!

A major hit was on its way and manifested itself like a fire-breathing dragon at this particular point in our mission. Unfortunately, the main challenge came from people and leaders back home who we loved and trusted, producing the kind of wounds that hurt the most.

A few days before Peter and I were to fly out of Johannesburg, we called back to California for a draw on our funds. We had almost run out of money. Between Peter and myself, we had less than five hundred dollars left. With half our trip left to go, we still had, thank

God, roughly half the funds that we had raised in the bank back home. We were not worried in the least.

When I called, however, I was told, "We are not sending you any more money until you reach Denmark."

"What?!" I yelled into the phone. "We still have Kenya and Israel and part of Europe scheduled before we even get to Denmark, and we're almost out of money! What's the deal? Listen! We raised a little over thirty thousand dollars for this mission, and you need to send us a draw *right now!*"

They said, "Sorry, you're not getting anything until you get to Denmark in June."

I flipped out, to no avail. June was over a month away. Believe me, I was so upset and *so* sorry that I trusted them with our funds. During the conversation, an accusation was also made that someone had seen us gambling in Las Vegas.

My response was, "You've got to be kidding! We went to the Billy Graham crusade and were there for one night!"

In all honesty, I *did* lose about thirty dollars on some hotel slot machine, God forgive me, but I am not a gambler and have never had that vice in my life. On top of that, we did not use any of our mission money. We went to Vegas on Peter's paycheck. By the way, where does it say in the Bible, "Thou shall not try a slot machine in Las Vegas?" But if you want a "true confession," the positively worst thing that we did in Sin City was go to a Jose Feliciano show. We did that—what a terrible transgression!

Nevertheless, we were faced with the reality that we were fourteen thousand miles away from home with practically no money in the middle of a huge foreign mission. We did have our airfare covered, but we needed everything else, including food, hotels, and local transportation. It was unbelievable, but we picked our emotions off the floor and took the situation to the Lord. He knows everything anyway, and we needed to trust him and pass this trial. All spiritual warfare can be reversed into an opportunity to grow as

God's children. However, sometimes it is not easy. I do struggle with forgiving some people when the knife sinks in the back.

We shared our dilemma with a couple of our pastor friends in Pretoria, and they took up an offering for us. They graciously gave us around three hundred dollars with the promise to continue to intercede for our mission. They added another blessing for us by saying that they would be praying for our soon return to South Africa. It was like healing balm applied to an open wound. Thank God for those whose hearts are yielded to him in times like these. Like I mentioned before, I have returned to South Africa every year since that time for sixteen years, so God definitely answered those prayers!

KENYA

Peter and I boarded a plane for Nairobi, Kenya, with bittersweet hearts. It took time to process our new situation. The first thing we discovered is that Nairobi is a very expensive city. The hotel was expensive, the food was expensive, *everything* was expensive. We realized that we were going to have to cut our visit short or we'd soon be on the street. We also decided to cut out part of Europe after Israel. On top of that, we had a few leads for ministry in Kenya, but every one of them turned out to be dead ends. No churches were interested in hosting us or having us share anything.

It was confirmation that we were to cut our visit short there. We spent only three days in Kenya.

Mount Kilimanjaro, Amboseli Game Reserve

There was one special plus side to my first visit to Kenya. In Nairobi, Peter and I ran into a couple of American marines on leave from Tanzania, and we all decided to pool our money together, rent a car (a little Fiat), and then go to the Amboseli Game Reserve. The park was 232 kilometers south of Nairobi, and it was definitely worth the trip. We were still in the "green season," with huge open plains of grasslands and the famous snow-capped Mount Kilimanjaro in the distance. As an artist, I cannot put into words how totally in awe I am of God's incredibly beautiful and majestic landscapes. Plus, consider the endless variety of birds and animals with such wild colors and details. I am one who always stops and smells the roses. We saw sunrises and sunsets in Africa that literally took my breath away! All creation declares his glory and reality.

When we were in Krueger National Park, our friend Sippy did all the driving, but here in Kenya, Peter was driving our little white rented Fiat all through the Amboseli. The landscape was so huge out there that we couldn't see another car or human from horizon to horizon, only herds of wildlife spread across the plains. At one point Peter got the John Wayne anointing and pulled off the road into the grasslands, then started beeping the little Fiat horn as he stampeded a big herd of zebras. It was crazy and beautiful, but pretty soon, while zipping across the tundra and chasing the herd, Peter stopped paying enough attention to the ground in front of us and buried the car in mud. I mean, we were *stuck*!

The marines and I pushed and rocked the little car back and forth, while Peter spun the tires forever and ever, covering the car (and us) totally with mud. Finally, we managed to get the car free, but the little white Fiat was now the little brown Fiat, inside and out. *Oh, John Wayne—get a grip!* We drove back to Nairobi, managing to find a little humor in our adventure, but then we pulled into the car rental place with their mud-caked victim. They didn't detect the humor at all and were not happy campers, adding a fifty-dollar cleanup fee to our bill. Oh well, we had it coming.

When we got back to the city, we met a friendly Kenyan guy, and Peter and I hired him to be our guide. We knew we had limited time, and he was taking us around the city before we had to leave for Israel. He showed us all over, pointing out this and that one afternoon. We bought a few souvenirs, and our guide helped me carry our stuff up to the hotel room while Peter took a short walk.

On his walk Peter was looking in a storefront window, when two black prostitutes walked up and boldly said, "Hey, boy, you want to have sex?" They went on and on about what they could do for him, but Peter told them, "No. I'm sorry, but no thanks!"

The two prostitutes would not take no for an answer, and it practically turned into a physical assault. It was definitely a spiritual assault. Peter kept saying, "No, no, no," and finally got away from them. He walked a couple of blocks back to the hotel. The interesting thing is that *exactly* when those prostitutes were assaulting Peter, our guide decided to rob me in the hotel room. It was shocking and unexpected from this guy, but I demanded that he get out of the room. Then the phone rang, and it was Peter calling from the lobby because I was supposed to meet him for dinner. I told Peter, "You need to get up here because this guy is trying to rob me!"

Peter came charging up to our room and helped confront the guy. Our guide was saying that if I didn't give him our money, he was going to say that I tried to solicit sex from him. You know, I shared in my story how as an eight-year-old boy I was molested by a male babysitter. I was completely honest about how it devastated my childhood and how the enemy seemed to put a mark on me that other pedophiles could see. The pattern followed me even after I surrendered completely to Christ, as the enemy of our souls tried to label me as a homosexual and discredit my ministry. Believe me, I see it! I have experienced it over and over again and know the strategy to label me. I will say it again here: I never lived the gay lifestyle or embraced homosexuality.

Peter told the guy, "You're going to get your butt out of here! Our God is gonna take a stand! He's going to fight for us, and you better get out of this room." Then we called the hotel security, and they hauled the guy away.

So Peter and I were both amazed at the recent turn of events. Our finances had been stripped away at the peak of success in South Africa, and for a kicker, we were assaulted with sexual advances and accusation separately, yet at the exact same time in Nairobi. Tell me that spiritual warfare is not real and that this is all coincidence! Nevertheless, God allowed it, and we had no choice but to trust him and move forward. And that's exactly what we did. We boarded a jet headed for Israel.

A SUNSET IN TIBERIAS

We flew on El Al Airlines into Tel Aviv and spent three weeks in Israel. I immediately discovered why so many people are radically impacted by even a short visit to the Holy Land. It's the atmosphere, the spiritual atmosphere. In Central and South America I could feel the spiritual atmosphere over those nations, and in Africa it hit me like a ton of bricks. More than anything else, I could feel the love and compassion of God for the people of those nations.

But in Israel it was different. It was like I could feel the presence and love of God for the entire universe—for all of creation in heaven and on earth. It was where heaven came down to earth in the form of a baby in a manger. It is where God became one with his creation to demonstrate his love and rescue us from a fallen world. It is the focal point of everything where God will soon establish his kingdom and, ultimately, create a new heaven and a new earth. It is the big picture! It is the plan of God from before the foundation of the world. It is where love will win, and Jesus will wipe away every tear in a perfected eternal universe.

We drove from Tel Aviv to Jerusalem and stayed in the local YMCA the first night. There were still bullet holes, or actually bullet pockmarks, in the side of the stone building from the Six-Day War of 1967. It had been the scene of some of the fierce fighting in that historic war as well as the 1973 Arab-Israeli War. Historic or not, we could not afford to stay there more than one night, because it cost almost fifty dollars a day. So we found a hotel in the Old City that cost only three dollars and fifty cents a night, which would allow us to stay in the country for three weeks before Denmark without having to become beggars. The Palestinian hotel was on one of the corners of the Via Dolorosa, the painful route that the Romans cruelly forced Jesus to walk through the streets of Jerusalem as he carried his own cross to his crucifixion. It was straight down from the Damascus Gate, catty-cornered from a Catholic convent. I stay there every time I go to Israel.

Soon we went to the Garden Tomb for my very first time, where I have subsequently had many visitations and divine appointments over the years. (You can read my "shiny Pat Boone angel" experience in the first volume of my story.) It was here in the Garden Tomb where death was defeated—**our very last enemy!**

After visiting such an incredible place, Peter and I rented a car and drove up to Tiberias, which is at the south end of the Sea of

Galilee. Everywhere we went, I was bombarded with the presence of God. We also visited Nazareth, then Capernaum, where Jesus healed Peter's mother-in-law. We went to Masada, where Roman legions finally defeated the last of the Israeli holdouts almost two thousand years ago in 73 AD. So much heart-wrenching history for God's chosen people!

One of the wonderful highlights of our pilgrimage was when we met a South African couple touring Israel. We hung out together, and I shared about the recent outpourings of God back in their nation. The presence of God fell on this couple, and we laid hands on them and prayed. They gave their hearts to the King of Kings and asked me to baptize them. Peter and I baptized them in the Jordan River. What an honor to baptize this humble couple in the same waters that John the Baptist baptized Jesus. It is written: "And Jesus, when he was baptized, went up straightway out of the water: and, lo, the heavens were opened unto him, and he saw the Spirit of God descending like a dove, and lighting upon him: And lo a voice from heaven, saying, This is my beloved Son, in whom I am well pleased."[12]

What a trip to walk where he walked and see what he saw. Israel probably wasn't a whole lot different in many places from the way it was two thousand years ago. We stood on the shore of the Sea of Galilee, possibly near the same spot where Jesus walked out in the midst of the waves to rescue his friends. Later we floated on the Dead Sea, which was not quite as supernatural as walking on water, but very cool. I remember sitting in a little café in Tiberias looking out over the Sea of Galilee as the sun was setting. The sky began to light up the clouds with brilliant colors until we witnessed one of the most moving sunsets of my life. It definitely took my breath away. God is the ultimate artist beyond comprehension!

FULL CIRCLE

I began this story, which is focused on missions and the Great Commission, in Gothenburg, Sweden, and after our stay in Israel,

Peter and I finally landed in Copenhagen, Denmark. Within a few weeks, Danny and Linda Lehmann joined us in Stockholm, Sweden, along with another couple, Neil and Rhonda, who flew in from California with them. We ministered together in meeting after meeting, and soon we were in a big tent with fifteen hundred Swedish Christians across the boulevard from the Bob Dylan concert in Gothenburg, Sweden. This first part of the story has come full circle, as we would soon be completing this around-the-world mission—but not quite yet!

In Denmark we immediately called back home to get a draw on our funds, and after more drama and delay, we did receive around three thousand dollars. It would take many years and the intervention of John Wimber for me to get the remainder of our funds. God help us in the church in this realm of integrity, control issues, and honesty in finances. It has been a black mark in the history of all religions, but we in the Christian church need to rise above the selfish defaults of our human nature and truly start reflecting Christ. This is especially a rebuke to leaders in the body of Christ. You dish it out, but can you take it? Listen: Jesus owns everything, but he gave it *all* up for you and me! It is the goodness of God that leads to repentance. We can do a better job!

They had arranged meetings for us up and down the country in Denmark. Peter and I shared in those meetings, which were so good that it would take forever to share all that God did in Denmark and then in Sweden, where we joined up with the Lehmanns and friends. It was all wonderful and powerful, and I'll never forget any aspect of the mission around the world in 1978. But like I said before, the main event of our mission was South Africa. God put an anointing on my life in Africa that has never lifted off of me. He put it there for me to give away, and I now offer it to you. It is an anointing to be a priest after the order of Melchizedek, King of Salem. It is an offer to be ordained in a royal priesthood that goes back four thousand years to the time of Abraham—and then back even further into eternity. It was our message from God to South Africa and the world about the priesthood of every truly born-again believer. We are destined to rule and reign with Jesus our Lord in his eternal kingdom! Realize that this is reality. **I pray by the power of the Holy Spirit in the name of Jesus that you see it—and receive the charge!**

EIGHT

Riley

AFTER OUR TIME in Denmark, an absolutely astounding "divine appointment" occurred on our mission trip around the world. For me, it was a very supernatural incident concerning a man I met in an airport in Greece. We were standing next to each other in a long line of passengers, waiting to board a plane to Israel. His name was Riley.

Before coming to Greece, I had decided to part ways with my traveling partner for a period of time because we had been on the road for nearly a year. Even best of friends can get on each other's nerves, and I confess that I can be very difficult at times. So can Peter. We decided to go on our own after Denmark and Sweden. In fact, we decided that we could hardly stand to be in the same country together. He went to Spain, and I went to Greece.

You know, when you're traveling, even if you're in beautiful, far away, foreign, exotic lands, it can be pretty darn miserable if you're alone. For one thing, I had my luggage to contend with, which was super heavy. I had collected a lot of things from Africa, and I carried this burden of luggage alone in Europe. Besides all that, it's just not as much fun when you're alone. ("Where are you, Peter? I'm sorry!") It's like a log that can't burn by itself. However, if it has another log or two, it can burn—the principle of burning.

So I didn't have a good time in Athens. Nothing was right. There even seemed to be a lot of confusion and unrest on the crowded streets. I could feel it in my spirit. Then to top it off, a Greek man in a uniform mugged me outside my hotel the first night in Athens. He was about twenty-six years old, and he beat me up for my money. He rolled me. He really beat me up and terribly upset me. My assailant lifted me up and shook me like a rag doll. He was about six foot two. He shook me just like that, just like a rag doll! I'll never forget it. He picked me up right off the ground, shook me, and told me to give him my flight jacket. I told him that he would have to kill me first. Then he tried to strip my jacket off, but it was soft leather. I clinched my arms together, and he couldn't get it off. He was furious!

He said, "I'll throw you off this ledge and get the jacket off."

"Do it! 'Cause I'm not going to give you my jacket! I don't care! You have to kill me before I'll give you my jacket!"

Then he took off.

The next day on the street, I passed him in a crowd. He was walking in the opposite direction. The guy who beat me up and mugged me smiled and put his hand out. He shook hands with me in broad daylight. It happened fast.

I didn't stay in Athens for very long, because it was just so traumatic having been robbed and beaten, so I decided to go back to Jerusalem, this time alone. I needed a touch from God like *right now!* There I was in the airport, standing in line in Athens, Greece, after being mugged. I was sore and scared, and that's what can happen to you when you go to exotic places by yourself. I never advise traveling alone.

As I was waiting in the airport line, this man started to talk to me. He asked me about some of the places that I had been, so I dropped Colombia and Brazil and Africa on him.

He was going, "Uh-huh, uh-huh," and then told me, "I've been traveling two years myself." He began to tell me his sad story of falling in love with a woman. He shared how he was absolutely enamored with her and how much he loved her. He said that their relationship was eventually ruined when she became a Christian back in the States and subsequently broke up with him.

"There was this church in California called Calvary Chapel," he continued, "and this hippie preacher named Lonnie Frisbee who prayed with my girlfriend to become a born-again Christian. I wasn't a Christian, so she broke it off with me."

I was absolutely shocked when he mentioned my name in the airport line. That would have astounded anyone, and it sure did me! It absolutely astounded me! His girlfriend had gone forward and accepted Christ in my meeting. She got involved at Calvary Chapel Costa Mesa and had come out of living in immorality. He named Calvary, and he named me!

I asked him his name, and he said, "Riley."

"Well, Riley, **I'mmmmm . . . LONNIE FRISBEE!!**"

Believe me, Riley got shocked beyond anything when he found out I was Lonnie Frisbee. He knew it was definitely a God thing, and so did I. He opened up and told me how he became hooked on traveling after the breakup. He was "wanderlusting" around the world, addicted to the road. He couldn't stop anywhere for long, because he had lost his love. We can all understand that, right?

Riley told me that in Australia he was tending bar at Christmas time. There was a series of bloody fights in the bar that he worked at, right in the middle of the Christmas season. It really turned him off, and he had a personal transformation somewhat like my experience. The Lord just spoke to him at the core of his being, and he changed his whole mind about everything. He had a miraculous conversion! He accepted Christ on Christmas Day in an Australian tavern.

He was now making a spiritual journey, hoping to find somebody to teach him about the Bible. He specifically prayed and asked God about it. He was going to Jerusalem, and that's where I was going. And so that brother and I flew to Israel and stayed in the same Palestinian hotel as I had before.

Here is a side note that is really important to me to mention in this book. When I go to Jerusalem, I always live with the Palestinians. One time I got very sick, and they nursed me back to health. I've now had twelve missions to Jerusalem. The Palestinians have *been* my mission in Jerusalem. The Word says, "First to the Jew and then to the Gentile."[13] Let me repeat that: First the Jew and then the Gentile. That's a very important revelation in the Bible.

Thank God he has not only come to reveal himself to the Jews, but Jesus is reaching out to save the entire world—including all of us Gentiles. He **loves** the Palestinians, and they have been very loving toward me!

Okay, so Riley said to me, "I was praying to God and asking him to lead me to someone who could teach me the Bible and teach me about him."

I was so touched that God chose me! It is amazing how he lined me up to be in the Athens airport to fly to Israel with this man who had been brokenhearted by his girlfriend's conversion in my meeting, a meeting that had happened years before. He named my church, and he named me in an airport line in Athens, Greece! I definitely pray for divine appointments all the time and expect them, but when God dramatically answers and sets things up, it continually blows my mind in a wonderful way!

I said, "Well, Riley, you'll have to come with me!"

You know, I was just so thankful to have a brother, a little brother to share Christ with.

And so we went to Jerusalem and stayed in my special Palestinian hotel. They always charge me three dollars and fifty cents a day. Riley and I worshipped God and studied his love letter together. It was a very special time! We walked on the streets that Jesus walked, and he walked with us in our hearts. Praise God!

So to wrap this up: Riley went to Israel with me, we roomed together, and on the last day I took him down into Solomon's Quarry, which is a big cave that goes under the ground. I prayed for him, he got baptized with the Holy Spirit, and **the power of God came upon him so strong** that he shook and spoke in tongues. He spoke in the most exotic languages! The languages would change; it would be one language, then another, then it would change again and be a completely different language. He spoke in tongues for two hours straight. He came up out of Solomon's Quarry covered in sweat, and he couldn't speak in English. He could only speak in tongues!

Finally, I had to catch a plane, so I flagged down a taxi. As I got in the cab, Riley was still going, "*Abba zabba abba zabba abba—zabba abba!*" It was really incredible!

The end of the story is that that man went back to Arizona to John Higgins's church, where his girlfriend had been attending. Riley got born again in Australia, baptized in the Holy Spirit in Jerusalem, and he went back to the States and found the girl he had been so desperately in love with. He married his old girlfriend, and now they're living happily ever after—if that could ever be true! **Hallelujah!**

NINE

They Screamed, "Lonnie!"

MY EYES HAD been opened to the whole world in wonderful
new ways on our adventure around the globe. Actually, God blew
my mind with everything that he did. My mind needed to be blown.
I've said it many times, but I think it's how I'm wired. I seem to need
dramatic, "for real" stuff to stimulate my life and keep me on track.
God definitely poured it out with every step that Peter Crawford and
I took on our trip. We were finally back in the good old USA, and I
practically kissed the ground we walked on when we arrived. You
don't truly appreciate what we have here until you see and
experience the rest of the world. Praise God for America!

I truly love my good friend Peter, but I knew we had maxed each
other out. The Lord showed me clearly that, at least for now, I had
taken him as far as I could in his walk with God. I told him, "My
friend Danny Lehmann heads up a super cool ministry up by Santa
Cruz called the Land, and I think that's your next assignment."

Peter prayed about my suggestion, and it turned out to be a
perfect fit! He met a beautiful missionary girl, Colette, up there, who
eventually became his wife. Even today, Peter is still serving God
with all his heart in Santa Cruz, California. Peter and Colette now
have five beautiful kids, and we get together frequently, talk on the
phone for hours, and have had many, many more ministry
adventures over the years.

After my sad experience with having others manage my ministry
affairs, I felt led to start my own ministry. Africa and Brazil were
suddenly calling all the time, and I started making plans for my next
mission trip. The Great Commission was front and center in my
heart and in my every effort. One of my good friends who always
supported and encouraged my ministry is Brent Higginson. He was
a successful businessman who, at the time, owned a couple of high-

end hair salons and was also a managing executive in the Thomas Kinkade art empire. He was a long-time Christian brother with Hollywood connections and also close ties to Calvary Chapel. Brent also happened to be a close friend of one of my favorite people in the world, Jeff Smith, the youngest son of Chuck Smith. Jeff was about seven years old when I first met Pastor Chuck and lived with them back in 1969. Jeff became like my little brother, and we have been constant friends ever since. Brent Higginson and one of his partners financed the next several foreign mission trips almost single-handedly, and we formed a ministry that I named World Outreach Ministries.

My good friends Fred and Ruth Waugh in Riverside, CA, continued to be a major part of my life. When I turned over the ministry at All Saints to Greg Laurie, Fred and Ruth stood with me in my vision for missions. When Peter and I went on our trip around the world, they held prayer meetings in their beautiful home every week to intercede for our mission the entire time we were gone! Just before we left, they invited us over several times to lay hands on us and pray. They filled their house up with friends, Ruth baked a cake and put out all kinds of delicious food, and they took up several offerings to help us. What wonderful and special people God has in his family. We are so blessed! When we formed World Outreach Ministries, I asked Fred to be on our advisory board, and he has been a counsel to me to this very day. Eventually, they both traveled with me to South Africa as well as to South America and Brazil. Praise God for Fred and Ruth!

Right about this same time period, after returning to California, my roommate Mike McCoy came to my house along with a friend of his. Mike had recently moved out of my ghetto house in Santa Ana, but his friend John Ruttkay was looking for a place to stay. This man, John Ruttkay, would become one of the longest lasting and closest friends of my life. At the time, however, *his* whole life was upside down, mainly due to a marriage breakup. He was bleeding internally, and I could see it clear as a bell. Been there, done that!

Mike McCoy had been telling John quite a bit about me as well as some of my history and exploits, and I guess he was expecting something a little different when I came walking out of the bathroom in my housecoat. I could see it on his face. I said, "Hey, brother, you can't read a book by its cover!"

I want to have John share his version of the beginning of our friendship and later about a few of our own exploits, which were definitely on the fast track for sure!

"MEETING LONNIE"
by John Ruttkay

I was in my final semester at Melodyland School of Theology, getting ready to transition into Vanguard University. This had to have been during the beginning of 1979. I was a relatively new Christian of about four years, although I was, at the same time, an "on fire" convert after having a radical conversion from a Buddhist lifestyle. Mike McCoy and a gentleman named Fred Waugh were classmates of mine, and both of these guys were also friends of Lonnie's. They had told me a lot about this Frisbee character, much of which was hard to believe. Nevertheless, both Fred and Mike are very credible people, and I was definitely curious about Lonnie, but not *that* curious, because I was probably at the lowest point of my entire life.

Due to a painful split with my young wife, I had actually been sleeping on a friend's couch for about two weeks. That gets old real quick. Mike McCoy had become a very bright light to me during this dark period, and he told me that his friend Lonnie might want a roommate since both Peter Crawford and he had recently moved out. Mike also felt that

Lonnie would be the perfect mentor for me at this point. He shared how Lonnie Frisbee had impacted his own life.

I was a little skeptical because I had also heard that Lonnie had come out of the Shepherding movement. The last thing I needed was some kind of control freak in my life, and I told Mike, "I really wish I could just rent a room in your place instead."

We were eating at a pizza place during this conversation, and Mike said, "Look, I feel like we're supposed to go over to Lonnie's right now."

I reluctantly said, "Okay, Mike. You win. Let's check out Lonnie Frisbee."

So we went over to Lonnie's house, and I'm telling you I'll never forget it. I walked in the place, and it was like an art studio pad, *completely* bohemian. I felt extremely comfortable there because my brother is a commercial artist and my dad was a commercial artist, and I've always been around art people with that kind of bohemian bend to their personalities. And Lonnie was definitely that. I thought, "Wow, this is really cool how this place is laid out." It was messy, with stacks of paintings—some were on the walls, some on easels—and a lot of art supplies, jars of brushes, and freshly stretched canvas. Most of the art was of American Indians and buffalos, with many painted on stretched deerskins. There were large and small sculptures, busts, and leather masks scattered around almost haphazardly. At the same time, it had a "hippie pad" feel, with beads and feathers and incense. I said to myself as I looked around, "This is a very cool atmosphere." The house itself was in the "hood," and that was kind of cool also. You could see that it was a gangbanging neighborhood with heroin addicts everywhere. For some unknown reason, I felt very comfortable there. It had to be the Lord.

Then Lonnie came walking out in his bathrobe. He's small, you know, really little. I was expecting some six foot three guy from the stories I had heard. He is about five foot seven, small-boned, and wears size five shoes. He immediately read my mind and challenged me with the "book cover" line. Then he looked at me, and I looked at him, and he said, "Hi, my name's Lonnie."

"Hey, Lonnie, I'm John."

"Well, sit down and tell me a little bit about yourself."

So I did, and he was very warm, very hospitable, very loving. Lonnie listened to my story for probably an hour, just listening and going, "Uh-huh. Uh-huh. I know. I know that place. I feel ya' man. I know what's happening here." And man, it was like he reached in and was able to cauterize my bleeding on the inside. It was very much supernaturally natural with Lonnie.

The next day I grabbed everything I owned, showed up at his doorstep, and knocked. Lonnie opened the door, and I said, "Hello, roommate!"

Lonnie and I were inseparable from that time on. We did everything together. The odd thing at the time, however, was that Lonnie was only there for probably seven days before he headed out to Africa, so I was there by myself. Well, not totally by myself since we had taken in a friend's dog, which was, of all things, a large pit bull. Man, it was a big dog and a great dog! His name was Butch, and I had an instant bodyguard for company. So we had this big backyard for Butch, and I had a room in Lonnie's little bungalow. Mike McCoy eventually moved back in, but he didn't move in for a few months, so I was just there by myself with my new dog while Lonnie went away.

Before he left, Lonnie told me, "Look, you just need to take care of everything. Oh, by the way, I've been sharing Christ with these heroin addicts, so if somebody comes here, they're on the verge of coming to Jesus. You know, they're guys who I'm sharing Christ with, but I'm sure they're going to come by—so don't get freaked out."

Sure enough, Lonnie left, and I heard a knock on the door a couple of days later. There were all these heroin addicts outside going, "Lonnie here?"

"No, man, Lonnie's not here, but come on in." I brought the crew in, and these guys were awesome. They were all gangbangers and drug addicts. Lonnie had tried to help the guy across the street who later committed suicide, and that young guy had also been a dealer and a heroin addict. People knew Lonnie in the neighborhood because he just helped out a lot of people. These guys told me that the night before they first met Lonnie, the cops were literally chasing them, so in the dark they threw their heroin stash in Lonnie's front yard. That's how Lonnie first saw them—on their hands and knees in his yard the next day, looking for heroin. And that's how Lonnie befriended them.

Anyway, Lonnie was gone in Africa for probably three or four weeks. On that trip he met and spent a lot of time with Dave Owens, a leader in South Africa. I couldn't have known it then, but Dave would eventually become very close to both Lonnie and me as time marched forward.

When I first met Lonnie, I felt like I heard the Lord say, "Stand by his side and walk with him through some of the things that are coming on his life." I had no idea what that meant. Little did I know what was coming. In my wildest dreams did I ever believe that we would soon be involved in such a powerful move of the Holy Spirit together.

So I (Lonnie) came back to California after about a month on the road again. It would take forever to tell all the details, all the divine appointments, and all the little and big miracles that God did on the next few mission trips. All I can say is that Africa continued to stay the main focus for me. However, on the way to Africa I would always stop in Rio. In Brazil God connected me to a well-known bishop who headed up a large number of churches. He allowed me to preach and minister in his churches all over the country. I witnessed in the marketplace as the Lord led, with signs and wonders following. I lie not! Like I said before, I had a huge burden for Brazil, but especially for the hundreds and hundreds of homeless children on the streets of Rio.

In Africa I especially remember being invited to minister at Ray McCauley's church in Johannesburg. Ray had been Mr. South Africa as a bodybuilding champion. He got saved and went off to Bible school in the seventies. In the beginning of his walk with God, he would visit churches and say, "If you only believe that sissies serve Jesus, just look at me!" Then he would take off his shirt, flex his huge muscles, and pose—you know, this way and that way—like they do in the big muscle competitions.

So here's Ray McCauley, "*Darrr* . . . Jesus loves me. *Darrr* . . . Jesus loves you!" (You know, they call bodybuilders "meatheads." They even call each other "meatheads.") But *many* started to come to the Lord with that simple message: "Jesus loves you!" He led lots of people to the Lord like that. He started a little church in his parents' home in 1978, with about a dozen people attending. By the nineties, God had made that man the pastor of the largest church in his country.

However, when I was invited to Ray's church, they had just recently outgrown his parents' house and were meeting in a theater. I could tell he was definitely worried about what I was going to do or say. He must have heard stories about my ministry. There was a nice crowd there in the theater, and he was walking back and forth, asking me, "What are you going to do?"

"I don't know." Even if I did, I wouldn't have told him anyway. Before I get ready to speak, I don't go over everything that I'm going to do or say just to relieve the pastor's nerves.

So he continued walking back and forth, asking, "What are you going to say?"

"I don't know!"

When we both went out on the stage, the Lord came on me so powerfully that I ended up doing a Kathryn Kuhlman performance! Listen to me, the presence and anointing of God came on so strong that I shouted, "Receive the power of God!!" Then I would point in one area of the theater and scream, "Over here!" and the group I pointed to would all fall down. Then I'd shout, "Now over here!" in a different section of the crowd, and they would all fall down over there. I must have scared those South Africans half to death.

Ray said, "*Where* did you get that anointing?"

"Here."

"*When* did you come into this?"

"Now."

He said, "Ohhh. Then that means we're both in it, huh?"

It was true. The evening that I "knew" the anointing of God more than I'd ever known it before was at Ray McCauley's church in that theater. I was fifteen thousand miles away in South Africa! It's a long way from home for me, but for Ray, it was right there, right then, and I am serious, he stood up and received from God that night in a certain way so that he went out and started working *mind-blowing* miracles all over Africa. He became one of the most dynamic evangelists in Africa, leading literally thousands of people to the Lord. He has cast demons out of people. He has pulled people out of wheelchairs. He has worked visible miracles in front of people. He is very, very powerful in God, and he is pastoring the largest church in South Africa!

Before all of this, Ray McCauley just flexed his muscles and said, "If you only believe that sissies serve Jesus, then look at me!" And he obviously was not a sissy. Kind of like what the Lord would later do with pastor Phil Aguilar. I do honestly believe that God is very tired of so many wimpy, sorry Christians representing him so *weakly*. God's grabbing hold of some macho men and pouring out his Spirit in them and on them.

In Cape Town I reconnected with Derek Morphew and stayed in his home with his beautiful family. Derek and Karen made me feel like part of the family, and I wish I could put into words how important and special that was and still is to me. Derek had me minister in his church again and connected me to many other churches and leaders. That's when I first met Dave Owens, who was a leader at the Invisible Church. We became great friends, although we also bumped heads a couple of times. Remember, we are all "works in progress." Nevertheless, the doors continued to fly open all across the world.

Some of the home meetings were more powerful than the big churches and big events. I never knew what God was going to do next. It is so exciting when you get into that kind of a flow! I mean, people were getting blasted, healed, and baptized in the Holy Spirit left and right. It was really overwhelming sometimes to keep up with everything. I would have to get away with Derek and other friends and just "chill" to try to process all that was happening. When the anointing is on you, it is like you become Clark Kent, stepping out of a phone booth with a cape on. Later you have to put your spectacles back on and figure out what in the world God just did!

At those times God would lovingly remind me, "As high as the heavens are above the earth, so are my ways higher than your ways! Lean not to your own understanding, Lonnie, but in all your ways acknowledge me, and I will direct your path!"

BACK HOME

When I returned from my second journey to Africa, John Ruttkay had taken good care of home base back in the hood. He was slowly but surely coming alive again after his failing marriage. It was a joy having John as a roommate and friend. I could see God's hand on him in a mighty way. He is so real, honest, and transparent and such a good communicator. I took John with me almost everywhere.

Even though I was no longer officially with Calvary Chapel Costa Mesa and still smarting from the continuing dispute over my mission funds, I still had many, many long-standing relationships and friendships with other Calvary Chapel pastors and churches throughout California and beyond. There must have been many hundreds or more Calvary Chapel offshoots by 1979, and I would get different invitations to come preach. In the past I was invited to big Calvary Chapel pastors' conferences where I met many of the new leaders, including John Wimber, the pastor of Calvary Chapel Yorba Linda. I was very impressed with John Wimber, and we talked for quite a while.

Between foreign mission trips, local speaking engagements, and ministry trips to Santa Cruz and San Francisco, I also helped a friend named Gerard Driscoll start a new work in Long Beach, CA, which we named "Wednesday Night Live." We quickly built a following of around two hundred Spirit-filled believers, whom Gerard pastored. A young gal named Jill Austin ran the overhead projector in those meetings, and she and I would become very close friends. She matured into a totally sold-out prophetic voice in the earth and eventually headed up an international ministry named Master Potter Ministries. God put an anointing on that girl—I am not exaggerating!

Mike McCoy moved back in my pad, and what a great friend he was over the years. So now it was John, Mike, myself, and our mascot Butch all living in our ghetto residence in Santa Ana, California. I love living in community with other believers, and believe me, there was never a dull moment. We all had super busy lives with tons of people coming in and out. At that time I also had several invitations from churches in Denmark again. It had been almost a year since I was there last, and we scheduled a return trip for June. Since John Ruttkay was graduating that spring, his time would finally be free, and I wanted to take him with me on this upcoming mission to Europe. It was the first of many foreign missions together, and what a fantastic time it was. Here is John's account of that first trip.

"THEY SCREAMED, 'LONNIE! LONNIE!'"
by John Ruttkay

Before I tell about our trip to Europe in 1979, I want to tell about the first time I ever heard Lonnie speak publically or preach in a church. When Lonnie returned from Africa after I moved into his place, he was all jet-lagged and trying to get back into the everyday flow in America. I was busy with school, and I remember one time we did something on a Saturday night and came home really late.

Lonnie said, "Oh man, I've got to preach tomorrow."

I kept thinking, "He's not getting anything ready. He's not prepared for nothing!"

Lonnie gave me an address in the morning and said, "Look, we've got to go to this place." He still hadn't prepared anything for the service by this point.

We were finding our way to this Calvary Chapel church, probably around ten in the morning. Lonnie was sound asleep in the front seat, and I thought, "Man, this will be interesting."

Remember, this is the first time that I saw Lonnie preach. We got to the church, he went in the bathroom, splashed

121

water on his face, brushed his hair a little, pushed his hair back, swished water in his mouth and spat it out, grabbed a Bible, walked out in front of the church . . . and I'm telling you, it was one of the most powerful messages I ever heard. The place got *lit up!* Words cannot describe what went on that day.

It was so interesting to me just to see how Lonnie navigated those waters. The next six months were some of the best months of my life. At the same time, it was one of the most difficult times of my life. I was working full time and still trying to patch things up with my wife, plus it was one of those seasons where I just *had* to get through school. Lucy, a former witch, became Lonnie's secretary, so she typed all my papers for me, which helped. We had such a close-knit community there. There was Mike and Lonnie and Lucy, and, of course, Butch the pit bull. There were all kinds of other people who were in our little circle. It was such a powerful time with people constantly in and out, along with great food and fellowship. Lonnie was like a gourmet cook. It was amazing and wonderful! Dietrich Bonhoeffer, one of Lonnie's heroes, would have been proud of us.

Then that June I graduated, and Lonnie wanted to go over to Europe. He said, "You're going with me, and we're going to go to Denmark and through Europe. We're going to go to Sweden, Germany, and then down to Italy and over to Greece." So we went and spent probably eight weeks in Europe, and *man,* was that fun. I took my savings out of the bank, and I think Brent Higginson financed Lonnie and most of the mission through World Outreach Missions. God met us there in some really awesome ways.

We got to Denmark, and I'll never forget it, people on the streets were yelling, "Lonnie! Lonnie!" People were actually screaming out to him. We were in this big city called Aarhus, Denmark, staying with this anesthesiologist. A decade before, back in the Jesus movement on Lonnie's first trip to Europe with Kenn Gulliksen and all those guys, and back when he first met Fred Waugh, Lonnie had a word of knowledge over this anesthesiologist. The word was that he was addicted to drugs and God was going to break off the addiction. We stayed at this doctor's home, and he said, "God met me so powerfully in that meeting with Lonnie that it changed my whole life!" This man became one of the leaders in churches in Denmark.

As we were walking through the streets one day, this other guy yelled, "Lonnie! Lonnie! Hi, Lonnie! We miss you, Lonnie!" So we all went to this guy's house to visit. He had an old vinyl 45 that they had made, and on it Lonnie was singing the song "Hallelujah" in a meeting from probably 1971. Lonnie sounded like a frog, you know, because he really could not sing. It was hysterical! But man, the people looked to Lonnie with such respect and love. He was really the catalyst of a genuine move of God in their midst.

We were in Europe for probably a little over two months and had an incredible time. Lonnie is just a fun person to be around. The meetings were powerful, the divine appointments so unbelievable, and we were just enjoying traveling and running into interesting people. He preached mostly in Denmark. Then we took off and went south through the rest of Europe and down through Italy. We went into the Greek islands and to the beautiful island of Corfu in the Ionian Sea. There is so much history in Europe going back thousands of years. It was so much fun, and such a great time! It was on this trip that I became hooked on missions forever.

∞

ANOTHER OUTPOURING

John Ruttkay and I (Lonnie) returned to America, and we didn't know it, but God was getting ready to initiate another mighty outpouring of his Spirit. It would be different than the Jesus People movement, but it would complete the birth of another "non-denominational" denomination that would impact the whole world!

TEN

A New Season

WHEN JOHN RUTTKAY and I came back from Europe, I entered one of the greatest seasons of my life. Denmark and the rest of Europe had been off the scale, as far as an exciting and productive mission trip goes. God *definitely* knows how to keep life interesting and more than fulfilling as we grab his hand and let Jesus lead us. Like always, it was so good to be "back in the USA." Chuck Berry and Linda Ronstadt tell us all about it. I love America. As time marched forward, I saw that there was a much-publicized "Washington for Jesus" rally happening soon on April 29, 1980. I knew in my heart that I was supposed to be there.

I told John, "Let's do another quick trip and check out this Jesus rally in Washington. God is telling me that we should go!"

John immediately responded, "Heck yeah, let's go! I grew up in Washington, D.C. We could stay with my family back there."

I was learning real quick that it was never hard to get John Ruttkay up for an adventure with Jesus. We were like the minutemen in Colonial days. You go about your regular life, go to the grocery store, pay your bills, and then someone sounds the alarm! You drop everything, grab your musket, and head out to the front lines of the battle. The battle might be in Denmark or in South Africa or right here at home.

In 1980, America was in trouble! We were taking God out of our history books, our schools and universities, along with everything else. The nation had taken a hard left turn. Some of us well-meaning hippies had unwittingly helped in the process! However, there was an important national election happening in November. The call was to fast and pray for our country in the capital of our nation.

When we arrived in Washington, D.C., I was amazed. Thousands and thousands of Christians converged on the capital.

The crowd estimates ranged from two hundred thousand to seven hundred thousand. It was at least a half a million or more. The mainstream media played it down, but the church sounded the trumpet—and the true believers rallied to the call. It was amazing. I told John, "We need to march at the front of this thing." They had a huge banner that said, "Washington for Jesus," and I grabbed a spot on one end, John grabbed the middle, and a very famous man named Harald Bredesen was on the other end. Every cell in my body felt the presence and power of God during that march. It was awesome!

I want you as the reader to get John Ruttkay's perspective again on this new season that we had just entered during late '79 and early '80. He is the one God chose to walk with me during the next few chapters of my life. As I mentioned before, John Ruttkay is such a good communicator, and I really want him to bring to life at least a little touch of what God was up to during this time period.

"CIRCLING THE CAMP"
by John Ruttkay

When Lonnie and I returned from Europe, it was going into the fall of 1979. We all stayed busy as usual. I worked on a few construction jobs. Lonnie planned another trip to Africa, worked with Brent Higginson putting together an advisory board for World Outreach Missions, and ministered to people and churches at every opportunity. I went with him to almost everything that I could. Lonnie Frisbee was my mentor, my friend, and my hero in the faith, all wrapped into one. There was never a dull moment, or if there was one, it was quickly dispelled by some dramatic God thing!

Our trip to Washington, D.C. was no exception. In fact, it was historic in the eyes of a multitude of people. And talk about a multitude of people! The massive crowd was jammed into the streets and venues of our capital as far as the eye could see. It was historic in the annals of America, and I believe it was historic in the annals of heaven. We fasted and prayed, marched, and cried out to God for our nation.

Many believe that the prayers and intercession during the "Washington for Jesus" event, which was totally non-political, nevertheless launched Ronald Reagan into the White House more than anything else. The Bible declares, "If my people, called by my name, will humble themselves and pray, then I will hear from heaven and heal their land."[14]

Washington for Jesus Rally, 1980

Six months and a few days later in November 1980, Ronald Reagan shocked the world by winning the election over Jimmy Carter by a total landslide.

President Carter's perceived weak and indecisive leadership had led to a bunch of Iranian students in Tehran taking fifty-two diplomats and American citizens hostage for 444 days. Iran released our hostages literally minutes after Reagan was sworn into office. Ronald Reagan turned our nation back to sanity and to godly principles for the next decade, and many people believe he was one of our greatest presidents.

While we were staying at my parents' home during this trip to Washington, D.C., we also decided to attend a meeting called TAG, or Take and Give, a ministry led by C. J. Mahaney and Larry Tomczak. There were at least a

127

thousand people at this meeting, which also included leaders like Lou Engle of The Call and Che Ahn, now the pastor of Harvest Rock Church in Pasadena, CA. The worship was awesome and the teaching was amazing, but the highlight was when someone in the congregation gave a message in tongues, and Lonnie stood up and gave the interpretation.

At the top of his lungs, Lonnie declared, "This is the word of the Lord for this season. It is for the church to come together," and then he quoted Psalm 133 word for word:

> Behold, how good and how pleasant it is for brethren to dwell together in unity! It is like the precious ointment upon the head, that ran down upon the beard, even Aaron's beard: that went down to the skirts of his garments; As the dew of Hermon, and as the dew that descended upon the mountains of Zion: for there the Lord commanded the blessing, even life for evermore.

I was just going, "Whoa, man!" I'll never forget it.

C. J. Mahaney stopped the meeting and said, "I don't know who you are over there—"

I thought to myself, "Oh boy, this will be interesting."

"—but," Mahaney continued, "I came here tonight asking the Lord something because I got Psalm 133 to preach on tonight. I was asking, 'Lord, could you confirm this?'"

The place just went *crazy!* It absolutely erupted. The anointing of God fell on that place so powerfully. It was also interesting because people had found out who Lonnie was and asked for a meeting with him the next day. I was *really* excited about it. I said, "Man, the Lord's already opening up doors here for you, Lonnie."

He said, "No, this isn't a door. This is a trap. These guys are not out for my good. These guys are out to trap me and destroy me."

"Really?"

"Yeah. I can tell you right now this is a trap!"

So we met with these Christian "brothers" at a Howard Johnson's in Washington, D.C. We sat there, and these guys came in, and we all had breakfast. It was small talk for a while, and then one of them said, "So, Lonnie, we understand that you're here—but *why* are you here exactly?"

All of these guys had come out of the Shepherding movement and apparently were afraid that Lonnie was coming in town and trying to take some kind of spiritual authority or something like that. They started to confront and attack him. I was flabbergasted at what I saw and kept thinking, "Are you kidding me?"

Lonnie simply said, "Okay, guys, great to meet you— goodbye! You have nothing on me, and there's nothing here that I'm interested in. I'm just passing through."

A couple of years later, I went to this church of a friend of mine, and this particular fellowship was one of the fastest-growing churches in D.C. A little of Lonnie's boldness must have rubbed off on me, and I had a prophetic word for the church, which they graciously allowed me to give. After I prophesied, this guy came up to me and asked, "Is there an opportunity for us to have lunch together?"

So we had lunch, and I soon recognized who he was. I said, "Oh, you were one of the guys here in D.C. who confronted my friend Frisbee."

"Oh my gosh!" he responded. "I am. And now I remember you also."

"Why did you do that?"

"Listen," he explained, "it was all part of the Shepherding movement. And you know what, John? Those same guys attacked me soon after. It was devastating for me."

My respect for Lonnie's discernment really soared with this additional confirmation. Lonnie had immediately seen a trap, while I was totally blind to it. Pray that God would give us all more discernment in the body of Christ! In fact, Lonnie was a champion for demonstrating, modeling, and advocating all the gifts of the Holy Spirit. There are nine spiritual gifts listed in the Bible in 1 Corinthians 12: words of wisdom, words of knowledge, the gift of faith, the gift of healing, the working of miracles, prophecy, the discerning of spirits, speaking in tongues, and the interpretation of tongues. I saw Lonnie Frisbee constantly operating in all of these gifts. He was definitely a man with a lot of flaws and failures, but he violently went after God and all that God wanted to do in his life. Lonnie would always tell me, "John, you can have all the gifts operating, but if you don't have love, you have NOTHING!" Now *that* is a word of wisdom!

Back in California, we began hearing a lot about this one particular Calvary Chapel in Yorba Linda. Friends of ours were raving about how special and powerful the worship was there, so Lonnie wanted to check it out. John Wimber, who had had a significant career in the secular music world, pastored the church. He played a mean keyboard and had been the manager for the Righteous Brothers, among other notable credits.

However, before we had a chance to check out John Wimber's church, we stayed pretty darn busy with Wednesday Night Live in Long Beach and other ministry tasks. It seemed to be unending. Sometimes when Lonnie would lead the Wednesday night service instead of Gerard Driscoll, he would cut me loose to preach. I had never preached before in front of a large group like that. In fact, it was the first time for me to see the power of God move while

I was on stage. That's how Lonnie worked—he would push you out into "that place." Whether you liked it or not, you were going!

Lonnie would instruct, "Well, you better listen to God, pay attention to what he's saying, and just do what he tells you to do!" (Simple? Yes and no!) If it got too goofy, he would come in and help finish the message. He was really gracious like that. Lonnie was a great teacher when it came to those aspects of the ministry. Anyway, that's the way Lonnie would disciple: He'd throw you out of the plane and yell down at you while you were free-falling, "Don't worry, you've got a parachute!" So Lonnie was good at developing preachers. I was very blessed to have had Lonnie Frisbee as a mentor. You can't help but get some of the DNA of whoever's influencing your life. I am grateful to God for Lonnie and the anointing that was on his life.

Even though we were super busy, and while I was, at the same time, very much trying to reconcile with my wife, we found the time to "circle the camp" of Calvary Chapel Yorba Linda. Lonnie told me, "If you really want to find out what's happening in a particular church, then get to know the intercessors."

We went to Calvary Yorba Linda on Sunday a couple of times and also went to several of the intercessory groups. It was in one of those intercessory meetings that a sweet lady said, "We're pressing in because we feel like we're on the verge of a move of God over this church, but there just needs to be a *pop* of that proverbial cork."

I asked what the problem was and who the cork was, and she said, "It's the pastor." I didn't really even know much about John Wimber. I just saw him preach a couple of times. Lonnie and I were only there at Canyon High School maybe two or three times at the most, but you could *feel* that there was something vibrant getting ready to happen. Lonnie would often put up his spiritual index finger to feel if there was any wind in a place. He would always do that, trying to gauge the spiritual temperature of a place, hot or cold. He got very excited because he felt a strong fresh wind blowing across Calvary Chapel Yorba Linda. The music was very powerfully anointed. It was definitely setting the spiritual atmosphere.

In addition to all these signals from the Holy Spirit, Lonnie had met John Wimber at a Calvary pastors' conference some time back, and they had talked about potentially doing a meeting in the future. Now, two or three years later, Lonnie's antennas were going way up! We went to this one youth concert at a high school put on by a band from Calvary Yorba Linda. Lonnie shared after the music and prayed for several of the kids. This one young guy named Ray Hersom, along with others, was mightily touched by the Holy Spirit!

It turned out that this particular young man, Ray, was close friends with the entire Wimber family and practically grew up with the Wimber kids. John heard about this encounter and asked exactly what happened. It was a big deal in front of a bunch of church members. The young family friend told John Wimber that it was about the most radical experience of his life and that the presence of God was like electricity and waves of power. John had known this kid all his life and that he was not some flaky person. John had already taken notice that Lonnie was coming around, circling the camp, and he finally called Lonnie up and invited him to a dinner at his home. It was really wonderful that I, being Lonnie's roommate, was able to tag along to this dinner.

"TEN THOUSAND VOLTS"
by Ray Hersom

In 1979, I was playing in a Christian band with Chris Wimber, about a month before a soon-to-be-famous Mother's Day meeting at Calvary Chapel Yorba Linda, our church. We were a youth band from the church, and we rented out the lecture hall at El Dorado High to put on a concert. A guy named Lonnie Frisbee (I had never heard of him before) spoke after we played. I was all sweaty after playing, so I went outside to cool off and did not even hear Lonnie speak. However, when I returned, Lonnie had called down some teens and those in their early twenties to the front. There were about twenty-five kids circling around him, so I went down to see what he was saying, standing just outside of the group. He pointed to me and said, "God wants to use you!"

I said to myself, "Whatever you want to do God, I say *yes*." Lonnie prayed a quick prayer for me and then told me to start praying for the other people. I had never seen any move of the Spirit before. I started to pray for the people and suddenly started to feel this power flow through my hands into these people. It was like ten thousand volts of electricity flowing through me. I was totally overwhelmed and amazed. I had never experienced the power of God or seen anything like that. Lonnie also prayed for Judy King to do the same.

My friend Chris Wimber went home and told his dad, John Wimber, "Ray amped out tonight!" John, knowing me well since I was his son's best friend, understood that I would not be emotional or make this up. He thought this might be God. So after praying about it and knowing Judy King and me, John invited Lonnie over to his house for dinner with some other church leaders to investigate further. God subsequently told John to have Lonnie preach on Mother's Day 1980. The power fell on the church that day, and the entire church has never been the same. So we started learning about God's power and the Holy Spirit.

Here is a short update: I was talking to God in 2012 and asked about that power encounter way back when I felt that power in my arms. Then I looked down at my arms, and it was suddenly like I could see—inside of my arms—the arms of Jesus! Then Jesus spoke and said, "That is what I want my church to know—that when they lay hands on people, they are my hands! I do not want them to know this theologically, but to 'know that they know.'"

Then I asked God, "Is there anything you want to say to me?"

"I love you, and you are my son with whom I am well pleased."

These are the two things that we need to realize in order to move and love like Jesus. He loves us more than we can imagine, and he is inside our hearts—and arms! After all these years, God is still using that experience for me to draw on God's power and love.

BLOW THE CORK

So John Wimber called and invited me (Lonnie) to dinner at his home. I knew God was really up to something during this season, but I didn't have a clue how it would all shape up. So much was happening with Africa and all our mission trips as well as our Long Beach fellowship. It was too many plates for me to spin. All I could do was flow with it. Also, right about this same time, Dave Owens from South Africa flew to America and stayed with us in my little home. He had been blasted by the Holy Spirit on a recent trip over there in South Africa and was seeking to find his way from the

Invisible Church into what the next move was, you know, that God had for him because he was a strong leader. You could tell that there was a gift of leadership on him. All this was happening fast—very fast! Sometimes you need to march with the cadence of the footmen, and then sometimes you need to run with the horsemen when the beat doubles! One thing was for sure: The beat was doubling in 1980, and I was excited about meeting with John Wimber at his home.

Little did I know that the cork was about to go *KABAM!*

ELEVEN
Mother's Day 1980

"Holy Spirit, Come"

JOHN WIMBER HAD invited me to his home for dinner, and I knew it was an important divine appointment, not just some ordinary dinner engagement. I told John Ruttkay, "Let's go!"

When we arrived at the Wimber residence, John was so warm and gracious, and his wife, Carol, was totally sweet and hospitable. Immediately, I felt very comfortable and, most importantly, I felt the presence of God. I definitely felt a sense of destiny in the air, which heightens all the senses, if you know what I mean. I love being in the center of God's will. There are those times when you absolutely know it for sure, and this was one of them. The center of God's will is where the action is! Several of John Wimber's leaders were also there, including Bob Fulton and Sam Thompson. We joked around with each other, and then they served up some incredible food. It was so much fun hanging out with these guys. They definitely threw the welcome mat out, and John Ruttkay enjoyed it as much as I did.

They collectively told me, "Lonnie, we know you've been coming around, and so if you feel led, we want to cut you loose! God is going to open some doors for you here. Let's pick a time for you to share your testimony and see where God takes us."

They were all laughing, but I kept thinking to myself, "Lonnie, you need this gig, and you're absolutely going to be on your *best* behavior from everything you've ever learned in the church. You're not going to screw this thing up!" I desperately wanted a healthy home church, a place I was welcome and could be part of the team. It was all I wanted, really!

As we walked out the gate from John and Carol Wimber's home, John Ruttkay told me, "Lonnie, they want to cut you loose, but they don't have a clue what they're asking for!"

"Listen, John, I'm going to behave and take it slow. Let's just keep praying. I need this!"

We eventually picked Sunday, May 11th, Mother's Day, for me to share. I was determined to be on my best behavior, to tone it down, to play it safe . . . but God Almighty had something else in mind!

So in the Sunday evening service on May 11, 1980, John Wimber introduced me to the congregation of Calvary Chapel Yorba Linda. The church met at a large local high school, which was named Canyon High, located in an eastern section of Orange County, California. There were at least three or four hundred people in the crowd, maybe more.

After the worship time, which was totally awesome, John addressed the church saying, "The Lord led me to have Lonnie Frisbee share, and so I want him to come now and conduct the meeting as the Lord leads him."

I'm going to quote some of the message that I brought to the people that Mother's Day evening directly, but it was also recorded on audiotape and pretty widely available if anyone wants to hear the whole thing.

MOTHER'S DAY

"A microphone and lights and people—what more can you want? When I was a kid, I was a frustrated Mouseketeer. I used to sit in front of a TV about *this* close, and they'd have 'roll call.' Because they had a Mouseketeer named Lonnie, I'd jump up and yell out my name and say, 'Lonnie!' And when my folks had company over, I'd get up and tap dance for all the company. It was a problem because I was born with clubfeet and could only tap dance with one foot good. But my parents were always saying, 'Sit down, sit down.' Well, I have to admit that I love to get up and talk before people, but it's a joy to be here tonight and represent Jesus Christ. I just want to say that I feel this is my new home here with you people. I travel a lot, but John and I decided that we're going to move together in the

138

Lord. He's going to help me when I'm down, and you're going to be my family in Jesus. I feel welcome here.

"I think the Lord's going to meet us tonight in a special way, so I want you to be in expectancy for a move of the Spirit of God. The Lord says, 'Wherever two or three are gathered in my name, there I am also in the midst of them. Wherever two or three will agree in touching anything, it shall be given unto them.'[15]

"This morning when we were coming to church, I was with a friend named Mark, and we got out of the car. All of a sudden, the word *Zion* came into my mind.

"I told Mark, 'We're going to Zion! We're marching to Zion right now! Zion used to be a mountain, a specific place, but now Zion is the mountain of God where the people of God gather. We're going to Zion right now!'

"We came in, John said, 'Turn to Hebrews Chapter 12,' and he preached on Mount Zion.

"It's a beautiful thing how the Lord gives you confirmations. John and I met three years ago at a pastors' conference, and the Lord told us that he was going to join us together. It has taken three years to do it because I'm a chicken. I kind of shy away from authority, but he's not too bad. He kind of reminds me of a teddy bear, you know what I mean?

"Some of you don't know me, so I'll just share a little bit about what the Lord has done. It's going to be a little smorgasbord. I started in the ministry twelve years ago in the Haight-Ashbury with a group of people called to serve the Lord outside of the 'organized church.' We weren't involved in any kind of church structure at all. We were just regular ol' roper dopers, and I was a nudist vegetarian hippie. I would go into the desert and take all my clothes off, and scream, 'God, if you're really real, reveal yourself to me!'

"One afternoon the whole atmosphere of this canyon that I was in started to tingle and get light, started to change, and I was there just going, 'Uh-oh.' I didn't want to be there!

"But the Lord identified himself. He said, 'I'm Jesus. I build nations and I tear them down. It's better for a nation never to have known me than to have known me and turned their back from me.'

"That's one of the first things that God told me. I didn't know what that meant, 'I build nations and I tear them down.'

"He said, 'I am the way, the truth, and the life. No man comes unto the Father, but by me. I am the door of the sheepfold. If any man enters in by another way, that man is a thief and a robber, and the gatekeeper will not open unto him.'

"I always thought that all roads led to Rome, but he explained to me that he was the only way to know God. So I accepted him (actually it was the *call* of God that I accepted, because I had previously, with partial understanding, received Jesus as an eight-year-old child).

"Then Jesus said, 'I'm going to send you to the people.'

"I saw a vision of thousands of people, all wandering around in a maze of gray darkness, bumping into one another with no direction or purpose for their lives. Then the Lord showed me that he was placing a light on me and on my life, and that light was Jesus Christ. I was going to bear the Word of the Lord.

"So I immediately started looking around for a staff because, you know, all prophets have staffs. In the movies they do. Charlton Heston did. I had a little taste for the flamboyant, so I got a staff. I also started to grow my hair a little bit longer than it was. I grew a long beard. You know, I couldn't tell a secret after the sixth grade— I just had a full beard at an early age—and so when I grew it out, I really looked like Isaiah's grandson. I was pastoring at Calvary at the age of nineteen, but no one knew how old I was because I looked like I just came out of a cave. I wore Saint Francis of Assisi shirts with hoods on them and robes and things like that.

"I was in a little Foursquare church when I got baptized with the Holy Spirit, and there was this evangelist from Texas, the kind of man who threw the microphone cord around and screamed, 'In the name of Jesus!'—you know, sweating all over the place. Well, I got it. I couldn't help but get it. It was like ten thousand volts of electricity. These people were falling down on the floor, and when they fell down on the floor, others threw blankets over them. I thought, 'That must be the mantle of the Lord,' like in the Old Testament when Elisha picked up Elijah's mantle and touched the stream. So I thought that that was the mantle of the Lord. I didn't know they were just modesty blankets that they were throwing on the women to cover up their knees. I thought it was the anointed mantle of the Lord. So I got my own. I didn't like the blankets they were using, so I got a deerskin to be my mantle. I painted a picture of Jesus on it and wore it like a cape. When I would pray for people and the Spirit of God would come on them, I'd take off my cape and throw the mantle over the top of them. When the ministry started getting good, I had to get two leathers.

"But the Lord started straightening me out, and he led Chuck Smith and me together. One night we were sharing our testimonies in the church for the first time, and at that particular point, there was a core of about thirty to ninety people attending the church. We had a little church. It was about as big as the corner of this room right here. It fit ninety people comfortably, a hundred tight. There were fifteen of us praying at the altar that night, and the Spirit of God prophesied through Kay Smith and said to us, 'Because of your praise and adoration before my throne tonight, I'm going to bless the whole coast of California.'

"I thought, 'Whew! She really thought of a dilly tonight!' But then I thought, 'The whole coast of California. That's got to be God!'

"When we started to receive the word as from God, the Spirit of the Lord fell upon us and we began to weep, and the Lord began to give people visions of that prophecy. The Lord continued on to say that it was going to move across the United States and then go into different parts of the world. That's when there was hardly any young people going to Calvary at all. From that day on, we went to the beaches and to the parks outreaching, taking on the Great

Commission as if it depended on *us!* Not relying on anybody else to do it—just us!

"I sense that we're experiencing a second wave of God. I believe that we're having an outpouring of the Holy Spirit, something similar to what I sensed back then eleven years ago. I sense it in the atmosphere. I sense it in the eyes. I sense it in the voices of the people I hear responding to the Lord in this hour. God is moving upon you in a very blessed way! Some of you are just new to it. You're just being introduced to it. I always thought that revival would continue on and on, that it was always going to be the same. But a revival doesn't always continue on, and I want to encourage you tonight to go *on* toward what God is doing. *Press into it!* Don't take for granted the timing or the season that we're in.

"One of the secrets, the reason why there are twenty-five thousand people going to Calvary out there now is because of a mixture of things. I think it's important to hear the story. When I first met Chuck Smith and the people who went to his church, they were mostly all John Birch-ers. I didn't know what a John Birch-er was. I used to go take Communion with the Mormons. I didn't know the difference between a Jehovah's Witness and a born-again Christian. I used to invite them in and talk about Jesus.

"But anyway, I was an extreme leftist, marching in the peace rallies, and I was against Vietnam. And here was a whole bunch of John Birch-ers, and they were inviting me in, and—you see how much of a miracle that was? To fellowship with a long-haired hippie when they believed in the John Birch Society type of doctrine or whatever you want to call it. But it was a radical accepting, the dropping of opinions. Then it was the 'wisdom of the age and the zeal of the youth' that was combined together. I think that you have that flavor here. I sense that.

"But you see, the young people were saying, 'Don't trust anybody over thirty!' Well, I'm thirty-one now, I have to change my doctrine. But that's what the young people thought, 'Don't trust anybody over thirty,' and there were good reasons.

"The adults at the same time were saying, 'Stupid kids. You don't have a brain in your head. Get over there!'

"And here these kids were coming up, saying, 'Let's see, I don't want to embrace materialism, because that destroys you, and I think we ought to be a little more free about the things that we think and say. There's a new thing happening—see?'

"But the adults were saying, 'Stupid!'

"It's a bummer to be rejected by adults, especially when you have something to say, even if you're confused about it. So the adults weren't accepting the young people. They weren't even *listening*; they weren't even paying attention, because the young people were saying good things!

"At that time there was a combination of 'the wisdom of the age' and 'the zeal of the youth,' combining the cross-culture of what was going on and accepting one another in love. The young people started receiving Christ, and the old folks started to see and listen!

"Then the Lord started to bless. There started to be a momentum in what God was doing. We had a mid-week service that started at seven o'clock, and the church was filled at four. It didn't let out until almost midnight. Kids coming from LA and Long Beach were getting back home at one o'clock in the morning, and their parents were saying, 'Where were you on Wednesday night?'

'Oh, we went to church.'

'Liar! Nobody can go to church from four o'clock till one o'clock. That's crazy!'

'Well, go down there and see for yourself.'

"The parents would come out, and they would get born again! That's how we started getting the older people to come: The older people came to the Lord through their kids. It used to be the other way around in the church. The parents used to pray for the kids all the time, but this revival was bringing in the parents."

OUTPOURING OF THE SPIRIT

Then that night at Calvary Yorba Linda, as I continued my little smorgasbord presentation, I went on to tell about some of my experiences with Kathryn Kuhlman and other stories. I told the story of trying to heal the young Mexican man who was wearing a neck brace in a coffee shop in Texas. I shared about my "wart healing" miracle ministry at Calvary Costa Mesa and a few other stories, which I already wrote about in previous chapters. The crowd was definitely with me, and from the moment I started sharing, I had them laughing and cracking up, which I love. I feel the Lord when the people laugh!

I shared a little about getting into some spiritual error in Florida and about Chuck graciously taking me back on staff before sending me off to Africa "by faith." I shared about the miracle provision and then my recent Africa stories. I shared it all, along with the healings and incredible outpouring of the Holy Spirit. The presence and power of God filled my body as I ministered that night.

I continued and told the people: "It has to be the body of Christ functioning together because the responsibilities in these days are too great for one man! It's crushing. I see ministers having nervous breakdowns because they didn't learn how to delegate authority. You are a model of what God wants to show the church in a lot of places. Learn, move, flow—it will be a little dangerous. Learn how to step out, you know, a little bit more when the Lord says, 'Come.' The Lord's saying, 'Come.' The Lord tonight is saying to you, 'Come, let's go into a greater dimension.' Now listen to this:

Arise, shine; for thy light is come, and the glory of the Lord is risen upon thee. For, behold, the darkness shall cover the earth, and gross darkness the people: but the Lord shall arise upon thee, and his glory shall be seen upon thee. And the Gentiles shall come unto thy light, and kings to the brightness of thy rising. Lift up thine eyes round about, and see: all they gather themselves together, they come to thee: thy sons shall come from far, and thy daughters shall be nursed at thy side. Then thou shalt see, and flow together, and thine heart shall fear, and be enlarged; because the abundance of the sea shall be converted unto thee, the forces of the Gentiles shall come unto thee.[16]

"Now we're living in the age of the Gentiles. We're coming to the close of an age. What you're experiencing is a period of grace; it's not going to last. The country is in severe trouble. Last week I was with seven thousand leaders from all over the United States, which included the largest assembly of cross-pollination of the body of Christ in the history of the United States. Every one of those speakers got up and said, 'We're really in trouble. The only help and the only hope for the country right now is how the church is going to respond to turning to God.'

"Christians in the United States are spoiled. They are in some other countries too. The enemy does it with prosperity. That's why people are trying so desperately to cling to the prosperity doctrines. I don't want to slam that too hard, but we're blinded by materialism. Now, notice how the verse says, 'Arise,' or 'Get up, make yourself available.' I think that the word for today is *availability*. I've heard the Spirit of God say that: 'Availability! I'll use *anyone*!'

"Now some of you may have a complex and say, 'Lord, you can't use me. I'm nothing.' You know when some of you struggle to get up and talk? Every time that you have an opportunity to share the Lord, remember it's not by your strength. It's not by might, nor by power, but by the Spirit of the Lord. And if the Lord can speak through a jackass, he can speak through you! Right? Now, it says, 'Shine.' This is the countenance of the Lord coming from us.

"I love to see freshly born-again believers. Can you see something about their countenance? Do you know when somebody *really* meets the Lord? When you look at them, they're *shining!* Everything's fresh, everything's new. Everything has so much hope to it. It's really the countenance of the Lord. The high priests of God used to stand up, lift up their hands to the people, and say, 'Let your

145

face be lifted up upon their faces, may your countenance be lifted up upon them.'[17]

"What happened to Moses when he went to the mountain? He encountered the living God! He came back to the people shining! His skin shined! Physically shined, it was *real*! It was something people could see—and it scared them. He had to cover his face, it was so real. We can read about it. It says, 'Shine, for thy light has come and the *glory* of the Lord has risen upon you.' Did you know that that can be a witness to people and you don't even have to speak a word to them? Have you ever had somebody come up to you on the street and say, 'What is it about you? Why are you so happy? Why are your eyes so shiny??'

"Well, if they had asked me years before, I'd have said, 'Acid!' But now it's the Holy Ghost! And it doesn't compare to anything that the world has. This is what the world *wants!* They want the peace. They want the radiance of life. That's what the Lord says, but then he doesn't promise you a rose garden. Like that country western song: '*I beg your pardon*'—sometimes I hear the Lord singing that to me in the Spirit—'*I never promised you a rose garden.*' Can you relate to that? 'Come to the Lord! He'll heal you, he'll prosper you, everything will be all right, and you won't have any problems, he'll take care of *everything*! Or go to hell and roast like a chestnut!' We get these ministers promising everything on a silver platter, and then you come along a couple of years into the Lord, the honeymoon's over, and you're going, 'What's this? Trials? Tribulations? Oh no! No fair! Oh, the rapture is coming, and it's—' We're becoming Christian escape artists!

"I have my hope in the Lord, and I have my hope in the second coming. But let me tell you something: 'Consider it not strange, brethren, the fiery trial that *will* test your faith as if some strange thing has come upon you.'[18] Look at what it says right there!

"We should be prepared. I don't think that the church is going to have to suffer God's wrath, but I think that the *pre*-tribulation to the *great* tribulation is going to be bad enough. I think it's already upon us with the marriage problems and the confusion in the head and all kinds of things that are coming upon Christians.

"Look at this: 'For, behold, the darkness shall cover the earth, and gross darkness the people.'[19] Isn't that what is happening? 'But the Lord will rise upon thee, and his glory shall be seen upon you.'

"There will come a blessing as we enter into covenant, as we enter into community, as we enter into the things of God! He shows us a freshness that his presence will come upon us and shine through us! He'll anoint our words. He'll anoint our efforts. Then it talks about world evangelism, about the abundance of the sea. The kings of the Gentiles will come unto you, and they'll be converted!

"The disciples said, 'Lord, is it now that you're going to restore the kingdom unto Israel? Is it now, huh, Lord? Huh, huh, huh?' And he said, 'The times and the seasons, which are set by the Father, they are fixed by him. Don't be concerned, **but ye shall receive** *power*, **after that the Holy Spirit has come upon you**: and ye shall be witnesses unto me in your town, and the towns around about, and into the uttermost parts of the earth.'[20]

"I believe that the Lord is going to put an emphasis on getting us together. It says, 'Then you shall see.' *Then* you shall see! And you shall flow together. The body of Christ is *not* flowing together, but is fragmented and split on opinions. We're coming into an hour now when we're going to see the Lord in our midst! We're seeing the Lord in our midst right now! He's moving down the aisles and healing people. He's moving down the aisles and baptizing people, and we shall flow together! That's the unity that Jesus spoke about in the prayer in John 17 and in Psalm 133: 'For there the Lord commanded the blessing, even life for evermore.'[21]

"The Lord wants us to act. He wants us to present ourselves so that we can become vessels of this power, because so many of us have tried in our own human effort to go out and serve God. It doesn't work! It fails every single time.

"Now let's enter into some ministry. I'm going to ask for you not to be concerned about yourself. The most anointed meetings that I have ever seen are where people are not asking for themselves. Not that that's wrong, but I want you to ask for the needs of the people who are here, all right? Can I ask for you to be a minister? A priest? I'm going to have the adults minister to the young people. I think there still needs to be healing between the generation gaps.

"There are some things that the Lord has pointed out to me. Hands are for healing. The gifts of the Spirit are ministered by the laying on of hands. The baptism of the Holy Spirit is ministered by the laying on of hands. There's impartation of authority by the laying on of hands. When Jesus left this earth, the last thing that he did was lift up his hands and bless the disciples. He went out of their sight with his hands lifted up, blessing them. The Old Testament priests used to raise their hands and bless the people. I don't think it was for no reason. That's why Jesus lifted up his hands, that's why the priest lifted up his hands, and Moses also. When Moses lifted up his hands during the battle, they won. When he put his hands down, they lost. It shows you something about authority. The authority figure lifted up his hands, and when he got tired they lost. He had body ministry. A brother propped up one arm and another brother propped up the other arm, and Moses was saying, 'What a glorious ministry the Lord has given me!' He couldn't hold his arms up by himself, the work was so great. But that's all he had to do was hold his hands up, and the blessing of God came out of him.[22]

"I'm going to ask the adults as we move into ministry to extend their hands toward the young people and really bless them like priests. It's your responsibility to get in your prayer closet. It's your responsibility to hold the young people of this church up before God because they're going to hold a key position in being evangelists and bringing the harvest in during the last time. We're going to give the adults an opportunity to minister to the young people. Let's start playing, 'His name is as ointment poured forth.' This is a beautiful song. It came out of the revival in Africa, and we'll just sing it one time or two times and enter into the atmosphere of the Lord.

Everybody stay in the atmosphere of prayer and expect the Spirit of God to move."

In the midst of this anointed song, I cried out, "Everybody twenty-five years old and under, come forward! Twenty-five years and younger. Okay, adults, lay your hands out toward the young people right now. Let's sing it again. Stretch it out toward the young people, right toward them. **Let him come! In the midst of the congregation, high praises to Jesus!**"

Then I addressed the crowd that came forward: "Young people, just hold your hands in a yielding position of availability. Adults, find a group of young people and stretch your hands out toward them, taking the authority in the name of Jesus. Begin to pray with faith and begin to believe God to use the young people in this church. There's a tremendous outpouring of the Spirit of God upon the young people here. Lift up your hands, open your eyes. Everybody keep your eyes open in this.

"The Spirit of the Lord is moving upon you right now in great power. Receive the power of God! The power moves in a chain reaction. Let the Spirit of the Lord move as the Lord fills you—let

the Lord *fill* you—because as the Lord fills you, he'll move on others around about you. The Spirit of the Lord is moving right here—the girl in the green sweater: I bless you in the name of Jesus. Let the power of the Holy Spirit come on your whole body right now! And now it's on the person next to her.

And now on this guy in the blue shirt right here! Receive the anointing and receive the power to be witnesses unto him. Let the power of the Holy Spirit come. You know, you cannot see the wind, but you *can* see the leaves as they rustle from the wind. You cannot see the Spirit of God move, but you can see the Spirit of God as he touches people.

"Let the Spirit of the Lord fill you so that he can fill others. The power of God is coming on this guy with a cast. Open your eyes! Let the Spirit of the Lord fill you all through your being in Jesus' name. The guy right here with the braces, keep your eyes open, look! Open your eyes, watch, watch! This is a class of the Spirit. Let the anointing of the Lord **fall**! Hallelujah! Let the power of the Holy Spirit *come*! This is like Pentecost!"

Over the noise of the crowd, and while I called down the presence and power of God on the people, the others were singing:

"Father, I adore you, lay my life before you. How I love you!"
"Jesus, I adore you, lay my life before you. How I love you!"
"Spirit, I adore you, lay my life before you. How I love you!"

While they were still singing, I went into the crowd, laying hands on some of the young people. Kids were on the floor crying, shaking, speaking in tongues. Chairs went flying as people crashed into them. They only recorded about half of the ministry time, but it went on and on. While people were singing one of my favorite songs, "Hallelujah," the Holy Spirit fell on the crowd in a fresh wave of power that was absolutely astounding. The place looked like a war zone. At one point a young guy was knocked to the floor by the power of God, and he started to speak in tongues loudly. The only problem was that one of the microphone stands was knocked over and landed right next to him. The microphone was right next to his tear-streaked face, blasting his new prayer language over the loud speakers. This was on top of all the crying and laughter and praises to Jesus. It was absolutely wild and absolutely glorious!

• • •

You know, the reason I'm writing this book is to reach as many people as I can with the message and reality of Christ. There were around four hundred people present in that gymnasium on Mother's Day 1980, but I'm praying that this "labor of love" will reach many, many more of you—and that the power and the presence of the

Holy Spirit will fall on you even *right now* wherever you are, just like he did in Canyon High School way back when. God is not limited by time, space, geography, or anything else, and he is only looking for those of you who have a hungry, open heart toward him. He loves each and every one of us and will take us on a radical custom-made ride that is beyond our wildest imaginations! Receive his love and all that he has for you in Jesus' name.

The Lord is saying to you, "Come, let's venture into a greater dimension."

Simply say, "**Yes, Lord!**" and watch what he does!

TWELVE

The Vineyard

THE OUTPOURING of the Holy Spirit upon the young
people of Calvary Chapel Yorba Linda that Mother's Day in 1980
was absolutely off the charts. It was just like some of the meetings in
South Africa—and then some! The presence and the power of God
was demonstrated in an awesome way that pretty much blew
everybody's minds, including my own. I had determined to play it
safe with this new church opportunity because I knew how much
controversy surrounded the outpourings that we had experienced in
Africa. Nevertheless, God has all the power, not me, and I simply
yielded to what he was doing—and loved it. That's ultimately the
secret: Just yield to him! It's all about "leaning not to our own
understanding"[23] and just flowing with the Holy Spirit. That's what
I ended up doing, and it was wonderful. Suddenly, it was truly like
Pentecost, with chairs flying and hundreds of piles of laughing and
crying young believers drunk in the Spirit, speaking in unknown
languages!

However, just like in Africa, not everyone was as thrilled as I
was. This included John Wimber, the pastor. He looked on in total
shock, while noticing many of his "highly offended" adults leaving
the building. In her book *The Way It Was*, Carol Wimber had this to
say about the meeting:

> You couldn't hear anything but the roar of the crowd, as
> hundreds were filled with the Holy Spirit at the same time and
> were shouting out loud in tongues. The chairs were falling over
> and the people were falling on top of the fallen chairs. The
> leaders that could still function were shouting at one another and
> it was complete pandemonium. Others were shouting that they
> were getting out of here. Young Tim Pfeiffer fell face down,

pulling the microphone down under him, and if we had ever entertained the thought of keeping any kind of reputation of respectability, it went up to the ceiling of the gymnasium along with Tim's voice—as he shouted uncontrollably in tongues with the volume turned all the way up—because someone had crashed into the soundboard.[24]

John went home and stayed up all night searching the Bible for some kind of scriptural context for what had just happened at his church. He prayed and prayed and looked through books on church history and on revivals. He read Acts Chapter 2 and many other references about the day of Pentecost, but was not convinced. When he later told the story to us, he said that he prayed and asked God, "Is this you or not?"

At something like five o'clock in the morning, the phone rang, and it was Tom Stipe, a Calvary Chapel pastor in Colorado. Tom reportedly said, "I don't know what's going on there, John, but the Lord woke me and told me to call and tell you that it's him. Does that make sense?"

Well, praise God, that conversation was definitely cool for John Wimber! It convinced him and answered his prayer that what happened to his church was orchestrated by the Holy Spirit, our guide. He was also reminded that it was not "his church." It was God's church. A lot of pastors forget that. John told us that in his frantic search for answers, he also found multiple accounts in church history of similar outpourings. John wrote about this in his book *Power Evangelism*:

> Then I remembered that I had read in *The Journal of John Wesley* about something like this happening. I went out to my garage and found a box of books about revivals and revivalists and began to read them. What I discovered was that our experience at the church service was not unique; people like John and Charles Wesley, George Whitefield, Charles Finney, and

Jonathan Edwards all had similar experiences in their ministries.[25]

However, not all Calvary Chapels ended up agreeing that what happened that night was from God. News spread like wildfire. There was a huge split of opinions. Other churches and individuals also weighed in on the controversy. People said it was pure emotionalism and accused me by saying, "Lonnie Frisbee uses mass hypnosis and crowd manipulation." No way could it be an anointing or an outpouring of the Holy Spirit of God! Many took the accusations several steps further and said, "It was the devil." The problem with that theory was that all the young people who were knocked to the floor said they had received the most powerful encounters with God of their lives. These kids had no grid for what happened to them. They came out of the experience in love with Jesus, on fire for God and the gospel, and were immediately blasted into his service full of energy and motivation. I don't think the devil is behind that kind of a response! Do you? We are to judge a tree by its fruit.

I want to humbly warn those who would make such foolish judgments to consider Matthew 12:24–33. Intentionally or ignorantly judging a work of the Holy Spirit as a work of Satan could lead someone down a very dangerous path. The Pharisees did that to Jesus, saying that he was casting out demons by the power of "Beelzebub, the prince of the devils."[26] Listen, we are supposed to judge the spirits, and I definitely encourage that. I do it all the time, but even I've made mistakes. I judged Derek Prince as a false prophet and a "wolf in the body of Christ." I was dead wrong, and I repented when God showed me my error. So if you happen to judge me wrong about bringing a fresh move of God to a meeting or to a nation, it is not the unforgivable sin. But Jesus warns us not to go down that path with a hardline, judgmental, Pharisaical attitude. At the end of that road, you will probably hear him say, "Depart from me, I **never** knew you!"

John Ruttkay was not able to make it to the Mother's Day meeting because of "life" (you know how that goes), but he was with me for a bunch of the aftermath. The church had a real big two-story house, which they named the Wagner House, which was used for offices and leadership meetings and so on. I want John Ruttkay to share about a meeting there immediately after John Wimber decided to embrace the Mother's Day outpouring as "from God."

"GAINING MOMENTUM"
by John Ruttkay

John Wimber wanted to bring some clarity and consensus to the craziness of the Mother's Day meeting, so he held a special meeting for the core leaders and members of Calvary Chapel Yorba Linda at the Wagner House. There were probably seventy men and women going up there. John asked Lonnie to share and maybe explain to his church so that they could understand better what God was doing.

I brought a friend of mine along, and we drove with Lonnie across the county to the Wagner House. I told Lonnie on the way, "Lonnie, man, A-game! Bring the A-game, please!"

By this time I knew Lonnie well. He never thought like a normal person. In the natural he could go on rabbit trails and detours that could be really confusing and sound totally crazy. On top of that, he had less "fear of man" than anyone I ever met. Whatever came into his mind came out his mouth! You never knew what was going to happen with Lonnie.

Anyway, there was absolutely no A-game! Lonnie started by getting up in front of everyone and kicking off his flip-flops.

I thought, "Oh boy, we're already starting to *descend* the hill of the Lord, not ascend the hill of the Lord."

Then he burped into the microphone.

I was like, "Okay, here we go!"

Next to me was a guy who looked like a nuclear physicist, with glasses on and his shirt buttoned all the way to the top. He was obviously agitated, tapping his foot on the floor as hard as he could.

I looked up and saw sweat beading up on Wimber's head and starting to trickle down his face. The more Lonnie talked, the stupider it got. I mean, he was not even connecting sentences! I kept thinking, "This is just a complete, total nosedive. We're in trouble!"

So John Wimber got up and said, "I think what Lonnie's trying to say . . ." and he tried to connect the dots about what Lonnie was saying, attempting to put some kind of theological context to the thing.

And Lonnie was in the back listening with his foot behind him up on the wall and his arms crossed, just listening to Wimber. Then he yelled out in the middle of the thing, "That's not what I'm saying at all! What *I'm* saying is everybody here needs to get touched by the Holy Spirit, and *you* need to start to surrender to Jesus on a higher level!"

I thought, "Okay, we're not even zero now. We're now in the negative bracket! Oh *man*, we're in trouble!"

But the next thing I knew, a wave of the glory of God just came into the Wagner House over us. The man next to me, the nuclear physicist guy, got knocked to the ground and started rolling under my feet. I mean, I didn't even know what a "holy roller" was until then, but this guy became one before my eyes. So he was on the ground rolling, and the presence of God had come in on us like a thundercloud! *Boom!* It was incredible! People were laughing and crying and

157

speaking in tongues. Lonnie yelled out super loud, **"Now** *that's* **what I'm talking about!"**

While in the absolute euphoria of the presence and power of God all over me and everyone else, I totally agreed with Lonnie. How could you not agree? God himself had decided to back Lonnie up with a mighty demonstration of what Lonnie was trying to say! We all need to get in touch with the Holy Spirit and go deeper!

We didn't get out of there until one thirty in the morning. It was mind-boggling! That's kind of how we did things. It started to progress very quickly. Lonnie was getting invited all over the place. He would visit a lot of other Calvary Chapels and other churches as well, and the presence of God would come wherever we went! So what Lonnie and I did, since he took me to everything, was just go in and share with people and say, "Hey listen, the Lord's been moving, and we're coming from some serious momentum," and then *Boom!* The presence of God would come down, usually touching the leaders first because, more often than not, they were the ones who were spiritually bankrupt. God was literally filling their accounts to overflowing.

That was one of the things about Lonnie: He understood about the river on the inside of you, and he would tap that river. He always connected the river of heaven with the river that's on the inside of you. He knew that once you had that moment of clarity with God, it was between you and him now. He just had the gift to push people into that river. I got to see him use that gift in churches all over Southern California at this time. We saw the Lord move very, very powerfully everywhere we went!

So I (Lonnie) was given the Good Housekeeping Seal of Approval by John Wimber and put on staff. The next three years or so were some of the most exciting and rewarding years of my life. But to get back to the immediate aftermath of Mother's Day, there was a tremendous exodus of long-standing, tithing members of Calvary Chapel Yorba Linda. People didn't like what was happening. It was very messy! It was outside their comfort zone. To John Wimber's credit, he cared more about obeying God than about the bottom line of the church budget, which was very refreshing. Then to everyone's joy, the young people started bringing their friends, leading them to Christ, praying for the sick, and casting out demons. Within two or three months, the church practically doubled. I don't know the exact numbers, but by fall, there were about two thousand mostly new believers and prodigals crammed into the gymnasium at Canyon High. It was wonderful and exciting and powerful.

Then the inquisition began. Chuck Smith called for a leadership meeting of the Calvary Chapel pastors to discuss the controversies surrounding all that was going on. Over the next year or so, I attended a couple of these sessions, and as much as I love Chuck, it was not pretty. At the end of the day, the official Calvary Chapel consensus was that John Wimber should take his church out on its own or under another umbrella. The split was to be explained as a matter of church direction, personality, and emphasis. The Calvary Chapel faithful were to continue to focus mainly on Bible teaching and church planting. John Wimber and his congregation were obviously more focused on the gifts of the Spirit and worship. So that was that! Chuck Smith made it crystal clear that we were no longer a Calvary Chapel. He said, "We are going a different direction than where John's going, so today everybody's going to make a decision whether they're going with him or they're going with me."

Guys were weeping in that room! You know, by that time we were all nearly fifteen years into a movement and had solidly embraced Calvary Chapel everything: teaching, doctrine, strategies, relationships. Following John Wimber meant disconnecting from that and stepping into something that no one knew exactly what was going on or where it would lead. Chuck was drawing a line in the sand, and it was decision time. Unfortunately, it was said by some that Lonnie Frisbee got John Wimber and his church kicked out of Calvary Chapel, but I like to blame God on that one!

I do want to say again that I still love Chuck Smith. He was definitely a father figure in my life when I really needed one. He discipled and schooled me in the Word of God. How could I ever stop appreciating that? I disagreed with him in a few things over the years, but so what! I also recognize the wonderful work of all the Calvary Chapels. There are hundreds, if not thousands, of sincere and dedicated leaders as well as a multitude of believers who have found Christ and grown in their faith through the powerful work of Calvary Chapels around the world. There is definitely a lot of "wood, hay, and stubble" in all our lives, but praise God that there is also much silver and gold in "them thar' hills" and hearts!

THE VINEYARD CHRISTIAN FELLOWSHIP

John Ruttkay and I went over to John's house right after that dramatic meeting, and there was a houseful of people and church leaders present discussing options. I think Blaine Cook and Jack Simms and the rest of the leaders were there. I remember my old friend Kenn Gulliksen was playing the piano, and at one point, which became a historic moment in church history, I heard him stop

playing and say to John, "Why don't you come under our umbrella in the Vineyard? I would be willing to turn the leadership of these churches over to you. You are more of a leader to the leaders than I am, and I recognize that. Pray about it, John!"

Lonnie and Kenn Gulliksen

160

To give a little background history, Kenn Gulliksen had been on staff at Calvary Chapel Costa Mesa for a relatively short time during the Jesus People movement. He had a secure ministry position in a huge, growing church, which was good for his young family. In 1974, Kenn felt like he heard the Lord call him up to the LA area to start a new work. He and his wife, Joanie, diligently prayed about it and obeyed the call. They left Costa Mesa with *no* salary, *no* benefits, and *no* visible security for their lives at all! They stepped out in faith, and eventually the Lord gave them the name Vineyard Christian Fellowship for the non-existent ministry that they were to birth.

Over the years I have been very good friends with both Kenn and Joanie, and—do you remember the story? I shared it already. Kenn and Joanie had just married in 1970. As a wedding present they received two plane tickets to go on a ministry trip to Denmark. Joanie was unable to go due to a scheduling conflict, so she prayed and felt led to give me her plane ticket to Denmark for the trip, and as a result, Kenn got stuck with me on what should have been his honeymoon! I've been forever grateful to Joanie for that incredible gift. This first trip to Denmark was very pivotal and rewarding in my entire life and ministry. Sometimes Joanie and I talk on the phone for hours to this very day.

But back to the Vineyard, Kenn Gulliksen moved his family to LA County, which is about a couple hours north of Orange County, California. They rented a little place for his family, and Kenn started his new church as a Bible study in the home of Chuck Girard, lead singer of Love Song. They were good friends from Calvary Costa Mesa. When Kenn was asked how the Vineyard started, he said:

"We were invited to Chuck Girard's house to start our new ministry, and we actually moved a block away from him specifically to plant a new church. We began the study in Chuck's living room, and it grew from there. We kept trying to come up with a name for the ministry, but we couldn't quite

161

land on the 'right' one. The Lord finally gave me 'Vineyard Christian Fellowship' about six months later. The Vineyard was conceived and born at Chuck Girard's home in the summer of 1974."

At one of those first meetings, Kenn shared his vision about being called to the LA area and his burden for people in the entertainment industry. He added, "We also have a burden for Beverly Hills, but don't have a place to meet yet over there."

A young beautiful actress named Pamela Norman was attending the Bible study, and she offered her apartment on 111 Doheny Drive just outside of Beverly Hills to Kenn for his growing meetings. John Travolta lived a couple of doors down, and other stars and celebrities lived close by as well. In addition to being an actress and a successful model, Pamela was also married to Larry Norman, who was, by then, a somewhat famous pioneer of contemporary Christian music. Larry Norman had multiple albums, traveled extensively all over the world, and was also a very eccentric and controversial personality. Pamela has a true, very outgoing evangelistic anointing on her life that is very special, and she invited her entire acting class along with everyone else to her home to attend this Bible study.

In a very short time, the infant baby Vineyard outgrew the existing Bible studies, and they met for their very first Sunday meetings at the Beverly Hills Women's Club. A pattern began to emerge as the crowds continually outgrew the venues one after the other. Kenn was offered a huge home on Coldwater Canyon Drive in Beverly Hills to meet, which was the home of Susan Stafford, the first hostess of the *Wheel of Fortune* TV show before Vanna White. It was in this beautiful home that Keith and Melody Green came to know the Lord.[27]

By the way, in addition to being a very anointed and loving pastor and teacher, Kenn is also a great worship leader in his own right. But by 1975, he had enlisted the twenty-one-year-old Keith

Green to be one of the Vineyard's worship leaders. Kenn guided this incredible talent for years and helped launch him out into his own Last Days Ministries, which grew to worldwide proportions. Keith Green's life, ministry, and music have become the "stuff of legends" since his tragic death at age twenty-eight in a plane crash in Texas in 1982. Read *No Compromise*, written by his wife, Melody, about our beloved Keith Green. It will challenge and inspire you, and break your heart. I only personally met Keith a few times, but how we all miss our bold young brother!

As the Vineyard grew, the leaders rented a church building in Sherman Oaks and grew to over a thousand on a Sunday night. They outgrew that venue in a matter of months. Kenn then moved the church to the beach near Santa Monica on the sands of the beautiful Pacific Ocean. Kenn loved taking the gospel to where the people were instead of waiting for them to stumble into a church "someday." I love that attitude! The Vineyard met for a year at Lifeguard Station 15. Only a couple hundred people followed Kenn to the beach, but by the end of the year, there were up to fifteen hundred enthusiastic believers meeting in bathing suits and on beach towels. The nursery kids were sent to garbage can number 9, and first grade met at garbage can number 10. Onlookers would move their towels closer and closer, and then they would get **born again**! He would even lead hecklers to Christ! Kenn is a great evangelist, among all his other gifts. When he rented a huge church building in the valley, Hal Lindsey (of *The Late, Great Planet Earth* fame) took over the beach church and continued that ministry for quite some time.

You know, I started this second book with a few stories about my times ministering to celebrities both directly and indirectly. Well, Kenn Gulliksen's vision of reaching out to the entertainment industry eventually took him and the early Vineyard on a wild ride—and into the lives of so many well-known stars and personalities. He did a Bible study in the home of Rosemary Clooney and became close friends with Pat Boone and his family among many others. Al Kasha and his wife accepted Christ at the

Vineyard in Tarzana and went on to closely fellowship with and encourage Bob Dylan in his new walk with Jesus. Robert Kardashian became a sincere believer and brought O. J. Simpson to the Vineyard and to Bible studies many times in the early days.

As Kenn described, "Al Kasha and his wife received the Lord at the Vineyard. I then led studies in their home and a lot of stars and sports people attended. Tony Dorsett came, and Bob Kardashian brought O. J. to the Bible study and to church. O. J. came only because he was Bob's best friend, and we were privileged to lead his first wife, Marguerite, to the Lord. I talked to O. J. numerous times and finally asked him, 'Why don't you come to the Lord?' His answer was simply, 'I don't see any difference between Jesus and Buddha and these other guys.'"

So Kenn asked him, "Then why do you keep coming?"

"Well," O. J. answered, "I like the music—and Bob's my friend."

Listen, we need to keep praying for famous people like O. J. Simpson who don't know the Lord. There is always hope. Kenn was in O. J.'s house many times and went to the hospital with him when his young two-year-old daughter tragically drowned in the family swimming pool in 1979.

Like with my experience, there were mountaintop highs in ministry and many heartbreaking lows. Kenn told us many amazing stories that only God could have set up because Jesus loves all people—from the richest most powerful star in Beverly Hills to every homeless child sleeping by a garbage pail in the alleys of Rio de Janeiro or Medellin, Colombia. Kenn Gulliksen needs to write a book for sure!

It would take a long time to tell all of the history of the early Vineyard, but to fast-forward a little, when they moved to the big church building in the San Fernando Valley, there was an explosion that happened. For one thing, God was sending many talented musicians besides Keith Green to lead worship and do concerts. Chuck Girard, Kelly Willard, Donn Thomas, Andy Park, and so many others led the way. Debby Boone had just released her "You Light Up My Life" hit and performed it live to over two thousand people in two back-to-back services at the Vineyard. In every single service Kenn gave an invitation to receive Christ, and hundreds came to the Lord in a very short time. It was during this season that Bob Dylan met Christ and went through the new believers' classes at the Vineyard. Tommy Funderburk helped take the music at the Vineyard to new heights by bringing in even more incredible talent. Three members of the Eagles participated. Kenn didn't even know who the Eagles were at the time. It was truly a blessed season. Kenn's vision of touching the lives of the entertainment industry had definitely come true. Here is another short snapshot from my friend Chuck Girard himself about this very exciting season of the early Vineyard.

"ANOTHER MOVE OF GOD"
by Chuck Girard

Love Song had disbanded after releasing two very successful albums. It had been a crazy, fast-paced ride through the Jesus People movement. By 1974, I was living in the LA area, still writing songs, and pursuing a solo career at the time. Kenn and Joanie Gulliksen were friends with my wife even before we were married, and Kenn called us up one day and said, "Can I meet in your house and do a Bible study?"

Chuck Girard

We agreed, and he came over once a week or so, and soon he and Joanie moved to our neighborhood. Kenn felt called specifically to Beverly Hills, but he didn't know anybody there yet. So the Vineyard Christian Fellowship could be traced back to that

165

Bible study in our living room. However, nothing much happened for a while, and then Kenn started doing meetings in Larry Norman's home in Beverly Hills. Soon other people opened their homes. They moved to a women's club for a few months, and then they leased a Methodist church over in Tarzana that became the mothership where Keith Green got saved.

I heard about Keith Green's salvation after people started coming up to me, saying, "Hey, a guy named Keith Green got saved and says he knows you." As a side note, I had worked with Keith when he was thirteen years old, before either one of us was a Christian. I was a studio singer, and Keith was under contract to Decca Records as the youngest person to ever be signed to a rock 'n' roll contract. His producer was Gary Usher, who happened to be the guy I worked for as a studio singer. Gary had organized the recording sessions and cut six singles with Keith. They were mostly songs that Keith wrote, and one was a Beach Boy song that he wanted to do. Keith did the lead singing and the piano, and that's where I met him. Well, I was just a work for hire, just another guy coming in to sing on his records, but he remembered me. Fast-forward to 1975: I didn't put it together right away. At first I was still thinking of Keith Green as a little kid, but then I realized, "He'd be almost ten years older, so in his early twenties now."

When we finally connected at the Vineyard, Keith remembered me, and I confirmed this was the same guy. I helped him get started in Contemporary Christian music. I'd give him bookings: When someone called me up and asked if I were available to play, I'd say, "Well, I'm booked, but I know this up-and-coming kid named Keith Green who I think you'll be real happy with. Here's his number." He opened for me a couple times, and in that way I helped him get started. It wasn't long before he was very well known,

166

and after he put his first album out, he skyrocketed past me, so the tables turned. Keith Green was a true man of God who we all miss. Keith led worship at the new Vineyard church, and from time to time I did also, along with many others. It was a great season with phenomenal growth.

Kenn had a vision to reach people in the entertainment industry, and he certainly achieved that goal. In fact, the guitar player in my Chuck Girard Band, Larry Myers, was also a counseling pastor at the Vineyard. He was counseling a young black girl who was in distress concerning a relationship she was in. She was working through some issues with her "musician boyfriend." That was all she'd ever call him. Then in one counseling meeting, she told him, "My boyfriend would like to speak with you about the Lord. Would you be willing to come up and talk with him?" Of course, Larry said, "Yeah." At that point she said, "I need to tell you my boyfriend is Bob Dylan."

So my friend and another pastor from the Vineyard went up and met with Dylan for about six hours in his home in Brentwood. They didn't push him for salvation, but at the end of the meeting, they shared how he could surrender his life to Jesus.

Love Song

Soon after that, Dylan started attending the Vineyard and went through a four-month discipleship school there. He also started going to a Bible study at the home of a man named Al Kasha, a two-time Academy Award-winning songwriter and a Messianic Jew (a born-again Jewish Christian). [28] God was bringing in many people from all different walks of life, including a lot of celebrities and sports stars. I had the privilege of briefly meeting with Dylan a couple times over the years.

I'd also like to share a little story about my friend Lonnie Frisbee. During the Jesus People times, he would have Love Song do little mini concerts at his Wednesday night meetings and take us with him to different outreaches and events.

Chuck Smith would also have us perform at Sunday services and take us with him to huge events. After about the first year or so, we became so busy that I didn't see that much of Lonnie. He was going a million miles per hour, and so were we.

Love Song played at Explo '72 in June of 1972 to a hundred and thirty thousand people in the Cotton Bowl. Billy Graham got up and spoke right after we played. It was amazing!

Explo '72 at the Cotton Bowl Stadium

But going way back, I definitely remember one special day as a baby Christian when I stopped by the Blue Top Motel to see Lonnie. I had only been a Christian about a month. At the time, he and his wife were basically overseeing the ministry at the Blue Top.

During our conversation we were talking about the Lord, and the subject of speaking in tongues came up. You know, Lonnie could be very direct. He didn't put any preamble on it. He didn't say, "I would like to pray for you to receive the baptism. How do you feel about that?" No—it was more like, "I'm going to pray for you to receive the baptism of the Holy Spirit, the Lord is going to touch you, and you're going to speak in tongues." It was like that.

When he said, "Speak in tongues," I resisted a little because I had had a negative experience under the influence of drugs a couple times when we lived communally in Laguna Beach. I'd go out back up in the hills there in South

Laguna, start playing my guitar, and I'd go off on these little languages, these kind of rambling, free-form, almost tongues-like riffs with my music. However, it would always end up in darkness, and the feeling was like, "This is not good." I'd put my guitar down, go in the house, and say, "Whoa. That was creepy." I did it a couple of times, and then I stopped because this dark thing would always happen.

I explained to Lonnie, "I've done this, and it's not a good thing. I don't think that God's happy with this."

Lonnie said, "No, no. This is a cool thing, and it'll be different." He prayed for me, and it hit me like lightning. The next thing I knew, I was speaking in tongues, and it was different from anything I had experienced before. Lonnie left the room, so I was there all alone for about a half hour, just babbling in tongues and praising God! I was still a new Christian when that happened—but that was typical Lonnie!

So that is a little bit about the birthing of the early Vineyard and a little about my times with Lonnie Frisbee.

MUCH GOOD FRUIT

Kenn Gulliksen turned his church in the San Fernando Valley over to Bill Dwyer and planted another Vineyard in Santa Monica, which was, again, a far-out church. Brent Rue, one of the assistant pastors, planted a Vineyard in Lancaster, CA. By the time that I (Lonnie) shared my testimony on Mother's Day 1980, there were at least six Vineyard Christian Fellowships going strong.

So that's what Kenn Gulliksen was offering to John Wimber when he stopped playing the piano that day at the leader's meeting in John's house right after Chuck Smith had made his "line in the sand" proclamation. I personally was super impressed with John Wimber and definitely excited to be a part of the team. Nevertheless, I initially thought that Kenn made a mistake to hand the entire

Vineyard over to John Wimber after working so hard to birth it and after producing so many leaders and churches in such a short time. But what do I know? Almost immediately, dozens of Calvary Chapels became Vineyards, and now, instead of just six Vineyards, there are hundreds and hundreds of Vineyards.

John eventually talked me into turning over my own ministry, World Outreach Ministries, to the Vineyard, which became the mission branch of the Vineyard. John and his board renamed it Vineyard Ministries International, or VMI. VMI has the same Federal Tax ID number as my original ministry. They only did a name change. No one really knows that, but now you do. I rejoice that much good fruit has been produced on the foundation that I birthed, so in that regard, I have much in common with Kenn Gulliksen.

I believe that I brought a move of God and an anointing back from Africa to the States and was able to help John Wimber take it around the world. If you detect a tinge of regret, I apologize. I don't want to get ahead of the chronology of events, and I definitely don't want to take anything away from the glorious work of the Holy Spirit that changed so many lives and churches worldwide. However, as my life story continues, you might come to understand my disappointment to have been COMPLETELY written out of the history of both the Jesus People movement and then this new Vineyard movement. Leaders had their reasons, some of which I have already alluded to and some that I will further disclose as the Lord leads.

Stay with me on this journey. In spite of some of the disappointments, there were mountaintop highs that were worth it all. Remember Romans 8:28: "And we know that all things work together for good to them that love God, to them who are the called according to his purpose." So to put things in perspective, God can even work good out of our failures as we humbly repent, speak the truth in love, and totally yield to Jesus. That's always been the goal of my life. Like I said concerning this powerful wave of God with the

Vineyard movement, the next few years were some of the most exciting and productive years of my entire life, and, as always, **unto him be all the glory!**

THIRTEEN

Jehovah Love

IN ALL SIGNIFICANT relationships, there is a honeymoon season. At least that is what I have observed and experienced. Of course, it happens in marriage, but it also happens in friendships, in a new job, and in many other life experiences. The most important honeymoon season is when we first come to Christ, when Jesus, our loving Bridegroom, sweeps us off our feet and takes each of us on our own special honeymoon. Sometimes it lasts a couple of months, and sometimes it can last for several years! He knows each of us inside and out and has planned every detail of this romantic season way ahead of time. He puts off dealing with hard issues because it's not time, and anyway, we can't handle everything at once. In fact, the

John Wimber

Bible says, "Before the foundation of the world he knew us and loved us."[29] In 1980, I absolutely loved my exciting new relationship with John Wimber and his church family—the honeymoon was on!

John had me preach and do ministry times, and we traveled together locally and eventually around the world. Right after Kenn Gulliksen made his gracious and honoring offer to have John come under his church umbrella, I remember going up to the Central Coast of California to some meetings. John had organized a worship conference in Morro Bay with a bunch of Calvary pastors and other leaders he had relationships with. I love eyewitness accounts, and here is a report from a young guy who was present in that meeting. I only briefly met this young worship leader a couple of times in my entire life. He lived in San Luis Obispo, a beautiful college town on the Central Coast, and his name is Kenny Morgan.

Before Kenny shares, I want to mention something important about meetings like Mother's Day and even the previous meetings in Africa and going forward. The Lord gave me the ability to see in the natural and in the Spirit, to see when the Holy Spirit is dealing with someone or resting on someone's life or imparting something. I believe it is a gift that is available to anyone, and I knew from the get-go that it was something the Lord wanted me to demonstrate and model for the whole body of Christ. It is not a gimmick to be copied, but a gift to seek and embrace. I think it is a combination of several of the spiritual gifts put into one: discernment, words of knowledge, wisdom, prophecy, and miracles all wrapped together. Like with all gifts from God, they are designed for us to become more effective in proclaiming the good news of the gospel of our Lord and Savior.

I am credited with coining the phrase "Come, Holy Spirit" on Mother's Day 1980, and many ministers have simply copied that phrase and used it extensively, expecting that the Lord is going to pour out his Spirit almost on demand. It doesn't work that way. I don't even remember saying, "Come, Holy Spirit," on Mother's Day. When I listen to the tape, I hear, "Holy Spirit, come!" So maybe people should try that one instead. But listen, about the time we think that we have God's program figured out, he changes everything! He wants us to stay yielded and to humbly allow him to lead the way. Consider how God has the ability to create billions of people over the centuries, and yet each person is totally unique and different with no fingerprint alike. The Holy Spirit can also minister to people in a million different ways. Don't copy anyone! The word is simply *yield!*

"THREE ENCOUNTERS"
by Kenny Morgan

I was part of a small Calvary Chapel on the Central Coast, and the very first time I met Lonnie Frisbee was way back in the late seventies at a Calvary pastors' conference. I wasn't a pastor, but managed to attend anyway. At the conference I looked across the room, and someone said, "That's Lonnie Frisbee, you know!" He was like a hero to me because I had read a lot about him through this little book called *The Reproducers*. At some point in the conference, I was going into the building through a sliding glass door, and he was coming out. He just stopped and stared at my face for quite a while. Then Lonnie said, "The Holy Spirit is resting on you," and he walked away. That kind of freaked me out. I was stunned. I didn't know what to do. I didn't feel anything in particular. That was my first encounter with Lonnie.

My second encounter happened like this. I was leading worship at a Calvary Chapel on the Central Coast when it was just getting started. I led worship there the first three years. I was terrible at it, but smart enough to always ask people for prayer and anointing. I was not a good singer and not a good guitar player, but the Holy Spirit would still show up occasionally. One day I called up John Wimber. This was back when he was still with Calvary Chapel, but after Mother's Day toward the end of 1980 or maybe early 1981. He invited me to come down and go to a seminar that he was hosting. I actually took the pastor from my Calvary with me, and we went down to Southern California.

My pastor knew Lonnie. As soon as we walked into the room, he introduced me with a simple, "This is Lonnie." Of course, instead of shaking my hand, Lonnie just came up very close to me. He had these really blue eyes, and he looked right into me in a very natural way. I didn't know if he remembered me . . . or what. Then he put his hand on my head and started prophesying over me—really loudly! The prophecy was all about me leading worship and the Holy Spirit coming upon me. He didn't know I was a worship leader. I never even had the chance to speak one word to him this time or the last, or ever for that matter.

Then my pastor and I went into the large main room. Lonnie started sharing—and all heaven broke loose! People were just getting whacked with the Holy Spirit! About a hundred of us were all sitting on the floor in the Wagner House. Blaine Cook was there, along with a lot of the early Vineyard people. All of a sudden, Lonnie just stopped in his tracks and pointed to this guy who was sitting cross-legged. Lonnie screamed out, "The Holy Spirit's on you!" The guy who was sitting cross-legged started gyrating about two feet off the floor. Not levitating, but just bouncing with his legs still crossed, without his hands. Just try sitting cross-legged and jumping a foot or two off the ground. It's impossible. This guy was bouncing off the ground, and then Lonnie went over and just prayed for him—still without touching him— while the guy bounced like a human beach ball. I remember thinking, "This is wild!" I'd never, ever experienced or imagined anything like it. We both, my pastor and I, just sat there with our mouths open, totally shocked. My pastor didn't like it. I loved it.

We drove back home that day, and I went to a prayer meeting that night. I brought my guitar and started singing, and I remember a guy got healed. Then the next day I went to church and was leading worship. Back then, you had a guitar, you had a microphone, and that was it. That was your worship band—*you.* But all of a sudden, I felt the Holy Spirit come upon me, and I became a different person. It was like slow motion. I could see things happening. As I was leading worship, I would say, "There's somebody here with ear trouble, somebody here with neck pain," and people would get sovereignly healed. From then on, I had a kind of prophetic healing ministry that would just show up. It was like I couldn't make it happen, but it would just show up. I really think I got an impartation from Lonnie. I don't know if an angel started following me around or what! Something started happening that was totally out of my normal experience. That was the second time I met Lonnie.

The third and last time I encountered Lonnie Frisbee was when I had a little home group. One night this kid named Chuck came to my meeting. He was twenty and fresh off the boat from the Presbyterian Church. We prayed for him and ministered the baptism of the Holy Spirit. He got totally filled with the Holy Spirit, spoke in tongues, the whole nine yards. It transformed his life!

Later that same week, because I was leading worship and kind of a leader at this new church in San Luis, Jack Little said to me, "Hey, John Wimber is going to be here this week with a bunch of people. We're just doing a little worship get-together in Morro Bay. Would you like to come?"

I was like, "Yeah, okay, sure." I was just this kid, twenty-four years old. I "didn't know nothing," but I'd had those experiences.

That night I called Chuck and said, "I think you're supposed to come with me. I'm barely invited myself, so I'm going to sneak you in the back."

So we went to this meeting in Morro Bay in a room that held about eighty people, almost all Calvary pastors, all close to John Wimber at the time. We just worshipped, and it was great. I was sitting in the back, Chuck was sitting behind me, and Lonnie Frisbee got up to talk again. He was telling just a little of his testimony and stories of people getting healed at

Calvary and thousands coming to the Lord. In the middle of sharing about a revival in South Africa, he stopped and interrupted himself, just like he had done in the Wagner House. He pointed at me and screamed out, "The Holy Spirit is on you!"

Again, I didn't feel anything, except embarrassment! Embarrassed because, of course, every eye in the room, all these Calvary pastors of huge churches, turned and looked at me. I was like, "Oh no, what do I do? Do I fake it? Should I fall on the floor or what?" All this was happening in an instant.

About that same time, I heard this noise behind me, and I turned around to see Chuck gyrating up and down about six inches off of his seat. Apparently, the power of God either went through me or went over my head. So when Lonnie pointed at me, he was really pointing at Chuck. Lonnie came back to him and started praying for him. Then he took Chuck's hand and pulled him up out of the chair by his hand and started using his hand like a fire hose. Lonnie held Chuck's hand and dragged him around the room, putting his hand on all of these people saying, "Come, Holy Spirit."

Everybody, and I mean *everybody*, got more than touched. The Holy Spirit was so thick that a couple of good friends of mine literally felt sick. Margie Crane was so overwhelmed with the Holy Spirit that she thought she was going to pass out! She kept saying, "What's going on?" Later she loved it, but the presence of God was initially so strong that it was affecting people's bodies. People were shaking and crying and in total awe of God. Some were hit with joy and started laughing their heads off! For me, the presence of the Holy Spirit felt like an electrical current starting at the top of my head and sweeping down over my entire body. Chuck got totally wrecked with the Holy Spirit and has never been the same. We have been good friends ever since. The whole experience was like a huge wave had crashed in on us and slowly subsided.

Finally, John Wimber got up and said, "Well, folks, the real reason we're having this worship meeting is that I'm changing the name on the bus. I'm no longer a Calvary. I'm a Vineyard, and I'm starting this movement. God wants his church back, so we're giving the church back to God. He wants people empowered. Those of you who want to come along and become a Vineyard, come with me."

Half the people were overjoyed, and half the people were really upset. And that's how the Vineyard movement was publicly birthed and announced right there. Chuck and I were like Forrest Gump in the back of the room at this historic meeting. It was just crazy.

THE MAT ROOM

John Wimber started to put together quite a few conferences and seminars right away. It was very impressive. John is quite the organizer and promoter. Before we really did any foreign ministry trips, he started bringing in leaders from England and South Africa and other parts. I (Lonnie) put him in touch with all of my contacts and leaders like Costa Mitchell, Dave Owens, and others from South Africa. I also had many contacts in England, Denmark, and so on. I think my good friend Derek Morphew also flew over here from Africa to attend healing conferences and meetings on the kingdom of God. The conferences themselves grew in size, and during the ministry times we saw the power of God hit huge crowds. Leaders were opened up to the gifts of the Spirit in new ways from new perspectives. The same thing was happening in our regular church services. The church was growing by leaps and bounds. It was a powerful season with many people getting saved, young and old—but mostly young!

John himself was growing in his ability to operate in and release the gifts of the Spirit to others. Many wonderful healings occurred during this time along with super accurate words of knowledge. While we were still at Canyon High School, John and other leaders, including myself, would sometimes get dozens of "words" for people in the congregation, and then we would send them into our own version of an overflow room. The overflow room at Canyon High School was actually the wrestling room, or "mat room," which was about a third of the size of the gymnasium. We would roll up the huge wrestling mats and stack them off to the side. In some services there would be a couple hundred or more people going back for healing or the baptism of the Spirit or deliverance from this or that. The young people were flocking to the church, and they were super hungry for everything that God had to offer.

During one of the overflow sessions that extended way past the regular Sunday evening service, I had an encounter with a young guy who was about thirty-three years old. Little did I know that this person would become a close friend and instrumental in my ministry and life in the future. In fact, the Holy Spirit showed me that he was bonding me together with this character for some unknown reason. The guy was standing off by himself on one side of the wrestling room with his eyes closed and his hands held uncomfortably out about waist level in a yielded way. I saw the Spirit of God over him and walked across the large mat room, where I had been praying for a growing crowd of people. Later I found out that his name was Roger Sachs. Almost exactly ten years later, I was doing missionary work with Roger and asked him to be the ghostwriter for this book. But right now, I want Roger to tell his version of that evening at Canyon High School.

"NOT OPENING MY EYES"
by Roger Sachs

The evening that I went for prayer at the church meeting in Canyon High School, I was a mess. I had been a Christian for a little over five years and knew enough by then to know that we cannot demand anything from God—but I was desperate. Before the service, as I pulled into the big parking lot, I told God, "You have to heal me tonight! I'm not leaving until you do something!"

I was a little late for the service, but as I walked in the dark by myself past the cars, I could hear the music coming from the gymnasium way in the distance. I had been coming to this church for over a year. Previously, I had been led to the Lord in Topanga Canyon, which is a neat canyon up by Malibu, by a country preacher and street minister named Rev. Glen Adkins who witnessed to me in a bar. The locals affectionately called him "Rev," but he was also the pastor of the little Topanga Community Church. God used Glen to help snatch me out of the drug scene here in California and to start putting my life back together. I really grew to love this devoted and generous man.

Actually, when I first met Glen, I had been hiding in Topanga for a couple of months after a series of big drug deals went bad. At the same time, I had been having a series of very strange coincidences for a couple years, which seemed almost spiritual and supernatural. I didn't know it, but it was the Lord reaching into my life.

I will try to condense a pretty long story. A dangerous drug lord in Tijuana, Mexico, had put a contract out for me after our group lost three loads of pot in a row to the border patrol. I was held responsible because I more or less headed up our operation in the States and had a partner in Mexico.

Between my Mexican partner and me, we were on the hook for six hundred kilos of marijuana that were on credit to us. On top of that, we had eleven of our workers locked up in San Diego, which included one of my close Mexican friends, who did over ten years in prison as a result of one of those three busts.

But that was not the main reason I was desperate for prayer that evening. My drug past was a contributing factor, but it had been over five years, and God had done quite a few miracles patching me back together after coming to Christ. In fact, several months after I was converted, I went back into the lions' den in Mexico and shared Jesus with my partner Ernesto Hernandez, who, I discovered, was also planning to kill me. He was very upset that I had disappeared for six months, leaving him on the hot seat to face our creditors. However, as in my case coming to the Lord, God began creating a bunch of strange "coincidences" in Ernesto's personal life—odd things that had him wondering what the heck was going on.

Instead of killing me, Ernesto heard me out and, to my surprise, got dramatically saved. A year later he went to Bible school in Guadalupe, Mexico. We stayed partners, but instead of smuggling and distributing drugs together, we started a prison ministry in one of the most dangerous prisons in the world, La Mesa prison just outside of Tijuana. Anyway, by 1980, I wasn't too worried about a drug cartel continuing to come after me. Most of the main players down there in Mexico thought that Ernesto and I had become crazy religious nuts and gave us a pass.

So five years into my Christian experience, I guess it was time for God to dig a little deeper into the roots of my brokenness and also to deal with some of the physical and psychological damage that the alcohol, LSD, and cocaine had done to my physical brain. The immediate problem was that I was having some very embarrassing panic attacks. These mental attacks would happen all of a sudden in public places, for no reason, in normal situations. I would turn beet red and feel like running or something. It made me very upset with myself, and I prayed, but they seemed to get more frequent and worse. It happened a few times at my bank, in restaurants, even in grocery stores. It affected my new construction company. I started to avoid any places where I would have these silent, but mentally screaming attacks. I became almost agoraphobic. It was crazy.

I said I was a mess, and I really was. In the past I had done a really good job screwing up my own life and many other innocent lives all around me. Other contributing factors were that I was divorced twice, going through a nasty custody battle over my young daughter, and I think I felt more normal around some of the cutthroat killers in La Mesa than I did on the streets of Orange County, California. I was holding in a lot of guilt, anger, and, at times, self-hatred. I wanted God to heal my mind and life—and to just make me normal without drugs or alcohol!

Hopefully that kind of sets the stage for me walking into Calvary Chapel Yorba Linda that evening. God had never let me down when I was desperate, and somehow I knew he was going to do something that night. He had to! I always sat way up high on the bleachers, and there must have been a couple thousand people there. Lately there had been a bunch of healings, and ever since Lonnie Frisbee became a part of the church, a lot of supernatural things were rocking the people. I really loved it when Lonnie shared and loved seeing God blow people's minds when miraculous things happened. That's what I was hungry for and hoping for, that God would do something radical in my case. I was just a face in the crowd, but what I was experiencing was ridiculous and crippling. "Please, God, deliver me from this bull!"

The first time I even heard of Lonnie Frisbee was at the original Vineyard church in LA. After Rev. Glen led me in a prayer to ask Jesus into my heart in August of 1975, he immediately told me about a new Bible study at a home up on Coldwater Canyon Drive where a young musician named Keith Green was leading worship and was quite a talent. I got the address and found the place, which was packed to the gills with mostly young people in their twenties like me. Kenn Gulliksen was speaking, and the new church he was pioneering had just moved from a women's health club to this huge house up in the Hollywood Hills. When I walked into the house, packed wall to wall with people sitting all over the floor, arms raised to the sky, listening to Keith Green pounding on a piano, it was the first time I felt the presence of God in such an incredibly powerful way. It gave me goose bumps from head to foot.

For the next four years, before moving to Orange County, I went to every service and every Bible study that this new Vineyard church put together. I followed them every time they moved locations, including to the beach in Santa Monica. When Kenn went to two services in a huge rented church building, I would stay for both services. The music was like going to a concert each week. I dragged everybody I could to the Vineyard. Many received Christ. I attended a new believers' class series about three times. Kenn Gulliksen is my all-time favorite Bible teacher and pastor combination ever. I still have boxes of his audiotapes of the weekly sermons and meetings and concerts.

I became very curious about Lonnie Frisbee when Kenn told us that he would actually be afraid to go places with Lonnie because God would show up in the streets and power encounters would take place everywhere he went. I heard a few other stories about Lonnie, but I never heard or saw him speak even once until he showed up at Calvary Chapel Yorba Linda many years later.

As I sat in the bleachers that evening waiting for a "word from God" about my situation, John Wimber started calling out healings and all kinds of specific words to people during the entire service. He would say, "If that's you, go into the overflow room at the end of the service, and people will be there to pray for you."

For the whole service John Wimber and other leaders kept getting words for people, but nothing even came close to addressing my request, and then suddenly . . . the service was over! I was shocked because God had never let me down since I surrendered to him. God didn't do anything. He was not answering my desperate prayer. I really just sat there stunned for a few minutes not knowing what to do. A big line of people had formed and was filing into the mat room.

John Wimber had completely walked off the stage, but then I saw him turn around and walk back up on the platform to a microphone. He said, "You know, I was leaving, but the Holy Spirit just showed me that some of you have been waiting for a word from God, and the word is: Just join the others getting prayer, and he will meet with you!"

That was the first and last time I heard a word like that, and I, along with about a dozen other people, grabbed it. We all headed for the overflow room, getting there last. Inside, there must have been a couple hundred people standing around, and one of the leaders was instructing everyone to hold hands and form a bunch of prayer circles just as I walked in. Very quickly, maybe six to ten circles were formed with probably twenty or twenty-five people in each one. A couple of people next to me took my hands, and we formed one of our own big circles. Someone was giving more instructions, and then people were praying out loud, but I don't remember any of what was said. I just remember that I shut my eyes and silently prayed, "God, I am not opening my eyes until you heal me!" I really meant it!

Well, not much was happening in my circle at all. With my eyes closed, I could hear several people pray near me, but from the other end of the wrestling room, I could hear all kinds of commotion. Some people were shouting, and I could hear crying and laughing, and then I heard Lonnie Frisbee's voice mixed in with everything. I was really wishing that I was in *that* circle, because nothing was happening anywhere near our side of the room. Even though nothing was happening, I was determined to keep my eyes closed, and pretty soon whoever was holding both of my hands let go. I felt foolish, but I just stood there by myself, continuing to wait for God to do something.

I don't know how long I stood there, but I got a taste of what it was like to be blind. Someone bumped into me. I could hear people walking around. I could hear bits of people's voices, some close, some far away. It seemed like my eyes had been closed forever. On top of everything, I continued to hear what sounded like a free-for-all on the other side of the room. It was the longest time I ever stood alone on my feet with my eyes closed in a public place in my life. Really, it was the *only* time, but I kept waiting, feeling foolish and all.

Then someone grabbed one of my hands and started pulling me forward. My eyes just instinctively popped open, and I could see Lonnie Frisbee leading me by the hand across the room to where all the noise was coming from. Everything went into slow motion. He led me into the center of a big crowd. In the middle was this beautiful, young blonde girl who had her hands raised to heaven, her head tilted back, and her face covered in tears as she cried out, "Thank you, Jesus! Thank you, Jesus! Thank you, Jesus!"

over and over while shaking. She looked like she was being joyfully electrocuted or something.

Next to her in the center was a young surfer-looking guy who was basically doing the same thing as the girl. His hands were raised as high as they would go, and he was also getting electrocuted with his eyes closed and tears streaming down his handsome face. Lonnie took one of my hands, connected me to the girl's hand, then took my other hand and joined me to the young surfer guy. Then Lonnie slapped me really hard in the chest with the palm of his hand and screamed, **"SPEAK IN TONGUES!"**

The only thing I can compare to what happened next is that it was like a good acid trip without drugs. It was like I stepped into another dimension. Whatever electrical current from God that was flowing through these two started flowing through my body like lightning bolts. I immediately started to speak in tongues, and wherever I went from there I can't really describe. I don't even know how long it lasted. I just remember as I was finally leaving the building and walking through the crowd, Lonnie appeared again and looked down at my Bible because on this particular used Bible someone had written on the closed pages in big bold letters: **JEHOVAH LOVE!**

Lonnie pointed to my Bible and asked, "What does it say?"

I turned the Bible sideways, opposite of the spine so he could read it, and Lonnie smiled and said, "Cool!"

That was the first and last personal contact that I had with Lonnie Frisbee for many years, until our paths crossed again later in England.

As I walked out to my truck, I reached up to take my hat off because I was sweating. I usually wore one of my Anaheim Angels baseball hats everywhere, but I discovered that I didn't have my hat on when I reached for it. As I was driving off, I realized that I continued to feel like I still had my hat on. I could distinctly feel it across my forehead and completely around my head, but I didn't have my hat on. For at least a couple of weeks, it was the same sensation, and I discovered that God was healing some of the damaged circuits in my brain. I never had those panic attacks ever again. Thank you, Jesus!

------------------ ⚬⚬ ------------------

NEW LIFE INTO DEAD BONES

So that's what it is all about: "Jehovah Love!" God delivered Roger that evening and answered his desperate prayers. See, sometimes it does help to get a little desperate! And God gave me the privilege of playing a small part in answering those prayers. That's our job: to simply partner with the Creator of the universe in whatever he is doing. In reality, Jesus has delivered us already on the cross, and we only need to humbly receive his love and salvation and healing. Listen, it is fun to see God move and to be a part of it. Come taste and see what I'm talking about. Let's all go on an adventure with the King of Kings and Lord of Lords. It's a simple "yes" away!

The honeymoon with my new church family was going great. John Wimber took this fresh outpouring of the Holy Spirit to a new level by introducing the gifts and the manifest presence of God to whole new segments of the church that were either asleep or completely dead. It is a wonderful thing to see God breathe new life into dead bones!

On our part, it's not about measuring up to some high religious standard. It's about seeking his face and not just his hand. It's about deciding to walk in the Spirit and to put God first in *everything!* He simply wants us to be his friends, to be real and honest and not phonies. He wants us to enjoy his presence and our relationship with him both now and forevermore! I absolutely loved this new wave that God was releasing upon California, and, believe me, this particular wave would again circle the globe and touch a multitude of people!

FOURTEEN

A New Wave

SO MUCH WAS happening in all of these transitions. John Wimber and Calvary Chapel Yorba Linda were in the midst of officially becoming a Vineyard. Lots of other Calvary Chapels decided to follow John and change their name to "Vineyard—this city or that." Suddenly, in a *very* short time, there were dozens of Vineyards in America, instead of just six or seven. Kenn Gulliksen completely turned over the leadership of this new movement to John Wimber and then continued his church-planting calling and went to the East Coast, starting a couple of churches over there.

We were also getting ready to go international. Being a missionary, I was definitely pushing for that. John was using me as a "point man" for bringing the gifts of God to the people, and I loved it. To put this into perspective and jump forward to the nineties, there are now probably over a thousand Vineyard Christian Fellowships worldwide. It became a true move of God! But in the beginning John put me on staff, paid me a modest salary, and eventually talked me into turning over World Outreach Missions to him and the church. At first I was reluctant and felt like the Lord was saying no, but I wasn't sure. Then John talked me into it for insurance reasons and whatnot. Like I already mentioned, he then formed a new board and renamed our ministry Vineyard Ministries International (VMI).

Before we took our new "brand" overseas, I was still getting invited to minister and share in churches here at home, including many Calvary Chapels. I knew there were hard feelings now between Vineyard and Calvary, which was really sad, and I wasn't trying to make it worse. I loved and still love them both. How could I not love them if I wanted to stay in tune with the Holy Spirit? I have been hurt by the church and leaders real bad many times—but

I try with all my heart to lay those things at the foot of the cross and move forward. That process can definitely be "a trial of faith" and very hard sometimes. Nevertheless, Jesus always rescues and heals me . . . eventually. So at the time, if I happened to be invited anywhere, I simply prayed about it, and if I got a green light from the Lord, I would go wherever he led. Believe me, I was not trying to get even for any mistreatment that I might have felt. Besides, John Wimber called Chuck Smith and demanded that they return the mission funds to me that I had raised for our Africa mission in 1978, which they finally did. Praise God!

I hope you, the reader, don't mind if I continue to have other people share from their vantage points concerning some of the seasons and events in my life. We can also benefit from their perspectives of a little twentieth-century church history mixed in. When putting my life story together, I gave Roger a pretty long list of people to interview. Most of the people who have shared and will share—John Ruttkay, Peter Crawford, Derek Morphew, Fred and Ruth Waugh, Kenn Gulliksen, Chuck Girard, Marwan Bahu, Gigi Gruss, Dennis Evans, Debby Kerner, Phil and Sandi Mahlow, Rich Buhler, Steve Zarit, Debbie LaMunyon, my brother Stan, and many others—are some of my closest friends and coworkers in the body of Christ. But for now, I want John Ruttkay to tell a little more about how things developed in this new Vineyard movement as it picked up speed.

"A POINT OF REFERENCE"
by John Ruttkay

Down in San Diego County, California, I had a lot of contact with different churches and friends since I lived there most of my life. I remember spending some time at one particular church, and the pastor and co-pastor had heard about some of the fireworks happening up north in Yorba Linda at John Wimber's church. They knew that I was closely involved and began asking me lots of questions.

They said, "What is all of this? Where are we supposed to go with these things?"

I told them, "Look, it's not easy to explain what's happening. It's easier 'caught than taught,' as they say in some circles. What you need to do is have my buddy Lonnie Frisbee come down. He'll explain things better than I can. Let's have him come for a Sunday night meeting. You guys just bring the church together and let Lonnie minister."

They all thought that was a great idea and agreed to have him come.

What I've found in trying to explain spiritual things to people, even though they are Christians and even though they have a great love for God, is that a lot of people don't understand the power of the Holy Spirit. This includes the baptism of the Holy Spirit even with people who have been baptized with the Holy Spirit and speak in tongues. They do not seem to have that much revelation on the power of the Holy Spirit, the different gifts of the Holy Spirit, and how much God wants to develop these realities. This pastor was one of those types. He was marginally on the edge of any kind of charismatic movement in the church. I find that kind of the norm in Calvary Chapel systems. They don't seem to stress the spiritual dynamics so much. It's not that they don't believe in those things; it's just that they don't emphasize those aspects of God. I think it's somewhat of a hindrance and doesn't allow people to come into the fullness of their walks with Jesus.

Then Sunday evening came around. I'll tell you something, we had a meeting where the presence of God came so powerfully! That night, Lonnie came and spoke at

Hornblende Hall down in Pacific Beach, and the pastor and some of the leaders were there along with a nice crowd. At about nine o'clock, as we were ending the service, Lonnie said, "Listen, we're gonna have a time of ministry, and the Holy Spirit's gonna touch many of the young people." Then he looked over to the pastor, and the presence of God hit the guy, and he literally flew up against the wall. Lonnie went over and laid his hands on him, and the power of the Holy Spirit came on him even more, and then suddenly, all of the other leaders got blasted! They were falling on the floor, shaking, and unable to function. These guys were fit to be tied. They didn't even know what hit them!

I was used to this by now. This kind of thing happened to people all over the world, and I'd been hanging around Lonnie long enough to see it happen wherever we went. But it was new to quite a few people at this time, and we had to have a special meeting the next morning just to explain what had happened. The following Sunday morning a week later—I'll never forget this—that pastor got up to start the service, and the only thing he could do was shake and sob. He couldn't even preach, because the presence of God came on him so powerfully. He finally said, "I don't know what this all means, but I know we're going in another direction."

That's when I took that whole group up to meet with John Wimber. Boy, those guys just hit it off and that church eventually became part of the Vineyard. There was just a tremendous amount of momentum that had followed this whole thing, starting with Mother's Day. The Vineyard movement was up and running! It was very dramatic, and I was blessed to be a leader in it. It was in this setting that I traveled to South Africa and other nations, following God's call. It was also in this time period during the early and mid-eighties that God really used Lonnie in influencing the whole church and this entire new move of the Spirit. Lonnie was probably the main catalyst for everything that was happening. John was using him as a point of reference. We loved every bit of it and were "in with both feet," extremely motivated, excited, and in love with Jesus and the wonderful Holy Spirit of God!

Here is one of my very best friends who has stood by my side through thick and thin over the years. Gigi Gruss probably knows me better than almost anyone on earth. She has a heart of gold and the boldness of a lion. She was just a teenager in 1980, and I'd like her to share a little about this new wave that hit us like a tsunami. She was right there in the mix, front and center!

"LIKE A WILD MAN"
by Gigi Gruss

"The Lonnie Phenomenon." Back in 1980, I was going to Calvary Chapel Yorba Linda and was under John Wimber's teaching. There were quite a few of us teenagers and young people praying for the sick, praying for everybody we came in contact with, because John taught us that the ministry was for everyone to take part in. He basically told us, "It's for the whole church to do. Come on, have fun! Join in and pray for people!"

John Wimber instilled a lot of confidence in us, reminding us that seeing healings and miracles

Lonnie with Gigi

wasn't for some special person or minister. If you just made yourself available to God and the Holy Spirit, you could pray for people. So we did it. We prayed for months and months before we started to see any healings at all. And then, slowly at first, some real healings began to happen.

I had been under that tutelage, that teaching, and then up came this wild man. Lonnie came to our church on what is now the famous Mother's Day meeting. I had never seen anybody preach like he did. I mean, he just spoke so simply, but so profoundly. I recognized the Holy Spirit because we were trained to recognize the Holy Spirit. As Lonnie shared, something so wonderful and so scary at the same time started to happen. People say, "The Holy Spirit is a gentleman. He doesn't force anyone to do anything, because he is a gentleman." But Lonnie began to show us that the Holy Spirit is not always a gentleman. Lonnie shouted out that you can't tame the Holy Spirit of God, and then something happened in that room.

Lonnie was talking about giving a life more fully to God. He was really calling out to those who are twenty-five and under. At the time on Mother's Day, I think I would've been nineteen. He yelled, "Anyone twenty-five and under, God wants to touch you!" All of us who were there just ran up to the front! We said, "Sure, we want more of God." We didn't know that it was going to be like a machete—or like being gunned down! The Spirit of God came so powerfully that people were screaming as though they were being shot down! At the same time, people were laughing ecstatically. Other people were crying. All we knew was that Jesus was present and the Holy Spirit was coming in his power. Lonnie couldn't knock down over a hundred or two hundred of us to the ground all at the same time. No man could do that—it was God!

This preacher man, Lonnie, like a wild man kept saying, "Come on! Jesus needs recruits. Jesus needs people who are going to do his work! Come on down! He wants you to be available to do his work!"

When the Holy Spirit came down on us like a hurricane, it was so powerful. I can feel the Holy Spirit by just talking about it. The whole thing was recorded. Anyone can go listen to it and even feel a touch of what it was like, though people can't really know the full extent of the presence of God unless they were there. There was such an anointing on this group of young people that it changed their lives forever. You can't heal or touch hundreds of people and have them all say that Jesus changed them forever unless something truly supernatural happened. We all said that Jesus reached into our hearts! He reached into my heart and took me to a higher place. I don't know any one of us who said a bad thing.

However, a lot of people left the church after that. Honestly, their hearts weren't really open to the things of the Holy Spirit. Like I said, I didn't know or even hear of anybody who had a bad experience. We need to take note of the fruit of everything we experience every time.

Before this, we were already praying for the sick, and now John Wimber was embracing the anointing that fell on us, so after that, there was a boldness that came in us. I think our church doubled the summer after Lonnie spoke. The young people of our church went out and evangelized. There was this radical boldness about it. We'd go to the malls and pray for the sick. We believed that wherever we went, we were carriers of Jesus and the Holy Spirit!

So there was this army that was raised up, that was mostly people under twenty-five. We'd pile in our cars, our little rabbit cars, and all go to meetings to hear Lonnie preach. No one laid hands on most of the people to receive the Holy Spirit, but my friends would get in my car after the meetings, all speaking in tongues. Their parents weren't even Christians. They'd say things to me like, "How do I explain this to my parents?" No one had ever told them about what receiving the presence of the Holy Spirit was. Can you imagine? You receive the gift of tongues without an explanation, and you're just a teenager!

It was such a beautiful, wonderful outpouring of the Holy Spirit that seemed so effortless. Of course, I came in at the end of it, not knowing any warfare or struggle that had preceded this outpouring. There is always a price to pay for advancing the kingdom of God. I was just a kid going, "Wow! We get to join in and be about Jesus and his kingdom!" We learned that from John Wimber, but now we received a power to carry it out. I think that's what it was: John had the teaching and the obedience, and Lonnie carried an anointing from God. We as young believers had the great honor to simply be a part of a special team. The Holy Spirit showed us that revelation—of how special and unique and important each and every one of us is to him. We can all experience the fullness of his presence by simply being available and opening our hearts, moment by moment.

When the Lord sent out workers into the mission field, he sent them out two by two, company by company, and mission by mission. One reference for this is Mark 6:7–13, but read the whole Book of Acts in the Bible. In fact, all of the epistles in the New Testament are filled with revelation, examples, and marching orders for the Great Commission.

About eight years ago, Jesus gave me (Lonnie) a missionary partner. He is a huge man over six feet tall and over two hundred pounds, which can be an asset in some of the more dangerous corners of the earth. He is also an electrical contractor by trade and a trusted friend in the Lord. His name is Dennis Evans. We have been through many battles and victories over the years, and at one of our meetings I asked him to share about missions and the Holy Spirit. I said to him, "Talk to the people about how God started to open your eyes as he took you on the mission field." Here is Dennis's take on his first experience seeing the Spirit of God move. In fact, this was on our very first trip together.

"A PENTACOSTAL BAPTIST MISSIONARY"
by Dennis Evans

My first missionary trip was to Hawaii. Lonnie and I were both at the Vineyard Christian Fellowship at that time, and he had been invited to speak at a Youth with a Mission event and also to share at a Full Gospel Business Men's Fellowship meeting in Hawaii. One of the pastors asked if I could go along because he didn't want Lonnie to go by himself. I thought, "Hawaii? Sure, no problem!" So we went to Hawaii.

The first stop was in the Manoa Valley in Oahu at the local YWAM base in Honolulu. We had a meeting that first night, and people came from all over—from the north shore and all over the island. We packed out the place. It was pretty dynamic.

The next evening we had another meeting. One of the local pastors attended, and the power of God was moving like the night before, even stronger, in a dimension that I had never seen before myself. Lonnie had the pastor come up and some of the other key leaders and laid hands on them. The power of God began moving on them. You could see it. You could tell that there were certain manifestations hitting almost everyone. Now, I was raised a Baptist, a fundamental Baptist, so I watched all of this happen from a Baptist point of view. I could see the shaking of the hands, which I now know is characteristic in Lonnie's ministry, and I thought, "Well, that's interesting." I became really excited as the meeting continued, because I felt the presence of God in a very special and powerful way.

The next day we went to the Big Island. We went way over to the huge main YWAM base out there on Kona, and we ministered. It was slow starting. Lonnie ministered for quite a while, when suddenly, one girl started crying. She started weeping—just wept and wept—and pretty soon, there were other people touched by God. *Everybody* started weeping; the whole room was weeping. I thought, "What is going on here?" Then it all subsided. It was quiet for a few minutes, and then laughter came. One person started laughing, and then everyone was laughing. I thought, "This is really bizarre!"

But that is how God moved in the meeting. He started by breaking hearts. *Everybody* felt the presence of God. As people focused on the Lord, he started breaking their hearts. He worked through them for fifteen or twenty minutes with tears. Then the laughter came—the joy of the Lord came. I was experiencing this dimension for the first time in my life. It was amazing!

Then we went to Maui and ministered at a church there, a pretty large church with hundreds of people. We met with some stiff opposition from the pastor there. The meeting started out great, but the pastor was the most difficult person in the whole building. However, by the end of the meeting, that same pastor and his wife and six kids were jumping around the room, crying, and laughing. It was amazing! Everybody in that room—and we're talking about hundreds of people—were crying and laughing and hugging and being baptized with the Holy Spirit. The pastor got just what he needed and what the whole church needed: He was baptized with the Holy Spirit! It was wonderful and powerful, and actually mind-blowing to witness.

But the thing that really stuck in my mind was that I saw the same manifestations—the hands shaking, the crying, the laughing, people being baptized in the Holy Spirit and speaking in tongues—in each place we went on the different islands. Now I'm a pretty logical person, so I said to myself, "Nobody could have made phone calls or seen this on video or found out what was going on in these meetings that quickly." This is how I think.

As we went on, we did more meetings, and the same things happened throughout. When I came back from that trip and started to digest all that I had learned from being on these different islands, in the different Full Gospel Business Men's Fellowship meetings, local churches, and Youth with a Mission meetings full of different types of people from all over the world, then I realized it all had to be real. The laughter and shaking and crying were all manifestations of the power of God working in these different groups, through these different people, and that revelation changed my life and put me on the mission field. I've been doing missions ever since. It would *so* be the Lord to have him break me in—in Hawaii of all places.

At one point Lonnie and I were standing outside the Pioneer Inn in Maui, and I blurted out, "Man, this is paradise! I love this place!"

I remember Lonnie saying, "The paradise that God has prepared for us is far better than this."

When he said that, I knew I needed to adjust my goal. My goal needed to be beyond my idea of paradise here on earth, because that idea changes. My goal needed to be centered on being with the Lord.

Now I focus on people and on the Holy Spirit, on how we can minister to the people and meet their needs. To truly meet their needs, the gifts of the Spirit are so important. This is a former Baptist speaking! I've learned that more gifts come as you get more involved. The Lord also gives you discernment in different situations and in different countries. It doesn't matter what country you are in, people are people. Whether you can speak the language or not, you can see people, and the Holy Spirit will give you his supernatural gifts and a genuine love for them—HIS LOVE!

THE WAVE

So this new wave, which would soon be called the Vineyard movement, was building up in California and moving eastward across the United States. It took about a year to reach the East Coast. In late 1981, the wave crossed the Atlantic Ocean and hit England with a mighty crash. A few months later, the wave turned south and hit South Africa even harder. It was so much fun riding this historic, absolutely "far out" spiritual wave of God that would eventually circle the globe!

FIFTEEN

A Team of One Hundred

WHAT A GREAT season we were enjoying during the early eighties! It was actually another revival. What does a revival look like? Well, the Lord was moving in all of the church meetings and conferences. Home fellowships were springing up all over. The Lord was using us on the streets and in the marketplace with divine appointments right and left. The music was super anointed. The prodigals and backsliders were coming home as their heavenly Father ran to meet them with a huge hug. God was anointing the new believers with "rivers of living water"[30] and *fire!* We certainly were not guilty of being lukewarm, as so many Christians are in their faith.

It's like the song "California Dreamin'" by the Mamas and the Papas, only with slightly refined lyrics: "*Stopped into a church I passed along the way. Well, child, get down on your knees—and don't pretend to pray!*"

Huge numbers of lost and searching people were doing exactly that: They were not pretending, as go the original lyrics of "California Dreamin'." Instead, they were calling out to God with all of their hearts. Our Papa God greeted them with a heavenly kiss and a gold ring for their finger. I love revival, and the Holy Spirit gave me the honor of participating in another one. It was so cool! Like I said, we were getting ready to take it around the world with a new emphasis. The message was still about the priesthood of all believers, but now it was coupled with signs and wonders and "doing the stuff." You know, John Wimber really grabbed hold of everything that the Lord was emphasizing. He became an expert at presenting these realities to the people. He would say, "Hey, folks, we *all* get to play in this!" I loved it!

However, we need to consider a couple of things about revival. They don't last forever. I found that out! Sometimes the fire slowly fades when we leave our first love or when trials and temptations confront our lives. Please remember the strong warning that Jesus gave to the wealthy church in the Book of Revelation. He said, "I know your deeds, that you are neither cold nor hot. I wish you were either one or the other! So, because you are lukewarm—neither hot nor cold—I am about to spit you out of my mouth."[31]

Listen, we need to balance this thing out with both the loving promises *and* the stern warnings. They are both designed for our good, to keep us on the right track. Sometimes we not only need to be delivered from the world and the devil, but from ourselves. It's true! I am often my own worst enemy. So are you! We shoot ourselves in the foot. We seem to sabotage our success and our own happiness way too much. We probably would all benefit from a good psychologist, don't you think?

Nevertheless, being lukewarm was definitely not our problem back in the early eighties. God gave me the privilege of modeling and demonstrating some of what the Lord wanted to pour out on the people. From the very beginning of my Christian walk in the Haight-Ashbury, God always gave me a few people to influence, disciple, or impart something to. It applies to all of us: There is always someone in your life who you are a little further down the road than. And Jesus continues to say to each of us like he said to Peter, "Feed my sheep!"[32]

In my case, like I have said before, whenever I find something good, I *immediately* want to give it away to all my friends. As a teenager, I thought LSD was super good, and so I turned on scores of people to that world. But then I found something that beat everything else. Of course, that something was Jesus Christ, and I have been giving him away ever since! It also says in the Bible, "Taste and see that the Lord is good!"[33] You know, there is something that is very, very special about God—he allows us to check this thing out. God doesn't expect us to keep going forward in blind faith forever. When he makes a challenge, he backs it up like only the God of the universe can do. He says, "Test me and see!"

Here at home in America, we were seeing God do amazing things with phenomenal growth and everything. I showed up on Mother's Day 1980, which was in May of that year, and then the following June of 1981—thirteen months later—we made our first overseas trip to England with a relatively small team from our church. Later that same year, we took a larger team to South Africa on the church's first mission to that nation. Both of these trips in 1981 were totally awesome, but the trip to Africa was such a joy for me. Every time I return to that country, I am blown away with the things that God does for us as a team and especially for the people we minister to. I often think to myself, "How could he top that one?" And then God blows my mind again and again with this miracle or that divine appointment or by letting me see with my own eyes an alignment of people and churches on a national scale!

Everything has been on a level that I never imagined. It is so rewarding and so much fun serving God to fulfill the Great Commission. I pray this book will inspire more of God's people to step out in faith and obey the command of Jesus to "go."[34] You will never be sorry. More importantly, I pray that many precious people will discover that it's not a bunch of fairytales, this thing about Jesus. I pray that you would simply surrender and say, "Yes, Lord!" It's the bottom line to the whole gospel. I believe that many of you will make that decision in your life before it's all said and done. For sure, you will be grateful *eternally* for that one!

In 1982, we took our second major trip to South Africa. This time it was advertised as a Vineyard "team of one hundred" ministry trip. There is a big dispute over the actual number of people who went. One person said it was fifty-four, another person said seventy-two, and others stand by the original one hundred. Anyway, it was a real big team with a lot of moving parts. Derek Morphew definitely had his hands full in South Africa organizing most of the trip. Believe me, it was a big job! By the way, Derek's church became one of the very first Vineyards in Africa, followed by a host of others. That mission trip in 1982 was probably the most remarkable of all, and it had the most permanent effect on the rest of my life. I will explain shortly, but first I want you to hear a couple more eyewitness accounts. Just as the Bible says, "None of this was done in a corner!"[35]

∞

"WHAT JUST HAPPENED?!"
by Carroll Childers

I was on the team of one hundred going to South Africa in 1982, but let me back up a few years. As a child, I grew up in a Baptist home, and then went completely wild as a teenager. When I was in my early twenties, I moved to Los Angeles. In August of 1980, when I was twenty-four, a friend invited me to the Vineyard. This was the West LA Vineyard that Kenn Gulliksen started. It had been seven years since I had been to any church. The first time I attended, there was a South African pastor named Dave Owens conducting the service because all the Vineyard pastors were in South Africa. The third week that I was at the Vineyard, I got saved in the middle of worship. I'd grown up a Baptist, but consider that day at the Vineyard while we worshipped the Lord, the day when I really got saved. I had heard all about it, but had never personally surrendered to Jesus in my heart of hearts. After worship, I thought, "I need to talk to somebody about this!"

There was this crazy, weird-looking guy who had just come back from South Africa named Lonnie. He was down in the front of the church, calling for people to come pray. Again I thought, "I need to talk to somebody about what's just happened to me!"

I went down toward the front, and Lonnie looked up and said, "That girl there, the Spirit of God's all over you! Come here and lay hands on this guy."

I'd never heard of the laying on of hands before since I had grown up Baptist, but I went over anyway.

Lonnie said, "Just put your hand on this guy's ear. He's deaf in this ear, and God wants to heal him."

I had been saved about forty-five minutes. I went, "Okay," and put my hand on the guy while everybody stood around us. Lonnie told me how to pray, and so I prayed a little bit, and the guy got healed. He could hear again out of that ear.

I said to myself, "What a cool church! This is kind of interesting," and I thought that this is what happened all the time at the West LA Vineyard. I thought it was normal. However, I went to my first home group that Tuesday night and started telling people what had happened. First of all, no one had ever even seen Lonnie before, at least nobody in that home group, and nobody had ever really seen any of that kind of stuff happen. I realized it was a new thing that was happening. So that was my introduction to Jesus, my introduction to Lonnie, and really, my introduction to the Vineyard all on the same day!

Two years later, our pastor Kenn Gulliksen decided to form a team from our Vineyard to join several other Vineyard teams going to South Africa. There were around fourteen from our Vineyard who made the trip. My roommate was the church secretary at that time, and I went in to visit her in the church office. I just happened to pass Kenn by the coffee area, and he said, "Do you want to go to South Africa?"

I went, "Hmm . . . sounds like a good idea."

So that was my call to missions! I didn't even know where South Africa was. I didn't have a heart for missions. I just had this thing about worship because it was the worship that drew me into the Vineyard. It was the worship that just transported me to Jesus. Everything that happened for me happened through worship. When I finally decided that I would join the team, Kenn asked me, "Why do you want to go to South Africa?"

I said, "I want to go anywhere they don't have this experience of worship. If that's South Africa or Afghanistan or China, I just want to go somewhere I can share this."

By that time I was kind of on the fourth-tier worship team, the ones who did everything that nobody else wanted to do, such as setting up for the Easter service at four o'clock in the morning or the Christmas Eve service at midnight. We were not the big guys. But I was doing worship a bit and also leading worship at a home group, so I thought, "I'll just go and do whatever they need me to do."

I ended up in Africa in October 1982. I was supposed to be there for two weeks and then go on with the rest of my team from West LA to Norway to work with Steve Sjogren. However, one of the guys from West LA's father was a missionary in South Africa and had a heart attack while we were there. He decided to stay behind and asked if I would stick around for a little while to help out, and that's what I did. Again, no great call. Just, "Hey, you want to hang out in South Africa?"

Yet there was something about the place that captured me. I was supposed to be there for two weeks, but could extend my visa for four months, so I thought, "Well, I'll stay for four months. That'll help out with the whole transition of the church."

However, I ended up staying for thirty-four years. I married, raised my family, and led worship in the South African Vineyard for almost all of that time. So that's my story. In many ways it all started with Lonnie Frisbee, but then again, Lonnie would always point to Jesus, the author and finisher of our faith!

—————————— ⚮ ——————————

I (Lonnie) want to share another very cool testimony from a young leader in the newly formed Vineyard under John Wimber. His name is Blaine Cook, and he went on to minister in amazing signs and wonders all over the world by the power of the Holy Spirit! He was on that very first Vineyard mission to England as well as to South Africa and most, if not all, of the following trips during this radical season.

—————————— ⚮ ——————————

"YOU ARE DEAD!"
by Blaine Cook

Back in 1982, I was at work in South Orange County, California, and I knew there was a church training class going on in the Wagner House. I wanted to attend, but I was working overtime to make money to go on an upcoming mission trip to South Africa with the Vineyard. Two or three hours into my workday, I just had this sense that God was telling me that I needed to get to the Wagner House, that Lonnie Frisbee was going to prophesy over me. It was a strong impression, a clear leading from God.

I went out and talked to my boss. He said, "You can't work half an overtime day and then expect to be able to leave."

I said, "I know, but I've got this personal thing that I have to do." I finally talked him into letting me go, and after working until the early afternoon, I got in my car and drove really fast to the Wagner House in Yorba Linda, about a forty-five minute drive. When I got there, I jumped out of my car and ran to the back door of the church offices. I didn't want to interrupt the meeting, so I walked around through the library because I knew the huge two-story house pretty well. However, when I went through the place, everybody was gone except for only four or five people.

As I was walking toward them, I thought, "I missed it! I missed the whole thing. It's not going to happen now."

Then I saw my mother-in-law, Ruth, my wife, Becky, Carol Wimber, and Lonnie walking across the room. I was probably thirty feet behind them, when suddenly Lonnie just turned around. I'll never forget it. He just turned around and yelled like he kind of did all of the time. I don't think Lonnie ever really whispered. He pointed at me, and the other people also turned around at that point because he yelled in a *really* loud voice, "This man right here is about to die!" He pointed at me and said, "You are dead!"

When he said that, my arms and legs collapsed, and I did a complete face-plant right in the carpet. I could not move my arms or legs at all! It was like they were completely numb or had fallen asleep. While I was lying on the floor, Lonnie said again, "This man's about to die! This man's about to die!"

I could actually feel life leaving my body, draining out my left heel. I don't know how that works, I just know that that's what happened! I started to sob and breathe really hard, and I actually thought I was literally going to die. Then Lonnie came over and laid on top of me, arm to arm and leg to leg, right on top of me. It was like in the Bible when Paul stretched out on the dead kid whom he resurrected. Lonnie put his head right near my left ear and then prophesied over me for probably about ten minutes. Even to this day, I don't have any idea what he said, because I was so overwhelmed!

He just prophesied. Finally, he got up and walked out. He was "done."

My mother-in-law, my wife, and Carol Wimber were there and waited for me to compose myself because I was really crying. It's interesting because it soon became obvious that some kind of impartation had taken place. There's no question in my mind that something dramatic happened. I don't know if Lonnie knew the extent of what the Lord did through him, but I definitely knew something radical had happened. But then again, I didn't know where to put the experience at the time. It was too wild.

However, I went on the South Africa trip shortly after this, and I don't know how to describe it, but there was an increase in everything. It was just a different level of spiritual acumen, and I operated in the gifts of God more effectively. I healed the sick in Jesus' name more frequently, with more power and more supernatural manifestations. I also noticed after that period of time that I had this gift of impartation, of imparting the Holy Spirit to people. I could lay hands on people, or sometimes I didn't even lay hands on them and only spoke to them, and the Lord would really show up and empower people. I can honestly say that I have a long trail of people who greatly benefited from the increased anointing on my life. It has been life changing for me, and I think for many others also.

I can trace all this back to the Wagner House, to that moment when Lonnie Frisbee was laying on top of a "dead man," prophesying in my left ear. When I look back, he was most certainly the one who initiated that whole side of my life. As a young leader, I was only starting to heal the sick and prophesy on occasion, but everything really intensified after that point. That's the story as I remember it. I've talked to my wife, Becky, about it because she was there and I needed to get her read on what happened. It's hard to remember exactly what goes on in those types of supernatural encounters, but it was a moment in time that changed my life, no question about it.

ENGLAND
(BLAINE CONTINUES)

Later in that same year, Lonnie and I were both on a ministry team to England. I have been asked what was the most astounding thing I ever saw in ministry over the years, and what happened in this one meeting in the UK definitely qualifies. At a church called Holy Trinity Brompton, the leaders of the church were a little concerned about having Lonnie Frisbee speak and had a very serious conversation about that with John Wimber. Lonnie was supposed to share one night and do his thing. John said, "You know what? I don't think you have to share tonight, Lonnie. I think I'm going to share instead."

Well, Lonnie wasn't really happy about that at all. He left the church and went outside to cool off. John got up and did the message and had an altar call at the end of the meeting. There was an area in the downstairs of the church where people went for prayer. It was a pretty big area. Now, these people in the church were *very* sophisticated, cosmopolitan, very staid, very English, all in coats and ties and dressed formally. When we had the altar call, a big crowd of people came filing down this stairway area from the auditorium and kind of packed wall to wall into a downstairs room. There were a few of our team members mixed in, and Becky and I were standing to the side after we had walked down the staircase.

Suddenly, I looked to my left up the staircase, and I could see Lonnie at the top. From the very top of the stairs, he just walked down, putting his hands straight out in front of him, just flat out in front of him, and started *yelling* in tongues at the top of his voice. When he reached the bottom, he started to walk through the crowd—and it was like the Red Sea parted! I mean, everybody went down! Everybody who was in front of him just went flying to the right and to the left. It was like a huge lightning bolt hit the people! They all fell down on the ground on top of each other, and *that* was the beginning of the ministry time. It was astonishing! Pretty much the entire room was on the floor. I was off to the side and behind Lonnie when he hit the crowd, so I didn't fall down, and maybe a couple of other people were still on their feet. But the piles of people on the floor literally looked like they had been struck by lightning. It wasn't like they just fell down swooning. They looked like they'd been tied to a high voltage electric wire. Some of them cringed and fell down, some of them fell straight back. *Nobody* broke their fall or anything. They just all piled up on the floor. A lot of them didn't get up for a long, long time. But Lonnie just turned around, walked out of the room, and disappeared up the steps. We were there cleaning up the wonderful mess with the ministry team afterwards for half the night! It's a great story that I will always remember.

Lonnie and I got to minister together quite a bit for about three years. It was a very interesting time and a great learning process for me. I believe that I learned how to move in the Spirit really effectively through Lonnie. I'm a pretty good student, so I watched closely and just wanted to *do* it. I thought it was a crazy-looking thing to be in partnership with Jesus! I enjoyed it then, and I still enjoy it. I still love to minister in the midst of the presence and power of God wherever I go. It's our calling and destiny.

"THE GIRL IN THE GREEN SWEATER"
by Debbie LaMunyon

Let me be yet another person to mention Mother's Day 1980, because when Lonnie gave his testimony and started ministering to the crowd, he pointed and yelled out, "The girl in the green sweater right here"—and that was me! I had a green sweater on, and he said, "Look at me!" I looked up and he said, "Let the power of the Holy Spirit come on your whole body *right now!*" I could feel the presence of the Lord. It was sweet and loving, and I felt the Father's love for me!

Then Lonnie yelled, "And now on the person next to you!" The person next to me was my husband, Alex, and *wow*, the Holy Spirit just leveled people all around us like in a chain reaction! Both Alex and I didn't fall down like hundreds all around us. It was different for us, but just as powerful. We were absolutely immersed in the Father's love. That was a very, very powerful night. None of us had seen the manifest presence of the Holy Spirit fall on people in such a way. To see all these kids that you personally know just go down like that was really something that I will never forget.

Right after the Mother's Day meeting, the Lord kept blowing our minds in church and everywhere else. The anointing fell on all of us. We caught it! Alex and I had a home group in our tiny 850-square-foot home, and it was packed every week. People were sitting up in the kitchen and everywhere because the Lord was showing up. One night at our home group, a friend of Alex's showed up whom he had gone to school with. This friend was now a professional golfer and also a very conservative Christian who didn't even believe in the gifts at all. But a girl he knew invited him, and he came along to our group.

I remember Mike Donaldson was leading worship that evening, and the Holy Spirit was there so powerfully. It was one of those nights where you're almost afraid to open your eyes during worship because it's just so heavy! You simply want to stay in that place in your heart and stay reverent and not look at anybody. The atmosphere was alive and almost magical with the power and peace of God shimmering in the air.

Our place was an old home with heavy wood floors. At one point during the worship, we heard this big loud *thump*! I was like, "Wow," and opened my eyes. There on the floor was the professional golfer, completely out of it, just lying there. He was totally out for thirty to forty minutes—I mean, *out cold!* When he finally got up, he was praising God. He went down a skeptic and a non-believer in the gifts, and he came up a man who was so hungry for God, so "on fire" and open to whatever God wanted to do in his life! It totally changed him. Nobody prayed for him, nobody. God was doing stuff like that almost daily. It was wonderful!

I remember saying to myself back then in my early twenties, "It's always going to be like this! There's no turning back. This is the life—to dwell in his presence." We all wanted to stay right there because when you are in his presence, nothing else matters. Nothing! You can have bills or other worries, but when you are in his presence, you know everything is going to be okay. God gives you the grace to get through whatever is coming your way. We so easily become bogged down in life and life's circumstances and overwhelmed with distractions that take us away from longing for God's presence.

I believe repentance is coming. Repentance for leaving our first love. Much of the church worldwide has strayed. We need to stay in his presence, where the peace and joy and the safety is. God will always be with us, but when our hearts are right, open, and desperate, God meets us in that place in a deeper, more rewarding way than ever! We need another Jesus movement!

But let me get back to the eighties because we were in the midst of a very special move of God then. I was just a little kid during the Jesus movement of the sixties, but the Vineyard movement was perfectly timed for my life. In addition, I grew up very close to the Wimber family. They lived down the street from me. John even hired me to work in his office. By 1981, Alex and I were invited to be part of the first mission team to England as well as the first Africa trip. These two trips were incredible! On a mission trip God speeds things up tremendously. Everything is accelerated because you have a smaller window of time and because you obeyed him to leave your home, comfort zone, and everything else to serve him. We had never been out of the USA, but we were ready to run with Jesus.

I remember at this one church in England, we prayed for a woman who had been a prostitute many years. She was a drug addict and had thirty-something demons inside of her. Her name was Libby. They took her into a back room of the church, like a church office, and we were in there for about an hour and a half. I got pulled in there to intercede, and John Wimber, David Watson, and Lonnie all led the meeting, but John led the deliverance. He did an incredible job with this woman.

Libby had been in the back of the meeting during the service when someone reached out to her. She wanted to be free. She was actually very pretty, but had that really troubled look about her. When John started praying, these demons started to speak in all different kinds of languages. It shocked me! But John took control of what was going on. He made the demons identify themselves and cast them out one by one in the name of Jesus. Lonnie was interceding and everything in there, but it was like this: I went in there as a young person, fearful of the spiritual darkness, of what was going to happen, and the unknown. But we all came out Ghostbusters! That is really the way I would put it. We were able to laugh at it and say, "To hell with you, darkness! You've been doing this to this woman for all these years!"

A light went on inside of my head. I finally understood that we do have power over darkness, but we've been ignorantly eaten up alive by it! We can't just stand by and watch people die around us and be swallowed up into this darkness, this hell that the enemy wants to suck all of us into. He's out to kill us! So that day a light bulb went on and not just in my heart and my mind, but in my spirit: the revelation of how the enemy is devouring us and how we let him devour us. I saw a demonstration of God's presence and power and deliverance.

As I was walking out of that back room, Lonnie turned around and pointed at me, saying, "From this day forward you will have discernment!"

I kind of gave a nervous laugh, and he yelled, "I am not joking! Did you hear me? You will have discernment from this day forward!" I had no idea what was getting ready to happen. A couple of days later, we were in another big church in Chorleywood, England, and it was Lonnie's turn to preach. He was up on stage sharing, and then he said, "I'd like to call Debbie up here right now." I looked at him and was like, "What the heck are you doing?"

I looked around and just sat there in my chair because I couldn't believe he was doing that. He called me up there and then handed me the microphone, wanting me to talk about asthma. I had been healed of asthma, so I did. I told my story the best I could, but I was feeling like I was almost being choked while I was up there. It was really bizarre. Back then, I would have rather had the stomach flu than be in front of a crowd like that, so for him to do that to me with no warning really shocked me. In my heart, which was beating a thousand miles per hour, I was going, "What the heck are you doing? Why are you picking me?"

After this, a lot of people came up to me, wanting me to pray for them. I was like, "Wait a minute. Now I see why John gets all these people who want him to pray for them." All of a sudden, you realize that people think you're "somebody." Well, the Holy Spirit showed me right away—because I know myself—that we all need to keep looking *up*, not at ourselves or anyone else. We are all just conduits of God's presence if we let God use us in that way. But for us to stay in an authentic, pure flow of his presence, we *have* to have the key ingredient of humility. Otherwise, we are polluted, and it's not a pure reflection of who is he is. Pride can grip people with the want, need, and desire to be on stage. It is an epidemic with many believers.

However, I will say that I never saw that in Lonnie. It was really key in looking back at that time in his life: He did not flow in that pride thing I see plaguing so many people. He'd pull up others and say, "Hey, let God use *you!*" In his mind he was probably thinking, "Little Debbie here can pray for healing!" He used me and wanted to take attention off of himself. With both John and Lonnie, it was their humility that allowed them to be used at that capacity. Lonnie had this simplicity and childlikeness that was very appealing and special. He knew he was a broken vessel, but Lonnie trusted the Lord wholeheartedly!

Praise God—revival was upon us!

SIXTEEN

Marwan

"My Palestinian Brother"

ONE DAY BACK in the wrestling room of Calvary Chapel
Yorba Linda, I noticed a young guy following me around and
watching me pray for people. For several weeks I would glance
around at the crowds of young people getting radically touched by
God—and there he'd be again, this young, dark-complected guy,
totally wide-eyed, just watching everything that was going on. I
finally went over to him one day and took him under my wing, so to
speak, because I saw how hungry he was for the things of God.

This young man was very interesting to me. We eventually
became best of friends and traveled the world together. His name is
Marwan Bahu. The "mar" portion of his name is just like in
"Marvin," and the "wan" is pronounced the same as in "wander."
Easy enough, but some people have real trouble with the name.
Marwan is a Palestinian, born in Jordan. His entire family was
forced to leave their homes back in 1948. His father's family had
lived for generation upon generation just outside of Jerusalem, and
his mother's family was from Jaffa. Both sets of his grandparents
owned businesses and were very successful. They all became
refugees in Jordan when they were forcibly evacuated because of an
impending war. At that time, Israel was becoming a nation again
after a couple thousand years. That is a modern miracle predicted in
Scripture. However, Marwan's family was never allowed back in
their homes. It was a total disaster for them.

Marwan's parents actually met in Jordan and were married
there. The entire family had always been Greek Orthodox
Christians living in an Islamic world. Not only did they lose their
homes and property in Palestine, but they also suffered rejection and
persecution from many of their new Muslim neighbors in Jordan.

Nevertheless, Marwan's grandfather pulled his family together, eventually started a business in Amman, the capital of Jordan, and was able to send two of his sons to America. These two sons, Marwan's uncles, were the first immigrants from his family to come to America back in the fifties. Marwan was later born in Amman, Jordan, on April 24, 1960.

I want Marwan to pick the story up from there and show how God brought a Jesus freak from the sixties and a wounded Palestinian immigrant together in the bonds of love. The Lord brought us together ultimately to serve our generation with healing and forgiveness, friendship and love. Jesus loves all the people of the world, and he certainly loves Marwan and all Palestinians! Jesus himself was beaten, tortured, and killed as a common criminal for every Palestinian as well as for every other human being on this planet. He gave his life willingly to provide all of us salvation and eternal life. He conquered death three days after his crucifixion to prove that he is the real deal. Marwan supernaturally encountered Christ shortly before we met—and believe me, he is the real deal also!

"I WOULD PUNCH YOU FOR NO REASON"
by Marwan Bahu

I was angry and didn't even know why I was angry. Maybe it was because of growing up as a refugee in Jordan. Maybe it was because I was really small when I was young and got picked on a lot. I didn't really start growing much until way after high school. I was five foot seven and weighed 125 pounds as a senior. I got in a lot of fights. However, when I was about twenty-two, I miraculously grew another three inches and quickly got up to about 190 pounds. I studied nutrition, sports, and exercise programs, and eventually opened my own health clinic. I could bench-press 455 pounds. But while I was growing up, I had a huge chip on my shoulder and was very mixed up inside.

I was seven years old when my parents brought us to the United States. I remember it very well because I actually turned seven on my trip to America. We flew TWA from Jordan. I also remember the stewardess gave me these little TWA wings to pin on my shirt, just like the captain wore, because it was my birthday. It was a two-day flight from Amman, Jordan, to California, where my uncles lived. We landed in LA on April 26, 1967.

My grandfather on my dad's side was responsible for sending some of my family members to America. According to my grandma, when they fled Palestine, they only had the clothes on their backs. That was it, nothing else, but my grandpa worked hard in Jordan and saved enough money to send two of my dad's brothers, one older and one younger, to the United States. My grandfather also borrowed money to pay their college tuition. My uncles then worked their way through college. One of them graduated from UCLA and the other from USC. When my grandfather passed away, they were still working out here in California after they graduated. They brought my grandmother over from Jordan, and then my father got sponsored by a close friend and borrowed enough money to bring my immediate family over. My grandfather never made it here, but he opened the door to my family moving to California. He died in Jordan in 1964.

My family on both sides had always been Greek Orthodox Christians, but I didn't know what I believed. When I was nine, I saw that movie *Jesus of Nazareth* and had a really powerful encounter in my room with the Lord. I yelled out to God, "Why did you let him die?" I couldn't understand why God would let an innocent man die. His presence came on me, and I started weeping. I tried to figure out what that was all about, but then nothing else happened for many years—until I was about seventeen.

By that time I was in Garden Grove, working at my dad's gas station. These two girls came in from Calvary Chapel, and I remember my brother and I were standing behind the counter. The pretty girls were talking and laughing with each other, and as they were leaving, one of them said to us, "Jesus loves you!" And, simple as it was, it impacted me. My brother made some remark to them like, "Okay, Jesus freaks, whatever," but what they said hit me! It stuck with me that Jesus loved me! No one had ever verbalized to me that they loved me. I knew my parents loved me by their actions, but they never said it. My mother was very nurturing, but I was especially trying to get my father's approval and love. So when these girls said, "Jesus loves you," it really impacted me because the very thing I was seeking was love. I didn't realize that I was also seeking God's love. Up until then, I had no clue that God loved me. There is power in our words!

Shortly after that encounter, I stopped working for my dad and started to work for this lumber company. That's where I met my friend Kevin. He was a real Christian who witnessed to me for a long time, until I finally went with him to Calvary Chapel. I was almost nineteen when we walked into the Costa Mesa church in 1978.

I watched the meeting at Calvary Chapel and thought it was really good because I had never been to a church service before in my life. It was actually a Thursday evening meeting in the overflow room. Chuck Missler shared, and at one point he said, "Okay, whoever wants to receive Christ come forward."

My buddy said, "Come on! Go forward!"

I said, "I already love God."

But Kevin continued, "Marwan, just go forward and receive Christ!"

I finally said, "Okay," and joined a bunch of people who went forward.

The speaker said, "Bow your head and repeat this prayer," so I sincerely prayed the prayer. Nothing exciting happened. It just felt like this gentle peace kind of settled over me. A couple of weeks later, my buddy moved back to Ohio where he was originally from. I was left alone, so I stopped going to church.

About a year later, I was driving my car in the fast lane down the 91 Freeway. My father had bought me this little two-seater Fiat Spider convertible, a nice little sports car. I was going home after an amazing workout—I had been training with a professional bodybuilder—when this thought came out of nowhere. It just came in and hit me on the side of my head, taking me back to the time when I had said that prayer in church. The thought was: "What have you done with Jesus?" In that *exact* moment, my windshield faded out—and I was traveling 70 miles an hour in the fast lane! The stereo faded out as well, and the Lord completely filled my car. He was sitting in the seat next to me. It was weird and is almost impossible to explain, but I'll try. His presence was so strong that I knew it was Jesus. I couldn't exactly see him because I was in another place, but I knew he was sitting next to me, and I could hear his voice. I was somehow caught up into some kind of dimension, and he said to me, "Marwan, it's time to come home." And then—*boom!* He disappeared.

The windshield came back into view, the stereo kicked on, and I noticed I had driven one full exit in the fast lane on the freeway, completely unaware of it. All of a sudden, I just began weeping uncontrollably. Mind you, I'd never read the Bible before. I had only had that one experience when I was nine years old and one prayer in a church. The first thought that came to my mind after the Lord lifted off my car was, "I've just been with Jesus!" That's what I said to myself. I had a visitation from God on the freeway!

I was about nineteen at this time, and my whole life changed just like that. I drove home, opened the door to my house full of excitement from meeting Jesus, ran in, and said, "Mom! Mom! You won't believe what just happened to me!"

My mom was in the kitchen doing dishes, so she came in the room. She didn't say a word. She looked at me, felt my forehead, smelled my breath.

I said, "Mom, come on. You know I'm a good kid. I don't do any of that junk."

She turned around without saying one word. She just had this perplexed look on her face and then walked back to the kitchen.

I went to my room and shut the door. I had dated a girl about two years before, and I don't know why, but she had given me her Bible. I never read it, but had put it in my nightstand drawer next to my bed. I went right to it. I remember this so clearly—I opened the drawer, pulled the Bible out, turned on the light, opened the Bible, and started reading. The scriptures just jumped off of the pages, and I just kept weeping and weeping.

My buddy Kevin had sent me a letter from Ohio some time before, but I hadn't opened it yet. That night, I quickly opened the letter up, and there was his phone number. So I called and got his sister-in-law on the phone. I just needed to share what had happened with somebody who understood.

When I asked if Kevin was there, she said, "No. Kevin moved back to Costa Mesa."

Once she gave me his new address, I immediately got in my car and went to Costa Mesa. I drove up to where he was living, walked down this alley, and there he was, working on his car.

I yelled, "Kevin!"

He looked up at me and said, "Marwan, it's like you've come back from the dead!" Those were the first words that came out of his mouth.

"Dude, you won't believe what happened to me!" And I told him my story.

I started going back to Calvary Chapel. I went seven days a week. Every day I'd find a Bible study. I was so hungry. Then I joined the church library. Chuck Smith had recorded his teachings on the entire Bible from Genesis to Revelation on tape. You could rent out seven cassettes maximum for free, and so I'd go rent out seven cassettes, take them home, and listen to them all in one day. Kevin had given me this little New Testament Gideon Bible, and I read through that New Testament every three days. It was just a little red New Testament with Psalms and Proverbs. I read it all the way, cover to cover. I couldn't get enough. I was *so* hungry for God.

I remember in my car I couldn't play a cassette or any worship tape from Maranatha Music without just weeping the whole time, wherever I was going. Sometimes I'd have to stop my car and gather myself before I could continue driving. I told everybody about Jesus! People would go, "Dude, I don't want to hear it!"

I would say, "No, no. You don't understand." Then I would tell them about Jesus, how amazing God is because he just *completely* transformed my life. Not only was I changed on the inside, but it quickly changed me on the outside also. For one thing, God knocked the chip off my shoulder—and then I physically grew three inches right after I started serving him on the mission field. Maybe it was a coincidence, but I don't think so! How many people grow three inches and gain over forty solid pounds after they're twenty years old? It was a brand new life in every way!

180 DEGREES

I had previously been the type of kid who was seen, but not heard. If guests came over, I'd cruise to my room and shut the door. I wanted to be alone. I was really timid and shy as a young person in most settings. At the same time, I was full of anger and really confused. But as soon as I got saved, you couldn't shut me up! It was like this guy who was locked up suddenly came out! From that moment on, my whole life changed and took a 180-degree turn.

After about six months of going to Calvary Chapel Costa Mesa, a buddy of mine said, "Hey, there's a Calvary Chapel in Anaheim Hills, and they meet in our old gymnasium." We both had gone to Canyon High School where Calvary Chapel Yorba Linda was meeting, so I started going there instead of driving to Costa Mesa because I lived right there in Anaheim Hills.

To my amazement, I immediately discovered that the Spirit of God was falling on that church. The first time I attended was just after the Mother's Day 1980 meeting when the Holy Spirit powerfully fell on hundreds and hundreds of young people. I walked in on a scenario where Jesus was not just revealing himself to one person driving down the 91 Freeway, but the Holy Spirit of God was revealing Jesus to a multitude of hungry kids! I heard Lonnie Frisbee share about God, and the anointing on Lonnie blew my mind! I instantly knew that this was where I was supposed to be. The first three or four weeks that I attended the church, there were around three hundred people in a Sunday morning service. Within nine months, there were about twenty-eight hundred people coming. We had to move three times within about a two-year period!

After I started going to John Wimber's church, I approached one of the pastors to go on a mission trip because they were going to England. They told me I wasn't ready.

I said, "Please let me go! I want to serve the Lord. You don't understand. I have this hunger to know God and to serve him with everything that I have within me!"

Yes, I was still only twenty-one years old or so. I didn't really know Scripture enough, but I did know that what was going on in my life was really real, and I wanted to give my life away to the Lord. Lonnie Frisbee saw me following him around, and he began to coach me about how to be available to the Holy Spirit, how to recognize what he is doing, and how to be open in order to learn how to operate in the gifts. I was like a sponge, soaking everything up. What an honor to have Lonnie take notice of me.

However, in June the church sent a team to England, and I wasn't allowed to go. Shortly after, we heard a lot of incredible reports and testimonies coming back from the mission to the UK. I was determined to go on one of the next trips. I signed up for all the seminars, for everything that I possibly could, in order to go on the next mission. I was there. I was faithful. I put my time in. I went through weekends listening to John Wimber tapes for ten hours in a row. That's dedication! And praise the Lord, I finally got to go! The leaders told me to "pray and ask the Lord if you can go."

So I prayed, and the Lord didn't say anything to me. Then I asked again, "Lord, can I go?"

He said, "I didn't tell you *not* to go."

I took that as a yes and committed to go on the very next mission.

At that time I began to have a deeper relationship with Lonnie because he was leading the group that was preparing to go to South Africa with John Wimber. Lonnie was more at an age where I could relate to him. God was really using him in a powerful way. It blew my mind over and over. The Lord placed me under his umbrella, under his discipleship, and I just started watching him, following him, and listening to him. He would take me along wherever he went and started to teach me about paying attention to the Holy Spirit, watching what the Holy Spirit is doing, and not to be too anxious to move because you don't want to be an opportunist, yet you want to be ready when the Holy Spirit tells you to jump. It's then that you want to go for it. You don't want to draw back. God wants people who will step up in faith and honor him. So I started to serve the Lord with more understanding.

I had been working for Butler's Shoe Corporation, the second largest shoe company in the world, for six months by this time. Then I got accepted to go to South Africa with the Vineyard (by this point, we had changed our name from Calvary Chapel Yorba Linda), so I was preparing to go overseas. One day the district manager showed up at our store, came up to me, and said, "Marwan, I want to talk to you." He brought me to the back room and then continued, "We want to offer you a store."

I said, "Wow!"

He offered me the whole package: medical insurance, a higher salary, benefits, paid holidays, and all this stuff.

I said, "That's amazing! Sounds like an incredible opportunity. But I've got to tell you something. I'm going to Africa because I want to serve Jesus!"

"Well," he said, "this is an amazing opportunity. It doesn't come by very often."

"I understand, but my number one priority is to serve God," and then I gave him my two-week resignation.

My district manager came back later and told me, "When you come back, if you want your job, it'll still be here." And that was that.

I had also bought this beautiful 1979 Yamaha 1100 XS Special motorcycle with a teardrop cherry red tank and all of that. It was decked out. Before I bought it, I had about two thousand dollars saved up, but I met a guy who was selling that bike for twenty-seven hundred. I told him I'd pay him in thirty days. That next month I made seven hundred and twenty dollars. I only spent twenty dollars on myself for the whole month. I didn't go out, I didn't do anything. I saved that seven hundred bucks and paid him. Then about a year later, the mission trip came up, so I turned around and sold that bike and used the money for my mission trip. It was a beautiful bike, but going to Africa was like a dream for me. When I was a little boy, I watched a movie about these nuns going down a river in Africa. They sang, "Michael, row your boat." I think God touched me way back then as a little kid with a dream to go to Africa. With this first mission trip, my dream had finally come true!

The trip was amazing. Every meeting the power of God just kept increasing. At one meeting the most radical thing I ever saw happened. We went to the Invisible Church in Johannesburg, South Africa. It was a pretty big church with three pastors: Dave Owens, Bushy Venter, and Costa Mitchell. There were about five hundred people there for the meeting that night. Lonnie took his friend Gigi, me, and a couple of other people with him. Lonnie got up and spoke for about thirty minutes, and then he said, "Okay, the Holy Spirit wants to move now. Everybody, stand up please."

This church building was all pews. There must have been thirty or forty pews deep, and they were all the length of the church. It was like a big movie theater setup.

Then Lonnie raised his hands and said, "Okay, Holy Spirit, come!"

Five hundred people went *boom!* They all fell down! They were on the floor between the pews, and many of them flopping under the pews, all by the power of God.

I lost it. I wept.

Lonnie came over to me and said, "Hey! Get a hold of yourself! You're not here to get ministered to. You're here to minister!"

So I wiped my tears and started walking over to different bodies, trying to figure out what to do.

Lonnie told me, "See what the Holy Spirit is doing and then just respond."

I started laying hands on people. People were getting healed, people were getting filled with the Holy Spirit, people started speaking in tongues! Demons were coming out of some. It was—*boom, boom, boom*—nonstop action. We had to crawl over the top of the pews because it was the only way to get to people. They were everywhere on the floor. Gigi was right with us praying for people, stepping over pews, and ministering in the power of the Holy Spirit! We were all mind-boggled!

At least an hour or so later, we finally left, and people were still under the power of God. We just left them there. Lonnie said, "Let's go," so we took off. It was pretty amazing! It was one of the most incredible moments of my entire life, and that church later became a Vineyard. We were in South Africa for a month and a half, and we had some incredible meetings. The Lord moved in *powerful* visitations.

We were in Cape Town at the church of a friend of Derek Morphew's. Alastair was his name.

Lonnie with Gigi in Africa

He had a church in the Cape, and it was a pretty good-sized congregation. As Lonnie did sometimes, he called the young children to come forward. I think the kids were from five to ten years old, something like that. Lonnie started to pray, and so we all started to pray for the kids. Suddenly, the power of God came on *all* of these little kids. There were three or four of them who went into a trance under the power of God, and it was a couple of days before they came out of it. Derek Morphew told us the parents called and were concerned because their kids hadn't woken up and it had been a day. Lonnie said, "Don't worry about it. Give it time. They're in a trance. They're before God right now, and they'll come back."

Pretty intense, radical stuff like that happened in one church after another. Hundreds and hundreds of people would come under the power of God and be healed instantly, born again instantly, or filled with the Holy Spirit. People would just be worshipping the Lord, and then all of a sudden, the presence of God would fall on them. It was effortless. And that's the type of ministry that I was raised on—watching God move effortlessly. I hate having to strive at something to make it happen. If we yield our vessels to the Holy Spirit, the Holy Spirit will do it all. He created the heavens and the earth and all the fullness thereof. God spoke, and the Holy Spirit performed it. So if God is speaking to your hearts about opening yourselves up to be missionaries here in America or abroad, then go for it! Believe me, it will breathe life into your bones!

I've had the opportunity to be right in the middle of what God was doing, and let me tell you, you will learn *so much!* You can grow by leaps and bounds just by being at the right place at the right time, in the very heart of what God's doing. It's incredible the vision that God will plant in your heart and in your mind and life. It's the kind of growth that you can't get in a Bible study or by going to Sunday service. It's beyond what you can experience here at home. There's a completely different anointing when you're away serving the Lord on a mission, even if it's only fifty miles away. I've gone to a lot of churches with Lonnie just to drive him there and back. Not to get up and speak or anything, just to make sure he got where he needed to go. I got blessed because I got to be a part of what God was doing. Even if it's that small, even if it's just supporting somebody with your prayers and your money, God honors that, and you receive whatever God gives to that individual.

I remember when I came back from South Africa, the Lord spoke to me, saying, "I'm going to send you back to your people!"

I said, "No way. You can't do that to me!"

I said that because my people are a hard people. I lived with my family, and that's how I came to know the Lord. They helped bring me to the end of myself because they're so difficult to deal with. They were traditionally supposed to be Greek Orthodox Christians, but none of them were living it. They had that hard-core Middle Eastern mindset. That's probably one of the reasons why not too many people are hip on ministering to the Arabic people—they're really difficult. But if we're going to minister to them, we're going to have to minister to them with power, right within *their* culture.

Paul said when he came to minister to people that he didn't come with persuasive words, but with a demonstration of power.[36] If you're going to convert Muslims and these tough Arabs, then you better have something that surpasses everything that they have. We need the power of God and to be supernaturally led by the Holy Spirit in order to reach them. *That's* what is going to shake their cultural mindset. The Middle East is where so many religions sprang up. It's where the roots are. They've heard it, seen it, and they've participated, so you're going to have to give them something more than what they have.

I'd like to encourage anyone who wants to reach people for Christ to give God whatever he is requesting of you. Be available. Say, "Here am I." Don't back up when the Lord says, "Okay, come forward." Take a step in faith. You're only going to gain. You're not going to know how to fight unless you get in the ring. I threw my hat in. Be encouraged because there are some incredible people in the body of Christ to help you grow in the Lord.

The Lord has given me the privilege to work with many Islamic people and see them come to Christ. I have traveled back to Jordan, and not only do I have a burden for my Muslim brothers, I have a burden for peace and salvation to come to my Jewish friends as well. I have seen the Lord do many miracles of reaching across the battle lines between Jew and Palestinian. The wounds are very deep, and I still feel the pain when I visit my grandparents' old homes. I saw the businesses that they started are still operating in both Jerusalem and Jaffa under new owners. How would *anyone* feel to have everything taken away from their entire family?

But again, Jesus gave up everything to rescue us. In my own case, he has not only brought salvation, healing, and new life to me, but has rescued and blessed my whole family, bringing

From left to right: Lonnie, Kevin Ross, Corne, John Ruttkay, and Marwan

us to a nation with the most freedom in the world. Jesus has given me a wonderful wife and five incredible children. Consider Joseph in the Bible. He was betrayed by his brothers, sold as a slave, taken to Egypt, and thrown in prison, but God delivered him by having him demonstrate supernatural gifts of the Holy Spirit to an entire nation. God used him to bless and deliver both Jew and Egyptian. That's what Jesus wants to do with each of us: have us come in a demonstration of his power and love—to rescue *all* the people of the world!

Since that first trip to South Africa, and after walking with Lonnie Frisbee all these years, I have dedicated my life to Jesus and the Great Commission. I traveled the world and made three more trips to Africa with Lonnie as well as many other trips to South America, England, Europe, Israel, and all over the place. It has been incredible, and I praise God for Lonnie and all that he has deposited in my life. But more than that, I have found the joy that comes from serving our King, Lord, and Savior, Jesus Christ of Nazareth.

HE ALONE IS WORTHY!

SEVENTEEN

Trouble in River City

THE GREAT COMMISSION has been the focus of this book as well as the season of my life right after the Jesus People movement—which, in turn, can be traced back to the Haight-Ashbury up by San Francisco back in 1967. By the mid-seventies, the Jesus Revolution had cooled off quite a bit, as far as thousands of young people getting born again month after month and mass baptisms catching the attention of the secular media around the world. However, a new denomination of Calvary Chapel churches and many offshoots emerged from that movement, and they continue to minister the gospel to millions of people all over the world to this day. I am forever grateful to have been a part of it from the very beginning. Hanging in my garage is one of the photos from the 1971 *Time* magazine story in which I am baptizing one of the thousands of young converts in the ocean at Corona del Mar. I took a copy of that photo to a local shop and had it blown up to a 5'x 3' poster.

They say a picture is worth a thousand words, and I agree. In fact, I think that some pictures could be worth *millions* of words, and that photo is one of them. My poster represents the bottom line to eternal life! It shows a repentant, humble soul coming to Jesus Christ and symbolically being buried into his death in the waters of baptism, only to be resurrected into a brand new life—a life in him—that will continue for millions of years in a universe filled with billions of breathtaking galaxies and unending wonders. It is the highest honor to have played a small part in that program. When my life on earth is over, it's what I would love to be remembered for. We all get to participate in this honor because, remember, "For God so loved the world that he gave his only begotten Son, that

WHOSOEVER believes in him shall not perish, but have everlasting life!"[37]

Immediately after the Jesus People revival, which they estimate brought in over two million new souls in America alone over a ten-year span, God sent Peter Crawford and me around the world in 1978 with a message of "the priesthood of all believers." That's what this second book has really been all about, along with the command of Jesus to "go to the uttermost parts of the world preaching the gospel of the kingdom of God."[38] As young ministers still in our twenties, we did our best to fulfill that call, and God allowed us, in his mercy, to be a part of another major movement. It was birthed in South Africa with signs and wonders, and then on Mother's Day 1980, the Holy Spirit poured out a powerful anointing on Calvary Chapel Yorba Linda, which shook up the entire church community in America and then abroad. I feel so blessed to have been able to participate in yet another major movement that brought in a multitude of believers and produced another modern-day denomination, the Vineyard. Presently, there are over a thousand Vineyard churches around the world. Only God could have done all of this, not Lonnie Frisbee or Chuck Smith or John Wimber or anyone else. It was our heavenly Father, sending Jesus and the Holy Spirit to execute his commands!

But—and there is a "but" to this story—it is also revealed in Scripture that before mankind was even created, there was a huge rebellion in heaven. A third of the angels turned against God and were cast out of his kingdom. We are not told all the details, because I don't think we can even grasp heavenly things very much with our finite minds. Nevertheless, it has been revealed enough to know that we are stuck in the middle of a gigantic spiritual war. We also know that it involves death because we see it all around us every day, and the Bible clearly teaches that death is a direct result of this rebellion. Each of us is destined to physically die unless Jesus returns first. So we would be very wise to pay attention to the reality that we are definitely in a war.

I have been asked the question a thousand times, "How can a perfect, all-powerful God create such an imperfect world full of starving children, injustice, death, and destruction?" Well, it might sound crazy, but it boils down to love. To experience real love, it must be given freely. That involves a choice, which, in turn, requires "free will." If God created everything perfect without giving anyone free will, then everyone would be a robot, and there would be no *real* love anywhere. How can you freely love someone if you don't even have a choice? God loves the birds and the animals, but he did not give them free will. They live by instinct. He loves the galaxies with all their beauty, but the galaxies cannot express love back to their Creator. God, however, did give the angels free will, but at some point many of them chose to rebel against God. Nevertheless, God had a plan already prepared from before the foundations of the world.

God used this rebellion as an opportunity to implement his master plan to create mankind, the pinnacle of his creation, and ultimately, to perfect his kingdom. We who were made "a little lower than the angels,"[39] but in the image of God were also created with complete free will. Yet mankind was also deceived and joined this rebellion. The First Adam miserably fell, but then out of God's love for us, he sent Jesus, "the Second Adam," to once and forever pay the price and penalty for all our transgressions. God became "one of us," took our place and our punishment, and conquered death. This is the heart of the gospel. We simply have a choice to accept or reject that sacrifice.

God also uses this war to develop each son and daughter who is adopted into his family. He develops and completes our faith, hope, and love. He teaches us to trust and prepares us to rule and reign with him throughout eternity. This is quickly summing up a very involved and supernatural story. But the end result of his plan is spelled out in the Book of Revelation where it says that every tear shall be wiped away and he will create a new heaven and a new earth. Jesus our King and Savior will rule eternally, **and there will**

be no starving children, death, and destruction! "Even so, come quickly, Lord Jesus!"[40]

Keeping this big picture in view, we were absolutely thrilled in the early eighties with all that God was doing. During the first three years with the Vineyard, I forget how many foreign trips we made, but it was glorious. I also made a few on my own, but God was pouring out "rivers of living water,"[41] just like he promised. Our big South Africa trip in 1982, with our "team of one hundred," was fantastic, but by the end of that trip, we got a little preview of some major warfare that was about to hit the camp. There was definitely "trouble in River City" brewing and a tremendous amount of warfare on the horizon. John Ruttkay was, once again, with me on that trip, and I want him to set up the scenario.

"AN OLD MAN WITH A PROPHETIC WORD"
by John Ruttkay

I want to mention a couple of things that God was using Lonnie for here in America just before we made our trips to South Africa and elsewhere with the Vineyard. My friends Bryan and Mercedes Marleaux are two young missionaries who Lonnie totally influenced and mentored before they even went into the ministry. Now they have been with Grace World Mission full-time for over twenty years and have gone all over the world. Back in 1980, Bryan was a professional surfer who had broken his leg. He thought to himself, "I hear people are getting healed at Calvary Chapel up in Yorba Linda. I better go up there. I want to get this cast off, and I need to get back to work." So he went up to Canyon High.

This was how the meetings were happening back then: Everything was very abstract! Lonnie wouldn't think twice about jumping up on top of a chair (even if he wasn't the speaker) and calling people out, and then the power of God would just—*POW!*—come on them so powerfully. So Bryan went up there, and at that time there were probably three or four hundred people in the auditorium. Lonnie saw Bryan in the back with crutches and yelled out, "You, in the back with the crutches! The Lord says he's got a plan for you!"

Bryan was immediately knocked straight up against the wall, screaming bloody murder like somebody was beating him with a rubber hose. He told me later, "My leg didn't get healed, but I got called to the ministry that day! I was on the floor for two hours with the presence of God on me. I had no choice but to make a decision on where I was going to go with that. I chose to follow Jesus! I chose to follow his plan!" We continued to see *that* kind of manifestation happening as the church grew, with a very powerful presence of God showing up time after time.

One of the things that Lonnie had on him was impartation. People got powerfully touched "impartation-wise." I would say Blaine Cook and, really, all the leaders got powerfully touched, and I know that I, along with Marwan Bahu, Bryan and Mercedes, Peter Crawford, Gigi Gruss, and many, many others, got an impartation from Lonnie. None of us can say that Lonnie Frisbee did not have a direct impact or influence on our lives. You model what you've been discipled under, and Lonnie was a good discipler. He was a hands-on leader.

The way that he did it wasn't, "Make an appointment with me at my office," because he had no office. Instead he would say, "You're my new roommate. You're living with me in community. Let's go do this thing!" That's how he discipled people. It was through osmosis that you caught it all. And that's exactly how Jesus did it, so I feel like Lonnie's model was very biblical. We really saw the presence and the power of God move in incredible ways.

Lonnie's influence in Africa was *so* strong. He convinced John Wimber to bring something like seventy-seven young people on a major mission trip to South Africa. I think that was the last count. Man, were we young back then. If someone was thirty or over, we were like "Whoa, we have an elder in the group here!" We went to South Africa with all of these kids and a couple of pastors mixed in who were kind of overseeing everything. Lonnie, Gerard Driscoll, and I were going to split off and minister in all of the Assemblies of God churches from the top of South Africa down to the bottom. Those particular churches had opened their doors and wanted God's Spirit to come with the "fire" that was coming from America.

One of the first things we did after arriving was plant a Vineyard in Johannesburg. We met in a park for a couple of team meetings. In just our team meetings alone, the power of God moved very dramatically. The presence of God would come in waves. It was in that park in South Africa where I first met Marwan.

Lonnie told me, "I see the Spirit of God resting on this young guy named Marwan Bahu."

I said, "Cool."

"I think he's supposed to go with us."

It would have been Lonnie, Marwan, Gerard Driscoll, and me on that team, but the elders who were over everybody said, "No, we're going to need to keep Marwan with us." So Marwan didn't get to go with us at that time, but he later joined us and became not just one of my best friends, but one of Lonnie's best friends also. We have served God both together and apart ever since!

We broke off as a sub-team and went from the top of South Africa to the bottom of South Africa. The Assemblies of God churches at that time were *super* religious, with doilies on their heads and stuff like that. The guy who picked us up to go to the first meeting was really something. After a while, I thought to myself, "I'd rather watch paint dry than listen to this guy talk anymore. We are in big trouble. There's *no way* the Spirit of God is going to move in this camp!"

When we got to the church, it was *dry bones!* I was like, "Oh, buddy, it'll be interesting to see how this goes down."

In the front row of the church was a whole line of old ladies—with their doilies and everything—sitting next to each other. Lonnie yelled out, "God is moving on these ladies in the front row!" Immediately, they all hit the floor in a chain reaction. We saw the presence of God come into that setting so powerfully. They were old saints who had that kind of religious thing on them, but man, when the Spirit of God came, you saw those doilies flying off like frisbees! Those old ladies hit the floor, one lady's false teeth fell out, people got delivered, and that religious spirit lifted off the people. People were dancing, and I mean, it was *on!* It was so much fun! After that, we went from one Assemblies of God church to the next. We did it for thirty days straight. It was crazy. The presence of God would come and blow everyone's minds, including mine!

I remember we were in this other church meeting in some obscure town in the middle of nowhere in South Africa. I was watching monkeys run through the streets in this place, that's how far out we were. There was a Christian school near the church, and these young kids in the school had to wear uniforms and little straw hats. They looked like Amish kids. That was how many of the white South Africans were back in '82: very conservative, very proper. A bunch of the young kids came from the Bible school to the church meeting. Instead of a row of old ladies with doilies in the front row of the church, there was a whole row of these kids with their little straw hats. The meeting was very traditional, and Lonnie was trying to encourage the worship to catch up to the twentieth century. The younger people were starting to open up, but they were very polite, very staid, and we needed a breakthrough.

As the meeting came to an end, we started to press in a little bit more, and Lonnie said, "Okay, this is the time now for ministry, and I see for every one of you in the front row that the Lord is about ready to touch you!" Then he walked by and flipped all of their hats off—*bang, bang, bang, bang*—right down the whole line. He took a big flask of anointing oil and threw it all over them—on their hair, their faces, their uniforms, all over the place, he didn't care. He just started pouring—*glug, glug*—and the power of God hit these youngsters *so* powerfully. We didn't get out of the meeting until one in the morning, and half of the kids had to be carried out. The presence of God just came with such power in all of these meetings. It was an awakening to the people of God. That's what it was. It was an awakening that God wanted to bring to his people in Africa and everywhere else. We were just in that moment.

As we moved further down south, ultimately to Cape Town, I met a very precious brother named Derek Morphew for the first time. Derek was one of the leaders for the Assemblies of God and actually a great theologian. Lonnie had known him since his first trip four years earlier in 1978, and they were great friends already. We stayed at Derek's house with his loving family. When we started to get into the Cape Town area and Stellenbosch and places like that, I could feel plenty of spiritual freedom. It was in the atmosphere! We started to see the Lord really lift this place up and do something very significant. Eventually, Derek Morphew became one of the Vineyard's top leaders in Africa and has actually headed up Vineyard Bible Institute, a worldwide school of biblical studies, for many years. The meetings in Cape Town were more of the same, with powerful demonstrations that we could write a dozen books about, not to mention the impact they had on thousands of lives. However, in one of these meetings, as we were coming to the end of our trip in 1982, there was this old prophetic man we ran into. I'll never forget it. He had kind of a weird eye, you know, and looked way "Old Testament" to me. He came up to us and said, "Brothers, I've got a word for you!" He was talking to Lonnie, Gerard, and me.

We were all like, "Man! This guy looks and sounds like the real deal. We better be careful!"

The tone of his voice had us all clinging to a life raft with one another. Then he said, "And I don't want to give it in the church. I want to do it in a park."

I thought, "Dude, we're in trouble. Oh, this is scary."

Still, we went and met the guy in the park anyway.

First he looked at Lonnie and said, "Brother, it's over for you in this movement. You're out."

Then he looked at Gerard and said, "Your church is finished. You'll no longer be pastoring."

Then he turned to me and said, "Your wife's going to leave you. Prepare yourself!" I had finally reconciled back with my then-wife, and we had a son. This news was gut wrenching.

We were all like, "AHHHH!"

Here we thought we were on the glory train after all that God had used us for, but we were all heading back to the States going, "Oh, it's going to be awful if this is really a true word!"

But it was like clockwork. Gerard lost his church. Lonnie was getting the right foot of fellowship from the church. I came home one night and had a note on the TV that said, "Can't handle it anymore. Moved in with my mom," and that was the last of that deal. I was devastated!

So a very difficult season had descended upon us. It was very disillusioning and painful to have to go through. You're on a spiritual high and being used of the Lord so powerfully, and then suddenly, everything that you have to walk through is painful. The Vineyard was just skyrocketing up, becoming the trendsetter, becoming the go-to place in the body of Christ for people to hear what the Spirit of God was really saying. John was one of the most in-demand speakers in the world. Blaine was also on that trajectory, and so those guys were heading up to the sky—while Lonnie and I were heading into Adullam's cave. It was just a really tough season.

A lot of accusations were coming at Lonnie. I remember when I first met him, I heard the Lord clearly say to me, "Stand by him and walk through all the things that you have to walk through with him." Well, it was "all good" when we were hitting that trajectory to the stratosphere with the Vineyard, but now it was total warfare, a real bummer. Nevertheless, the Lord allowed this season, even warned us ahead of time. Please remember this wonderful promise: "And we know that all things work together for good to those who love God, to those who are the called according to his purpose."[42]

Believe me, Lonnie, Gerard, and I each love God with all our hearts, and our friend Jesus would eventually pull us out of Adullam's cave, just like he rescued David from King Saul a few thousand years before. God knows how to prepare us for eternal living, even with the hard things, as the **real** kingdom of God quickly approaches!

GUNS BLAZING

When I (Lonnie) returned to California from South Africa in 1982, all kinds of things began to happen. I was very familiar with spiritual warfare, especially when you attempt to serve God, but I was not prepared for the intensity of a totally new onslaught. It was not just one thing, but a series of things. For starters, there were accusations about my sexuality and rumors that I was gay. Throughout my entire ministry, the enemy has tried to label me. I will address that accusation now, but will also explore the whole subject of homosexuality in the final volume of my life story.

If you have read the first part of my story, then you know that I was molested by a pedophile as an eight-year-old child, which extremely traumatized me. When I told my parents, they didn't believe me, and this person continued to have access to my life, threatened me, and continued to molest me as a little child for several more years. I was filled with shame, terror, guilt, and self-loathing. I look back and see how the enemy put a mark on me that other pedophiles could see. One of my art teachers molested me and tried to convince me that it was normal, just alternative. A dance instructor did the same when I was on Casey Kasem's popular TV dance show, *Shebang*, as a fifteen-year-old.

I admit that as a young teenager I willingly explored my sexuality a few times, but I rejected that world. It was the early sixties, and besides, I was girl crazy and a hopeless romantic. On top of that, we were in the midst of the drugs, free sex, and rock 'n' roll generation. I became a nudist vegetarian with a very active sex life. I participated in multiple orgies and had a series of girlfriends and "puppy love" relationships. Being somewhat of a teenage star on *Shebang* opened me up to a whole world of promiscuity and the party life.

When I went to the art academy in San Francisco and lived in the Haight-Ashbury, I saw the militant gay movement get birthed, along with several other movements that swept across our nation. During that time, I was supernaturally led back to Christ and wholeheartedly dropped my net, left college and everything else behind, and followed Jesus. I'm not saying that as a young eighteen-year-old Jesus freak I never smoked another joint, never dropped another tab of acid, or never stumbled sexually, but I *am* saying that God lovingly cleaned up my life and showed me a more rewarding and powerful way to live. Jesus met me in such wonderful, real ways that he captured my heart, and **I am forever his**! I serve him because I want to, not because I have to.

I met and married my wife, Connie, while I was still a teenager and loved her with all my heart. I still love her, even after an adulterous affair destroyed our marriage years later. I told that story already. But after that, I suddenly became a single Christian, still in my twenties, who God had given great favor and visibility in the ministry. Believe me, I did not feel called to celibacy and really wanted to remarry and have a family. I was engaged twice over the next eight years to two wonderful Christian gals who I still love dearly, but it wasn't in the cards for us. The ministry kept me traveling the whole world on a super fast-paced trajectory. The enemy kept after me, but the truth is, I was daily serving God with all my heart.

There did come a time a little later, when I *did* get a root of bitterness against the church and did severely backslide. It was the most painful season of my life. I knew better, which made it even worse. You will hear all about it. I will be confessing a lot of my failures and sins, baring my soul. That period of my life mainly came after all of these allegations and warfare hit my life in the mid-eighties. But let me mention this one huge reality as we examine one another here: Every human being sins every day. How do we sin? We sin every day in "thought, word, and deed!" I don't deserve it, but my report card simply says, "FORGIVEN," because God, in his love and mercy, only sees the "righteousness of Christ" on me—and hopefully on you—as well as on every other repentant believer! That's a very good deal that cost Jesus everything!

Come now, and let us reason together, saith the Lord: though your sins be as scarlet, they shall be as white as snow; though they be red like crimson, they shall be as wool![43]

As far as the allegations that I am a homosexual, I will emphatically say right here, up front that I have *never* lived the gay lifestyle. At the same time, I have a ton of compassion for people who have been drawn into that world. They are some of the most interesting, creative, and gifted people. It's a huge and controversial subject, but I have my personal experience and have witnessed many others who have walked down that road. I have also seen much of the fruit of a life "coming out of the closet." It's usually not a pretty picture once you get past the thin veneer covering the brokenness of a very hurting person. I also have the revelation from the Holy Spirit and the Word of God that homosexuality is a counterfeit. Don't believe the lie of a third sex, you know: male, female, and homosexual.

Up in Tahquitz Canyon when I was eighteen, I cried out to Jesus to reveal himself to me—*if* he was really real! I was, at that time, still spiritually confused about everything. Well, you heard the story: I had the most radical encounter with God of my young life. He supernaturally manifested himself and placed a call and anointing upon me, which changed my direction forever. I have done my best to fulfill that personal call with many successes and many failures. I am writing these words right now because of that very day when Jesus commanded me to "tell the people that I am coming soon!"

I have delivered that message in full-time ministry for the last twenty-four years, and I will continue to proclaim the good news of the gospel until my dying day. But do you know and see that the spiritual warfare doesn't stop when you decide to serve Jesus? It didn't stop for Jesus either until he cried out from the cross, "It is finished."[44] The *resurrected Christ* instructs each of us to "pick up your cross and follow me!"[45] That means we still have challenges to face in our present lives. I certainly had some facing me for about a five-

247

year period starting in 1983 or so. But praise God, we live in a dispensation of time when Jesus has sent the Holy Spirit to guide us, heal us, and prepare us to eventually rule and reign together with him in an eternal kingdom. God even uses this spiritual war that we are in the middle of to develop us into the image of his Son! Remember, we have been given authority "in his name"—over *all* the works of the devil!

You know, it should be encouraging to everyone that God did all these mighty things in the Jesus movement and in the Vineyard movement through such a broken vessel such as me. If he can use me, then he can use any one of you. One of my favorite passages in the Bible goes like this:

> For ye see your calling, brethren, how that not many wise men after the flesh, not many mighty, not many noble, are called: But God hath chosen the foolish things of the world to confound the wise; and God hath chosen the weak things of the world to confound the things which are mighty; And base things of the world, and things which are despised, hath God chosen, yea, and things which are not, to bring to nought things that are: That no flesh should glory in his presence. But of him are ye in Christ Jesus, who of God is made unto us wisdom, and righteousness, and sanctification, and redemption: That, according as it is written, He that glorieth, let him glory in the Lord.[46]

"Onward, Christian Soldiers!"

EIGHTEEN

Devil's Food Cake

IN THIS CHRONICLE of my life experiences, I love to jump back and forth in time a bit. Therefore, allow me to end this part of my life story by transporting us back to the late sixties, when we were quickly moving into the Jesus People revival. The Lord was about to give me a mighty lesson on obedience and the power of God, a lesson that has helped guide me throughout my life and calling.

I was having a very large home group meeting, and there were about 120 people attending. We decided to dedicate the time one evening to seeking the Lord with prayer and worship (mostly worship) and a little bit of Bible instruction. We also were taking Holy Communion.

It was back then when the Lord showed me the importance of taking Communion for the cleansing of sins. He emphasized that Communion is not just a symbolic ritual, but there actually is healing in the elements, even though we as Protestants do not believe in the transubstantiation of the Eucharist. In other words, we do not believe that the bread and wine actually turn into the physical blood and physical flesh of our Lord Jesus. At the same time, we have a lot of love and acceptance for Catholics, who do teach that. We all have wrong traditions that we're blinded to, I'm sure. We are very pro-Catholic in our fellowship because, again, remember it says, "Behold, how good and how pleasant it is for brethren to dwell together in unity! It is like the precious ointment upon the head, that ran down upon the beard, even Aaron's beard: that went down to the skirts of his garments; As the dew of Hermon, and as the dew that descended upon the mountains of Zion: for there the Lord *commanded* the blessing, even life for evermore."[47] It is one of my favorite scriptures that I strive to live by.

According to church growth statistics or by the observations of religious people studying the situation, "power ministries" supposedly have a ten-year life expectancy. Today I'm celebrating my forty-second birthday, and I've had twenty-four years of ministry. The Lord has given me a "demonstration of God's power" anointing for most of those twenty-four years. I've outlived the statistics already! However, it has not been without a lot of trials and tribulations, as you have been learning. The enemy has attacked me with everything that he was allowed to. On this particular occasion at our home fellowship back in the late sixties, he was using a big slice of devil's food cake.

Like I mentioned, that particular evening we as a company of believers were seeking the Lord, worshipping, and preparing our hearts to take Communion. The Lord was reminding me of the verse, "He who's been forgiven much loveth much."[48] That was *supposed* to be the focus. All of us have been forgiven much, especially me, and I was trying to focus on the Lord. So here we were, a group of people huddled around Communion, and then suddenly, I was reminded that this sweet mother in the Lord had baked me a devil's food cake from scratch, homemade frosting and everything. It was waiting in the kitchen.

While I was serving communion to these 120 people, I started to see a bright, shining vision of this particular devil's food cake. I was seeing it right in front of me. Instead of seeing the Lord and his instructions, I was seeing the cake. It was too easy for the enemy and my human weakness. If he can't use food, he will use a woman dressed loosely, and if he can't use lust, then the check that was in the mail from the last meeting never came. I think there is a particular demon out there who has intercepted dozens of my paychecks. It's kind of like when you go to the laundry mat with a bag full of socks, but you leave with every single one mismatched. Total distraction and frustration!

As I saw this vision of the chocolate cake, I heard a voice say, "There's not enough, Lonnie. There's not enough. There's 120 people here in this meeting, and there's only one cake."

That's *exactly* how the devil got on me that night. "You'd better hurry up! You'd better hurry this Communion service up, 'cause if you don't get in there and get a piece of that cake, it's gonna be all gone—because you know Christians!"

I thought, "Yeah, how many times have I been to a Christian potluck and so many of the brethren came, but they didn't bring anything in their own pots. No casserole or anything." And then I remembered being in potlucks where Christians would jump in line to get seconds before some people were served firsts. Of course, everybody pretended like they weren't seeing how rude that was.

Anyway, the enemy was talking to me when I was ministering in front of those 120 people. I just kept hearing this voice say, "You'd better get in there and get that cake before it's all gone." Let me remind you that I had been doing one meeting after another. I decided that I deserved and wanted that cake—and I wanted it now! Scripture also says, "Grieve not the Holy Spirit."[49] This is one particular place in my public ministry that I would like to point out when I really grieved the Holy Spirit (pretty severely). I shut down the Communion service. Oh, don't ever do that! I quickly served the people the Communion elements, totally left the anointing of God that was present in the room, and closed the meeting. You know, it's like confessing that you had a fight with your wife—and that in that fight you were totally wrong.

But there I was, standing in front of the cake. I have to confess that I cut a piece of cake as big as the Bible I was carrying. I thought, "This is mine, and all 120 of you can fight for the rest of it." See, I had this need to have *mine*, to have more than what my proper share should have been. The brethren were looking at me with disgust. I had this embarrassingly huge piece of cake on my plate. I had an attitude of "let them eat cake," but they had to divide the rest of it up among 120 of them. We didn't have 120 pieces of cake. The enemy had been clearly speaking. I could hear (and listened to) every word he said.

I sank a fork into this large piece of cake like a Betty Crocker commercial on Saturday morning TV. The fork went slowly down into the cake. I was focused on all of the senses—the sight, the touch, the smell—and just as I lifted that large, gluttonous piece of cake to my mouth, the voice of the Lord came to me.

The moment that cake *almost* reached my mouth, the Lord said to me, "Lonnie, what would you rather have? That cake or me?"

I said, "Why, you, Lord."

And then I wolfed the piece of cake down like a frog snapping a fly out of the air. It's true. I hate to say it, but right now I feel the urgency of the Holy Spirit telling me to definitely share this story. As I put the cake in my mouth, brethren, I had one of the most exciting and most powerful encounters with God through the Holy Spirit that I had ever experienced up until that time. The power of God struck me with a gigantic mouthful of devil's food cake. Doesn't God have a sense of humor?

Because the experience was so overwhelming, it's hard to put into words. I had never imagined that anybody could ever have the power of God come on them the way that he was coming on me. It was as dramatic as the day I was baptized in the Holy Spirit at Pastor Chuck Kruse's church. The Spirit of God knocked me to my knees on the ground in front of the people! The experience was so overwhelming that all I could do was moan and choke and groan! It's out of the eighth chapter of Romans where it says, "We do not know how to pray [with a mouthful] as we ought. But the Spirit of the Lord will intercede through us with groaning of utterances that cannot be expressed."[50] And I began to have groanings of utterances that could not be expressed with a giant mouthful of devil's food cake in front of 120 people.

I had left the Spirit of God in the living room to go into the kitchen to get *my* cake (because she made it for me!). I was being a child about it. Yet here the Lord taught me one of the greatest lessons of my young twenty-year-old life. As I continued to experience the supernatural encounter with the Holy Spirit, cake and frosting went all over my face, all down the front of me. I cried out to God to forgive me. At the same time, I was "somehow" thanking and praising him, with chocolate flying and dripping everywhere. It was not unlike the oil coming off of Aaron's beard—but much sweeter. I realized that I needed to get back into the room where I had left the Lord. God cleansed my heart as I wiped off my face and went back to the living room to minister to the Lord's precious children with a mighty outpouring of love and forgiveness. I shared from my heart with a fresh new revelation that "he who's been forgiven much loveth much!" The Lord met us with an outpouring of his wonderful presence! I will never forget that devil's food cake, but more than that, I will never forget the wonderful cleansing power of the Holy Spirit!

Listen, my friends, I have grieved the Holy Spirit much more in my life since the time I was a twenty-year-old youth pastor in the late sixties. The enemy has relentlessly pursued and tempted me with much more than a big old piece of cake. I confess that there were times when I failed the test. I will also confess that I love Jesus with all my heart, mind, and soul—and he has never given up on me. He will never give up on you either! That doesn't mean that God will not take us to the woodshed and severely discipline us. Out of his love, he disciplines us. In the mid-eighties I was about to enter the most difficult and darkest season of my life. It almost did me in!

I will graphically share more than many will want to hear, but I believe at this juncture in my life, God wants me to help a bunch of people with my personal experience. He wants me to help a multitude of victims. I am not pointing the finger at everyone else, playing the victim card. I take complete responsibility for my failures. I am willing to do that, as humiliating and humbling as it is and has been. But as I stand here today on my forty-second birthday, God has shined a marvelous light on me and done a deeper work than I ever dreamed possible. Praise God!

God used a wonderful man named Rich Buhler to help pull me out of the dark season that I had descended into after leaving the Vineyard in early 1984. Years later, someone gave me his book *Pain and Pretending*, and that book opened my eyes to some of what I was experiencing. In about 1989, I ran into Rich at a restaurant, and we had a real long talk. I had never met him in person, but had listened to his radio program for years. After he patiently listened to me pour out my heart for a couple of hours, he recommended that I consider talking to a good Christian counselor. Listen, I was desperate and open to anything. Rich suggested that I meet with a close friend of his who is a very experienced and well-known psychologist, and I agreed.

After many sessions with this professional man, he told me that in all of his years as a counselor, I was the most severe case of physical, sexual, emotional, and spiritual abuse of anyone in his entire practice. He helped me tremendously to get in touch with many of the roots of my brokenness so that God could start healing me even at this late date. God also used many of my close friends who never gave up on me. Thank you, God, for friends!

This volume of my life story has been overall super positive, truthful, and focused on the Great Commission—and my attempt to obey the call. I pray it will challenge and inspire you and many others to step out of your comfort zone and rise up to the challenge. I loved every second of the wonderful adventures that God took us on around the world. There were challenges and a lot of warfare, but it was totally thrilling! I am actually going to Brazil and Africa again in a couple months. The final volume of my story, which is the last installment of this three-part series, will be subtitled *Set Free*. God has shown me, by his grace, that he will use my story as a roadmap—a roadmap to recovery, a roadmap to healing, and ultimately, a roadmap home. The roadmap is a person. The roadmap is Jesus, our King and Savior!

Remember, my brothers and sisters:

"IT IS NOT BY MIGHT, NOR BY POWER, BUT BY MY SPIRIT, SAITH THE LORD!"

Lord Jesus, please touch every reader with the loving presence of your Holy Spirit. I pray to the Lord of the harvest that you will send out workers into the Great Commission. The fields are definitely white already for harvest! I pray that EVERYONE will open their hearts and receive all that you have for them and all that you have for their families. Out of your love and mercy, grant them salvation, healing, deliverance, provision, and revelation, as they simply say yes to YOU!

"In the name of the Father, the Son, and the Holy Spirit—Amen!"

Postscript

by Roger Sachs

What a joy it is to finally be releasing this second installment of Lonnie Frisbee's life. Thank God it didn't take another twenty years—only four. I want to thank all of Lonnie's friends who have helped so much in the process. I especially want to thank Peter Crawford, Fred and Ruth Waugh, Marwan, Gigi, John Ruttkay, Lonnie's brother Stan, Chuck Girard, Kenn Gulliksen, James Goll, Jeff Jansen, and so many others who contributed. I also want to thank Jason Francia for his technical gifts and our new editor, Jennifer, who has been with us for a whole year now. I wish we had had her professional talents back in 2006, when I received the green light to continue working on Lonnie's story. However, we were on a very "low-budget show" back then, along with all the other warfare that comes along with *everything* concerning Lonnie Frisbee.

Nevertheless, as I learned as a baby Christian back in 1976 from my favorite pastor, Kenn Gulliksen: "Every obstacle in life can be an opportunity to overcome by the power of the Holy Spirit in the name of Jesus!" That truth has stuck with me for the last forty years or so, and I am thankful to our Lord for pushing this second book across the finish line! I pray that the power of the Holy Spirit will be all over Lonnie's testimony as it goes out.

I have also made this a little bit of a "family affair," as my wife, Roxanne, is a leader in our ministry, my son John, who just obtained his master's degree in English, has come aboard to help in many ways, and my daughter Jenna has been endlessly transcribing Lonnie tapes and interviews. I'm sure Lonnie is thrilled in heaven because he loved John and Jenna very much. They were just toddlers back when Lonnie was with us, and he told me one time on an outing with the kids to Balboa Park in San Diego, "Roger, it is one of my biggest regrets that I never had children of my own, and I have really enjoyed watching the interaction between you and your kids."

Lonnie was such a special, "for real" person, and we miss him so much! The Holy Spirit is hitting me with a dose of nostalgia right now.

Personal prophecy seems to be a big thing now in segments of the church. Lonnie moved in all the gifts of the Spirit, and he gave me a personal prophetic word a couple of years before he died concerning this project and a bit about my involvement. In part he said, "Out with the old and in with the new. You have a tendency, Roger, to try to figure things out," and then he screamed Lonnie style, "**but you won't be able to figure it out!**" He added, "And it is bigger than your wildest imagination!" There was a lot more, but that was the gist of the word. Obviously, I still haven't figured it out, and I don't even try. I believe, as many people around the world have come to believe, that Lonnie Frisbee had a genuine prophetic voice, so I have simply tucked that word away and trust that God is up to something radical with Lonnie's testimony—that will continue to play out in his timing. More than anything, I hope that our involvement will at least be a small part of a huge ingathering of souls.

I know that God is in control and that we need him more than ever. Our nation needs him more than ever. Our world needs him more than ever. It is getting really, really dark out there, and we need another revival to turn America and the world back to God and to Jesus, our Lord and Savior. Only he is the answer!

We are currently working on the final installment of Lonnie's story, which will be subtitled *Set Free*. I feel it will be the most controversial of the series, as Lonnie tells us about his own "dark season of the soul." But he also tells us about the God of the universe who steps in and rescues him—as he does for everyone who turns to Jesus. And believe me, Lonnie again turned to God with all his heart. As the Holy Spirit started showing Lonnie the roots of his brokenness, Lonnie went "all in" for healing because he desperately wanted to be free and whole—and pleasing to his friend Jesus. He was "set free" in ways that are absolutely inspiring and then ultimately taken to his eternal destination, where I'm positive he heard the Lord say, "Well done!"

Lonnie has been set free forever because:

"IT IS NOT BY MIGHT, NOR BY POWER, BUT BY MY SPIRIT, SAITH THE LORD!"

Endnotes

1 Daniel 5:27

2 Psalm 139:8–9

3 John 4:35; Matthew 9:38

4 Matthew 28:18–20

5 Ephesians 6:13–18 NKJV

6 1 Corinthians 13:12

7 John 10:10 CEV

8 John 8:36

9 1 Corinthians 2:4–5

10 2 Corinthians 2:11

11 John 10:10 CEV

12 Matthew 3:13–17

13 Romans 1:16 NIV

14 2 Chronicles 7:14

15 Matthew 18:20

16 Isaiah 60:1–5

17 Numbers 6:26

18 1 Peter 4:12

19 Isaiah 60:2

20 Acts 1:7–8

21 Psalm 133:3

22 Exodus 17:11–12

23 Proverbs 3:5

24 Carol Wimber, *John Wimber: The Way It Was* (Hodder & Stoughton, 1999), p. 147.

25 John Wimber with Kevin Springer, *Power Evangelism* (HarperCollins, 1986), p. 25.

26 Matthew 12:24

27 Verified in an interview with Kenn Gulliksen, June 2016

28 Kasha attended Rosemary Clooney's Hollywood Bible Study before it relocated to his own home, with stars like Bob Dylan and

Donna Summer regularly turning up. According to Kasha, Dylan wrote his first Christian album, *Slow Train Coming*, there in 1979. See Dan Wooding's "Al Kasha, the Man Who Prayed the 'Sinner's Prayer' with Bob Dylan, Says the Singer-Songwriter is Still 'Saved'" in Assist News, June 7, 2014, www.crossmap.com/news for more information.

29 Ephesians 1:4–5

30 John 7:38

31 Revelation 3:15–16 NIV

32 John 21:17

33 Psalm 34:8

34 Mark 16:15

35 Acts 26:26

36 1 Corinthians 2:4

37 John 3:16

38 Acts 1:8

39 Psalm 8:5

40 Revelation 21:4; Revelation 22:20

41 John 7:38

42 Romans 8:28

43 Isaiah 1:18

44 John 19:30

45 Matthew 16:23 VOICE

46 1 Corinthians 1:26–31

47 Psalm 133

48 Luke 7:47

49 Ephesians 4:30

50 Romans 8:26, with author addition

About the Authors

Lonnie Ray Frisbee (1949–1993) was an evangelist, missionary, and artist known to many as the "hippie preacher" who helped launch the Jesus People movement in the early 1970s. Raised in Southern California, Lonnie played a major role in the expansion of Calvary Chapel with Chuck Smith and Vineyard churches with John Wimber. Lonnie Frisbee influenced ministers and ministries around the world.

Roger Sachs is the founder and president of Freedom Crusade, the final ministry Lonnie was involved with before his death in 1993. He is the ghostwriter of Lonnie's authorized autobiography, *Not by Might, Nor by Power*, and has written his own life story, *Fire on the Mountain*. Roger currently lives with his wife, Roxanne, in Santa Maria, California.